500 Recipes

Cupcakes

igloobooks

Published in 2013
by Igloo Books Ltd
Cottage Farm
Sywell
Northants
NN6 0BJ
www.igloobooks.com

Copyright © 2013 Igloo Books Ltd

Food photography and recipe development: PhotoCuisine UK
Front and back cover images © PhotoCuisine UK

SHE001 0913
2 4 6 8 10 9 7 5 3 1
ISBN: 978-1-78197-897-9

Printed and manufactured in China

500
Recipes

Cupcakes

Igloobooks

CONTENTS

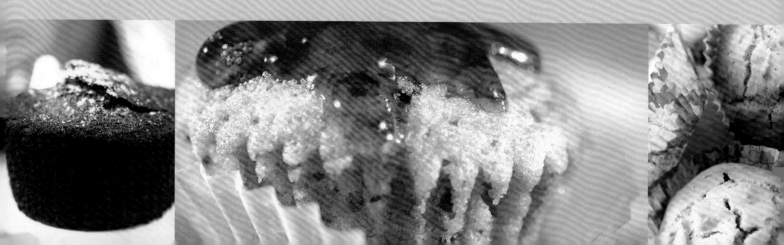

CUPCAKES

Chocolate-topped Mini Cupcakes

Double Chocolate Mini Cupcakes

2

Replace the vanilla extract in the cake mixture with 2 tbsp of unsweetened cocoa powder and add 75 g of chocolate chips. Sprinkle the cakes with white chocolate chips instead of chopped hazelnuts.

White Chocolate Mini Cupcakes

3

Replace the dark chocolate with white chocolate.

Chocolate-topped Coconut Cupcakes

4

Add 2 tbsp of desiccated coconut to the mixture before cooking.

PREPARATION TIME: 25 MINUTES

COOKING TIME: 15 MINUTES

INGREDIENTS

110 g / 4 oz / ½ cup self-raising flour, sifted
110 g / 4 oz / ½ cup caster (superfine) sugar
110 g / 4 oz / ½ cup butter, softened
2 large eggs
1 tsp vanilla extract

TO DECORATE

110 g / 4 oz / ½ cup dark chocolate, minimum 60% cocoa solids, chopped
2 tbsp hazelnuts, chopped

- Preheat the oven to 190°C (170° fan) / 375 F / gas 5 and line a 36-hole mini cupcake tin with paper cases.
- Combine the flour, sugar, butter, eggs and vanilla extract in a bowl and whisk together for 2 minutes or until smooth.
- Divide the mixture between the paper cases and bake for 10 – 15 minutes.
- Test with a wooden toothpick, if it comes out clean, the cakes are done.
- Transfer the cakes to a wire rack and leave to cool.
- Melt the chocolate in a microwave or bain-marie.
- Dip the top of each cake in the chocolate and sprinkle with nuts, then leave to set.

MAKES 24

Raspberry Mini Cupcakes

- Preheat the oven to 180°C (160° fan) / 350 F / gas 4 and line a 24-hole silicone mini muffin tin with paper cases.
- Beat the egg in a jug with the oil and milk. Mix the flour, baking powder, sugar and raspberries in a bowl, then pour in the egg mixture and stir to combine.
- Divide the mixture between the moulds then bake in the oven for 15 – 20 minutes. Transfer the cakes to a wire rack and leave to cool.
- Beat the butter with a wooden spoon until light and fluffy then beat in the icing sugar a quarter at a time.
- Use a whisk to incorporate the raspberry syrup, then whisk for 2 minutes.
- Spoon the icing onto the cupcakes and scatter over the cake sprinkles.

PREPARATION TIME: 25 MINUTES

COOKING TIME: 15-20 MINUTES

INGREDIENTS

1 large egg
120 ml / 4 fl. oz / ½ cup sunflower oil
120 ml / 4 fl. oz / ½ cup milk
375 g / 12 ½ oz / 2 ½ cups self-raising flour, sifted
1 tsp baking powder
200 g / 7 oz / ¾ cup caster (superfine) sugar
150 g / 5 oz / 1 cup raspberries

TO DECORATE

110 g / 4 oz / ½ cup butter, softened
225 g / 8 oz / 2 cups icing (confectioners') sugar
1 tbsp raspberry syrup
red cake sprinkles

Orange Mini Cupcakes

6

Try adding 1 tbsp of finely grated orange zest to the muffin mixture and buttercream.

MAKES 12

Baby Girl Cupcakes

- Preheat the oven to 190°C (170° fan) / 375 F / gas 5 and line a 12-hole cupcake tin with pink paper cases.
- Combine the flour, sugar, butter, eggs and vanilla extract in a bowl and whisk together for 2 minutes.
- Divide the mixture between the cases, then transfer to the oven and bake for 15 – 20 minutes. Transfer the cakes to a wire rack and leave to cool.
- To make the buttercream, beat the butter with a wooden spoon until light and fluffy then beat in the icing sugar a quarter at a time.
- Use a whisk to incorporate the milk and vanilla extract, then whisk for 2 minutes.
- Spoon the buttercream into a piping bag fitted with a star nozzle and pipe a swirl on top of each cake.
- Sprinkle with edible glitter and top each cake with a sugar baby girl head.

PREPARATION TIME: 30 MINUTES

COOKING TIME: 20 MINUTES

INGREDIENTS

110 g / 4 oz / 1 cup self-raising flour, sifted
110 g / 4 oz / ½ cup caster (superfine) sugar
110 g / 4 oz / ½ cup butter, softened
2 large eggs
1 tsp vanilla extract

TO DECORATE

110 g / 4 oz / ½ cup butter, softened
225 g / 8 oz / 2 cups icing (confectioners') sugar
2 tbsp milk
1 tsp vanilla extract
Edible glitter
sugar baby girl heads

Strawberry Baby Cupcakes

8

Replace the milk with 2 tbsp of strawberry syrup to add a pink tint to the cakes and give a fruity flavour.

9

MAKES 12

Simple Vanilla Cupcakes

PREPARATION TIME: 25 MINUTES

COOKING TIME: 20 MINUTES

INGREDIENTS

110 g / 4 oz / 1 cup self-raising flour, sifted
110 g / 4 oz / ½ cup caster (superfine) sugar
110 g / 4 oz / ½ cup butter, softened
2 large eggs
1 tsp vanilla extract

- Preheat the oven to 190°C (170° fan) / 375 F / gas 5 and line a 12-hole cupcake tin with paper cases.
- Combine the flour, sugar, butter, eggs and vanilla extract in a bowl and whisk together for 2 minutes.
- Divide the mixture between the paper cases, then transfer to the oven and bake for 15 – 20 minutes.
- Test with a wooden toothpick, if it comes out clean, the cakes are done.
- Transfer the cakes to a wire rack and leave to cool.

Vanilla Cupcakes with Buttercream Frosting

10

Decorate these cakes with a simple buttercream frosting.

11

MAKES 12

Sugar Pearl Cupcakes

PREPARATION TIME: 25 MINUTES

COOKING TIME: 20 MINUTES

INGREDIENTS

110 g / 4 oz / 1 cup self-raising flour, sifted
110 g / 4 oz / ½ cup caster (superfine) sugar
110 g / 4 oz / ½ cup butter, softened
2 large eggs
1 tsp vanilla extract

TO DECORATE

110 g / 4 oz / ½ cup butter, softened
225 g / 8 oz / 2 cups icing (confectioners') sugar
28 g / 1 oz / ¼ cup unsweetened cocoa powder, sifted
2 tbsp milk

- Preheat the oven to 190°C (170° fan) / 375 F / gas 5 and line a 12-hole cupcake tin with paper cases.
- Combine the flour, sugar, butter, eggs and vanilla extract in a bowl and whisk together for 2 minutes.
- Divide the mixture between the paper cases, then transfer to the oven and bake for 15–20 minutes. Transfer the cakes to a wire rack and leave to cool.
- Beat the butter with a wooden spoon until light and fluffy then beat in the icing sugar and cocoa a quarter at a time.
- Use a whisk to incorporate the milk, then whisk for 2 minutes.
- Spoon the chocolate buttercream into a piping bag fitted with a small star nozzle and pipe small stars to fill the surface of the cupcakes.
- Top with the sugar pearls.

Sugar Pearl Fruit Cupcakes

12

Add 75 g / 3 oz of dried fruit to the cupcake mixture before cooking.

MAKES 24

13

Cheese and Almond Mini Cupcakes

Cheese and Nut Mini Cupcakes

14

Try this recipe with Roquefort and walnuts instead of Reblochon and almonds.

Cheese and Tomato Cupcakes

15

Add 2 finely chopped sun-dried tomatoes to the mixture before cooking.

Cheese and Bacon Cupcakes

16

Add 100 g / 4 oz of cooked chopped bacon pieces before cooking.

PREPARATION TIME: 25 MINUTES

COOKING TIME: 15 MINUTES

INGREDIENTS

2 large eggs
120 ml / 4 fl. oz / ½ cup sunflower oil
180 ml / 6 fl. oz / ¾ cup Greek yogurt
75 g / 2 ½ oz / ½ cup flaked (slivered) almonds
110 g / 4 oz / 1 cup Reblochon cheese, cubed
225 g / 8 oz / 1 ½ cups plain (all purpose) flour
2 tsp baking powder
½ tsp bicarbonate of (baking) soda
½ tsp salt

- Preheat the oven to 180°C (160° fan) / 350 F / gas 4 and oil a 24-hole silicone muffin tin.
- Beat the egg in a jug with the oil, yoghurt, almonds and cheese until well mixed.
- Mix the flour, raising agents and salt in a bowl, then pour in the egg mixture and stir just enough to combine.
- Divide the mixture between the moulds, then bake in the oven for 10 – 15 minutes.
- Test with a wooden toothpick, if it comes out clean, the cupcakes are done.
- Serve warm.

MAKES 36

Chocolate Caramel Mini cupcakes

Chocolate Fruit and Caramel Cupcakes
18

Add 75 g / 3 oz dried fruit to the cupcake mixture.

Peanut and Caramel Cupcakes
19

Add chopped peanuts to the mixture and sprinkle on top.

Pecan and Caramel Cupcakes
20

Add chopped pecans to the mixture and sprinkle on top.

PREPARATION TIME: 20 MINUTES

COOKING TIME: 15 MINUTES

INGREDIENTS

110 g / 4 oz / ½ cup self-raising flour, sifted
28 g / 1 oz / ¼ cup unsweetened cocoa powder, sifted
110 g / 4 oz / ½ cup caster (superfine) sugar
110 g / 4 oz / ½ cup butter, softened
2 large eggs
36 chocolate caramels

- Preheat the oven to 190°C (170° fan) / 375 F / gas 5 and line a 36 hole mini cupcake tin with paper cases.
- Combine the flour, cocoa, sugar, butter and eggs in a bowl and whisk together for 2 minutes.
- Divide the mixture between the paper cases and press a chocolate caramel into the top of each, then transfer to the oven and bake for 10 – 15 minutes.
- Serve warm

21

MAKES 36

Red Iced Mini Cupcakes

- Preheat the oven to 190°C (170° fan) / 375 F / gas 5 and line a 36-hole cupcake tin with paper cases.
- Combine the flour, sugar, butter, eggs and vanilla extract in a bowl and whisk together for 2 minutes.
- Divide the mixture between the paper cases and bake for 10 – 15 minutes.
- Test with a wooden toothpick, if it comes out clean, the cakes are done.
- Transfer the cakes to a wire rack and leave to cool.
- Sieve the icing sugar into a bowl, then slowly stir in the food colouring and boiling water a few drops at a time until you have a thick icing.
- Spoon the icing over the cakes and sprinkle with hundreds and thousands and cake sprinkles.

PREPARATION TIME: 25 MINUTES

COOKING TIME: 15 MINUTES

INGREDIENTS

110 g / 4 oz / ½ cup self-raising flour, sifted
110 g / 4 oz / ½ cup caster (superfine) sugar
110 g / 4 oz / ½ cup butter, softened
2 large eggs
1 tsp vanilla extract

TO DECORATE
225 g / 8 oz / 2 cups icing (confectioners') sugar
red food colouring
boiling water, to mix
coloured sprinkles

Mini Rainbow Cupcakes

22

Use lots of different food colouring and make small amounts of icing in each colour. Drizzle a bit of each coloured icing onto the cupcakes to create a rainbow effect.

23

MAKES 12

Chocolate and Cream Cupcakes

- Preheat the oven to 190°C (170° fan) / 375 F / gas 5 and line a 12-hole cupcake tin with paper cases.
- Combine the flour, cocoa, sugar, butter and eggs in a bowl and whisk together for 2 minutes.
- Divide the mixture between the paper cases, then transfer to the oven and bake for 15 – 20 minutes.
- Test with a wooden toothpick, if it comes out clean, the cakes are done.
- Transfer the cakes to a wire rack and leave to cool.
- Whisk the cream with the icing sugar and vanilla until thick then spoon on top of the cakes.
- Top each cake with a cherry and some chocolate flakes.

PREPARATION TIME: 25 MINUTES

COOKING TIME: 20 MINUTES

INGREDIENTS

110 g / 4 oz / ½ cup self-raising flour, sifted
28 g / 1 oz / ¼ cup unsweetened cocoa powder, sifted
110 g / 4 oz / ½ cup caster (superfine) sugar
110 g / 4 oz / ½ cup butter, softened
2 large eggs

TO DECORATE
225 ml / 8 fl. oz / 1 cup double cream
2 tbsp icing (confectioners') sugar
½ tsp vanilla extract
12 glace cherries
chocolate flakes

Double Chocolate and Cream Cupcakes

24

Add 2 tsp of cocoa powder to the cream mixture to create double chocolate cupcakes.

25

MAKES 12

Peanut Butter Cupcakes

PREPARATION TIME: 30 MINUTES

COOKING TIME: 20 MINUTES

INGREDIENTS

110 g / 4 oz / ½ cup self-raising flour, sifted
110 g / 4 oz / ½ cup caster (superfine) sugar
110 g / 4 oz / ½ cup butter, softened
2 large eggs
2 tbsp crunchy peanut butter

TO DECORATE

110 g / 4 oz / ½ cup butter, softened
2 tbsp smooth peanut butter
225 g / 8 oz / 2 cups icing (confectioners') sugar
2 tbsp milk
2 tbsp chopped peanuts

- Preheat the oven to 190°C (170° fan) / 375 F / gas 5 and line a 12-hole cupcake tin with paper cases.
- Combine the flour, sugar, butter, eggs and crunchy peanut butter in a bowl and whisk together for 2 minutes.
- Divide the mixture between the paper cases, then transfer to the oven and bake for 15 – 20 minutes.
- Transfer the cakes to a wire rack and leave to cool.
- To make the buttercream, beat the butter and smooth peanut butter together with a wooden spoon until light and fluffy then beat in the icing sugar a bit at a time.
- Use a whisk to incorporate the milk, then whisk for 2 minutes.
- Spoon the buttercream into a piping bag fitted with a star nozzle and pipe a swirl on top of each cake.
- Sprinkle with chopped peanuts.

Cupcakes with Caramel Sauce **26**

Put 2 tbsp each, of: butter, double cream, golden syrup and brown sugar in a pan and boil for 2 minutes, stirring. Leave to cool before drizzling over the iced cakes.

27

MAKES 12

Cinnamon Cupcakes

PREPARATION TIME: 30 MINUTES

COOKING TIME: 20 MINUTES

INGREDIENTS

110 g / 4 oz / ½ cup self-raising flour, sifted
110 g / 4 oz / ½ cup caster (superfine) sugar
110 g / 4 oz / ½ cup butter, softened
2 large eggs
2 tsp ground cinnamon

TO DECORATE

225 ml / 8 fl. oz / 1 cup double (heavy) cream
2 tbsp icing (confectioners') sugar
1 tsp ground cinnamon

- Preheat the oven to 190°C (170° fan) / 375 F / gas 5 and line a 12-hole cupcake tin with paper cases.
- Combine the flour, sugar, butter, eggs and cinnamon in a bowl and whisk together for 2 minutes.
- Divide the mixture between the paper cases, then transfer to the oven and bake for 15 – 20 minutes.
- Test with a wooden toothpick, if it comes out clean, the cakes are done.
- Transfer the cakes to a wire rack and leave to cool.
- To make the topping, whisk the cream with the icing sugar until it forms soft peaks.
- Spoon the whipped cream into a piping bag fitted with a large star nozzle and pipe a swirl on top of each cake.
- Use a small sieve to dust each cake with cinnamon.

Cinnamon Cupcakes in Syrup **28**

Put the juice of 2 lemons in a pan with 2 tbsp of caster sugar and 1 tsp of ground cinnamon and heat until the sugar dissolves. Spoon the syrup over the cakes as soon as they come out of the oven.

MAKES 12

Blackberry and Raspberry Cupcakes

- Preheat the oven to 180°°C (160° fan) / 350 F / gas 4 and oil 12 muffin tins.
- Beat the egg in a jug with the oil and milk until well mixed.
- Mix the flour, baking powder, sugar, raspberries and blackberries in a bowl, then pour in the egg mixture and stir just enough to combine.
- Divide the mixture between the tins, then bake in the oven for 20 – 25 minutes.
- Test with a wooden toothpick, if it comes out clean, the cakes are done.
- Transfer the cakes to a wire rack and leave to cool completely before dusting with icing sugar.

PREPARATION TIME: 25 MINUTES

COOKING TIME:
20 – 25 MINUTES

INGREDIENTS

1 large egg
120 ml / 4 fl. oz / ½ cup sunflower oil
120 ml / 4 fl. oz / ½ cup milk
375 g / 12 ½ oz / 2 ½ cups self-raising flour, sifted
1 tsp baking powder
200 g / 7 oz / ¾ cup caster (superfine) sugar
75 g / 2 ½ oz / ½ cup raspberries
75 g / 2 ½ oz / ½ cup blackberries

Blackberry and Blueberry Cupcakes

30

Replace the raspberries with the same amount of blueberries.

MAKES 24

Wholemeal Almond Mini Cupcakes

- Preheat the oven to 180°C (160° fan) / 350 F / gas 4 and oil a 24-hole silicone mini muffin mould.
- Beat the egg in a jug with the oil, milk and almond essence until well mixed.
- Mix the flour, baking powder, sugar and ground almonds in a bowl, then pour in the egg mixture and stir just enough to combine.
- Divide the mixture between the moulds and sprinkle with chopped almonds, then bake in the oven for 15 – 20 minutes.
- Test with a wooden toothpick, if it comes out clean, the cakes are done.
- Transfer the cakes to a wire rack and leave to cool.

PREPARATION TIME: 25 MINUTES

COOKING TIME: 20 MINUTES

INGREDIENTS

1 large egg
120 ml / 4 fl. oz / ½ cup sunflower oil
120 ml / 4 fl. oz / ½ cup milk
1 tsp almond essence
375 g / 12 ½ oz / 2 ½ cups wholemeal flour
2 tsp baking powder
200 g / 7 oz / ¾ cup caster (superfine) sugar
55 g / 2 oz / ½ cup ground almonds
75 g / 2 ½ oz / ½ cup blanched almonds, chopped

Wholemeal Walnut Mini Cupcakes

32

Replace the almonds with the same amount of crushed walnuts and the almond essence with vanilla essence.

MAKES 6 33

Chocolate and Hazelnut Cupcakes

PREPARATION TIME: 45 MINUTES

COOKING TIME: 25 MINUTES

INGREDIENTS

110 g / 4 oz / ½ cup self-raising flour, sifted
28 g / 1 oz / ¼ cup unsweetened cocoa powder, sifted
110 g / 4 oz / ½ cup caster (superfine) sugar
110 g / 4 oz / ½ cup butter, softened
2 large eggs
110 g / 4 oz / ½ cup chocolate and hazelnut spread

TO DECORATE
whole hazelnuts
summer berries
strawberry and caramel sauce

- Preheat the oven to 190°C (170° fan) / 375 F / gas 5 and oil a 6-hole silicone large cupcake tin
- Combine the flour, cocoa, sugar, butter and eggs in a bowl and whisk together for 2 minutes.
- Divide half of the mixture between the moulds, then add 2 tsp of chocolate spread in the centre of each one.
- Top with the rest of the cake mixture then transfer the mould to the oven and bake for 20 – 25 minutes.
- Serve the cakes warm, garnished with your choice of summer fruits and strawberry sauce or whole hazelnuts and caramel sauce.

Fruity Chocolate and Hazelnut Cupcakes
34

Add 75 g / 2 ½ oz / ½ cup of raisins to the cupcake batter before cooking, to add a fruity flavour.

35

MAKES 12

Strawberry and Rose Cupcakes

PREPARATION TIME: 30 MINUTES

COOKING TIME: 20 MINUTES

INGREDIENTS

110 g / 4 oz / ½ cup self-raising flour, sifted
110 g / 4 oz / ½ cup caster (superfine) sugar
110 g / 4 oz / ½ cup butter, softened
2 large eggs
110 g / 4 oz / ½ cup strawberry jam (jelly)

TO DECORATE
110 g / 4 oz / ½ cup butter, softened
225 g / 8 oz / 2 cups icing (confectioners') sugar
2 tbsp rose water
pink food colouring
flower-shaped cake sprinkles

- Preheat the oven to 190°C (170° fan) / 375 F / gas 5 and line a 12-hole cupcake tin with paper cases.
- Combine the flour, sugar, butter, eggs and strawberry jam in a bowl and whisk together for 2 minutes.
- Divide the mixture between the paper cases, then transfer to the oven and bake for 15 – 20 minutes.
- Test with a wooden toothpick, if it comes out clean, the cakes are done.
- Transfer the cakes to a wire rack and leave to cool.
- To make the buttercream, beat the butter with a wooden spoon until light and fluffy then beat in the icing sugar a quarter at a time.
- Use a whisk to incorporate the rose water and food colouring, then whisk for 2 minutes.
- Spoon the buttercream into a piping bag fitted with a star nozzle and pipe a swirl on top of each cake.
- Sprinkle with flower-shaped cake sprinkles.

Raspberry and Rose Cupcakes
36

To maximise the rose flavour of these cakes, replace the strawberry jam with rose petal jam and decorate with a single fresh rose petal instead of the cake sprinkles.

MAKES 12

Mixed Pepper Cupcakes

Mixed Pepper and Pesto Cupcakes

 38

Add 2 tbsp of pesto to the mixture before baking.

Cheesy Mixed Pepper Cupcakes

39

Add 5 tbsp of cubed mozzarella to the batter before baking to add a cheesy flavour. Sprinkle with Parmesan before serving.

Courgette and Mixed Pepper Cupcakes

40

Replace one of the peppers with grated courgette to add extra flavour.

PREPARATION TIME 25 MINUTES

COOKING TIME 25 MINUTES

INGREDIENTS

1 red pepper, deseeded and sliced
1 orange pepper, deseeded and sliced
1 green pepper, deseeded and sliced
2 tbsp olive oil
2 large eggs
120 ml / 4 fl. oz / ½ cup sunflower oil
180 ml / 6 fl. oz / ¾ cup Greek yogurt
110 g / 4 oz / 1 cup Parmesan, grated
225 g / 8 oz / 1 ½ cups plain (all purpose) flour
2 tsp baking powder
½ tsp bicarbonate of (baking) soda
½ tsp salt

- Preheat the oven to 180°C (160° fan) / 350 F / gas 4 and line a 12-hole muffin tin with paper cases.
- Fry the peppers in the olive oil for 10 minutes or until soft.
- Beat the egg in a jug with the oil, yogurt and cheese until well mixed then stir in the peppers.
- Mix the flour, raising agents and salt in a bowl, then pour in the egg mixture and stir just enough to combine.
- Divide the mixture between the paper cases, then bake in the oven for 20 – 25 minutes.
- Test with a wooden toothpick, if it comes out clean, the cupcakes are done.
- Serve warm.

41

MAKES 12

Chocolate Meringue Cupcakes

PREPARATION TIME: 35 MINUTES

COOKING TIME: 30 MINUTES

INGREDIENTS

110 g / 4 oz / ½ cup self-raising flour, sifted
28 g / 1 oz / ¼ cup unsweetened cocoa powder, sifted
110 g / 4 oz / ½ cup caster (superfine) sugar
110 g / 4 oz / ½ cup butter, softened
2 large eggs
28 g / 1 oz / ⅛ cup desiccated coconut

TO DECORATE

4 egg whites
110 g / 4 oz / 1 cup caster (superfine) sugar
110 g / 4 oz / ½ cup dark chocolate, minimum 60% cocoa solids, chopped
2 tbsp desiccated coconut

- Preheat the oven to 190°C (170° fan) / 375 F / gas 5 and line a 12-hole cupcake tin with foil cases.
- Combine the flour, cocoa, sugar, butter, eggs and coconut in a bowl and whisk together for 2 minutes.
- Divide the mixture between the paper cases, then transfer to the oven and bake for 15 – 20 minutes.
- To make the meringue topping, whisk the egg whites until stiff, then gradually whisk in half the sugar until the mixture is very shiny. Fold in the remaining sugar then spoon into a piping bag fitted with a plain nozzle.
- Pipe a mound of meringue on top of each cake and return to the oven for 10 minutes or until the topping is golden brown, then leave to cool completely.
- Melt the chocolate in a bain-marie, then dip the top of the cupcakes so that the meringue is completely coated.
- Sprinkle some of the cakes with shredded coconut before the chocolate sets.

Walnut Meringue Cupcakes

 42

Replace the desiccated coconut in the cake mixture with 5 tbsp chopped walnuts and decorate the chocolate-coated meringue with a walnut.

43

MAKES 12

Chocolate and Strawberry Cupcakes

PREPARATION TIME: 30 MINUTES

COOKING TIME: 20 MINUTES

INGREDIENTS

110 g / 4 oz / ½ cup self-raising flour, sifted
28 g / 1 oz / ¼ cup unsweetened cocoa powder, sifted
110 g / 4 oz / ½ cup caster (superfine) sugar
110 g / 4 oz / ½ cup butter, softened
2 large eggs
110 g / 4 oz / ½ cup strawberry jam

TO DECORATE

110 g / 4 oz / ½ cup butter, softened
225 g / 8 oz / 2 cups icing (confectioners') sugar
pink food colouring
coloured sprinkles

- Preheat the oven to 190°C (170° fan) / 375 F / gas 5 and line a 12-hole cupcake tin with paper cases.
- Combine the flour, cocoa, sugar, butter and eggs in a bowl and whisk together for 2 minutes.
- Divide half the mixture between the paper cases, then add 1 tsp of strawberry jam in the centre of each one.
- Top with the rest of the cake mixture then transfer to the oven and bake for 15 – 20 minutes.
- Transfer the cakes to a wire rack and leave to cool.
- To make the buttercream, beat the butter with a wooden spoon until light and fluffy then beat in the icing sugar a quarter at a time.
- Use a whisk to incorporate the strawberry syrup, then whisk for 2 minutes.
- Spoon the buttercream into a piping bag fitted with a star nozzle and pipe a swirl on top of each cake.
- Sprinkle with coloured sprinkles.

Strawberry-Topped Cupcakes

 44

Instead of decorating the cakes with hundreds and thousands, top each one with a whole strawberry dipped in dark chocolate.

Carrot and Orange Cupcakes

- Preheat the oven to 190°°C (170° fan) / 375 F / gas 5 and line a 12-hole cupcake tin with paper cases.
- Whisk the sugar, eggs and oil together for 3 minutes until thick.
- Fold in the flour, baking powder and cinnamon, followed by the orange zest and carrots.
- Divide the mixture between the paper cases, then transfer to the oven and bake for 20 - 25 minutes.
- Transfer the cakes to a wire rack and leave to cool.
- To make the icing, beat the cream cheese and butter together with a wooden spoon until light and fluffy then beat in the icing sugar a quarter at a time.
- Add the vanilla extract then use a whisk to whip the mixture for 2 minutes until light.
- Spoon the icing onto the cakes and finish with a sprinkling of orange zest.

PREPARATION TIME: 40 MINUTES

COOKING TIME: 25 MINUTES

INGREDIENTS

175 g / 6 oz / 1 cup soft brown sugar
2 large eggs
150 ml / 5 fl. oz / ¾ cup sunflower oil
175 g / 6 oz / 1 ¼ cups wholemeal flour
3 tsp baking powder
2 tsp ground cinnamon
1 orange, zest finely grated
200 g / 7 oz carrots, washed and grated

TO DECORATE

225 g / 8 oz / 1 cup cream cheese
110 g / 4 oz / ½ cup butter, softened
225 g / 8 oz / 2 cups icing sugar
1 tsp vanilla extract
1 orange, zest finely pared

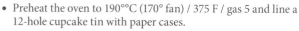

Chocolate Clock Cupcakes

PREPARATION TIME: 35 MINUTES

COOKING TIME: 20 MINUTES

INGREDIENTS

110 g / 4 oz / ½ cup self-raising flour
28 g / 1 oz / ¼ cup cocoa powder
110 g / 4 oz / ½ cup caster sugar
110 g / 4 oz / ½ cup butter, softened
2 large eggs
110 g / 4 oz / ½ cup dark chocolate, chopped

TO DECORATE

110 g / 4 oz / ½ cup butter, softened
225 g / 8 oz / 2 cups icing (confectioners') sugar
2 tbsp milk
110 g / 4 oz / ½ cup dark chocolate, chopped

- Preheat the oven to 190°°C (170° fan) / 375 F / gas 5 and line a 12-hole cupcake tin with paper cases.
- Combine the flour, cocoa, sugar, butter, and eggs in a bowl and whisk together for 2 minutes. Fold in the chopped chocolate and divide the mixture between the paper cases.
- Transfer the tin to the oven and bake for 15 – 20 minutes. Transfer the cakes to a wire rack and leave to cool.
- To make the buttercream, beat the butter until light and fluffy then beat in the icing sugar.
- Use a whisk to incorporate the milk, then whisk for 2 minutes.
- Spoon the buttercream onto the cakes and spread out with the back of the spoon.
- Melt the chocolate in a microwave or bain marie and pour into a piping bag with a small plain nozzle.
- Pipe each cake with a chocolate number, 1 – 12, then arrange the cakes on a large serving plate and use 2 small spoons as the hands of the clock.

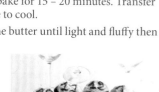

Salmon and Cream Cupcakes

PREPARATION TIME: 25 MINUTES

COOKING TIME: 15 MINUTES

INGREDIENTS

2 large eggs
120 ml / 4 fl. oz / ½ cup sunflower oil
180 ml / 6 fl. oz / ¾ cup soured cream
110 g / 4 oz / 1 cup smoked salmon, chopped

225 g / 8 oz / 1 ½ cups plain (all purpose) flour
2 tsp baking powder
½ tsp bicarbonate of (baking) soda
½ tsp salt

TO DECORATE

60 ml / 2 fl. oz / ¼ cup soured cream
2 tbsp salmon roe
handful fresh chervil

- Preheat the oven to 180°°C (160° fan) / 350 F / gas 4 and line a 24-hole muffin tin with paper cases.
- Beat the egg in a jug with the oil, soured cream and salmon until well mixed.
- Mix the flour, raising agents and salt in a bowl, then pour in the egg mixture and stir just enough to combine.
- Divide the mixture between the paper cases, then bake in the oven for 10 – 15 minutes.
- Test with a wooden toothpick, if it comes out clean, the cupcakes are done.
- Transfer to a wire rack to cool, then top the cupcakes with a spoonful of soured cream, a few salmon eggs and a sprig of fresh chervil.

48

MAKES 12

Black Forest Gateau Cupcakes

PREPARATION TIME: 30 MINUTES

COOKING TIME: 20 MINUTES

INGREDIENTS

55 g / 2 oz / ½ cup self-raising flour, sifted

55 g / 2 oz / ½ cup ground almonds

28 g / 1 oz / ¼ cup unsweetened cocoa powder, sifted

110 g / 4 oz / ½ cup caster (superfine) sugar

110 g / 4 oz / ½ cup butter, softened

2 large eggs

350 g / 12 oz / 1 cup morello cherries in syrup, drained

110 g / 4 oz / ½ cup dark chocolate, minimum 60% cocoa solids, chopped

TO DECORATE

225 ml / 8 fl. oz / 1 cup double (heavy) cream

2 tbsp icing (confectioners') sugar

2 tbsp dark chocolate curls

12 fresh cherries, stoned and halved

- Preheat the oven to 190°C (170° fan) / 375 F / gas 5 and line a 12-hole cupcake tin with paper cases.
- Combine the flour, almonds, cocoa, sugar, butter and eggs in a bowl and whisk together for 2 minutes.
- Fold in the drained cherries and chocolate and divide the mixture between the paper cases.
- Transfer the tin to the oven and bake for 15 – 20 minutes.
- Transfer the cakes to a wire rack and leave to cool.
- To make the topping, whisk the cream with the icing sugar until it forms soft peaks.
- Spoon the whipped cream into a piping bag fitted with a large star nozzle and pipe a large rosette on top of each cake.
- Top each cake with 2 cherry halves and sprinkle with chocolate curls.

Double Chocolate Gateau Cupcakes

49

Make a chocolate ganache to replace the whipped cream. Heat 225 ml / 8 fl. oz double cream until boiling then pour over 225 g / 8 oz chopped dark chocolate and stir until the mixture has cooled and thickened.

50

MAKES 12

Strawberry Cupcakes

PREPARATION TIME: 30 MINUTES

COOKING TIME: 20 MINUTES

INGREDIENTS

110 g / 4 oz / 1 cup self-raising flour, sifted

110 g / 4 oz / ½ cup caster (superfine) sugar

110 g / 4 oz / ½ cup butter, softened

2 large eggs

1 tsp vanilla extract

TO DECORATE

110 g / 4 oz / ½ cup butter, softened

225 g / 8 oz / 2 cups icing (confectioners') sugar

2 tbsp strawberry syrup

2 fresh strawberries

6 sugar paste roses

- Preheat the oven to 190°C (170° fan) / 375 F / gas 5 and oil a 12-hole silicone cupcake mould.
- Combine the flour, sugar, butter, eggs and vanilla extract in a bowl and whisk together for 2 minutes.
- Divide the mixture between the moulds, then transfer to the oven and bake for 15 – 20 minutes.
- Transfer the cakes to a wire rack and leave to cool.
- To make the buttercream, beat the butter with a wooden spoon until light and fluffy then beat in the icing sugar a quarter at a time.
- Use a whisk to incorporate the strawberry syrup, then whisk for 2 minutes.
- Spoon the buttercream into a piping bag fitted with a star nozzle and pipe a swirl on top of each cake.
- Cut each strawberry into 3 pieces and use to top 6 of the cakes. Top the other 6 cakes with a sugar paste rose.

Strawberry Jam Cupcakes

51

Cut each cake in half horizontally and fill with strawberry jam and whipped cream before icing and topping for an extravagant treat.

MAKES 12

White Chocolate Cupcakes

White Chocolate and Orange Cupcakes

Try adding a little grated orange zest to the cake mixture to balance the sweetness of the white chocolate.

White Chocolate and Lime Cupcakes

Try adding a little grated lime zest to the cake mixture to add a citrus kick.

PREPARATION TIME: 20 MINUTES

COOKING TIME: 20 MINUTES

INGREDIENTS

110 g / 4 oz / ½ cup self-raising flour, sifted

110 g / 4 oz / ½ cup caster (superfine) sugar

110 g / 4 oz / ½ cup butter, softened

2 large eggs

1 tsp vanilla extract

150 g / 5 oz / 1 cup white chocolate chips

TO DECORATE
white chocolate flakes

Preheat the oven to 190°C (170° fan) / 375 F / gas 5 and line a 12-hole cupcake tin with paper cases.

Combine the flour, sugar, butter, eggs and chocolate chips in a bowl and whisk together for 2 minutes.

Divide the mixture between the paper cases, then transfer to the oven and bake for 15 – 20 minutes.

Test with a wooden toothpick, if it comes out clean, the cakes are done.

Transfer the cakes to a wire rack and leave to cool completely, then sprinkle with white chocolate flakes.

55

MAKES 12

Hot Chocolate Cupcakes

PREPARATION TIME: 45 MINUTES

COOKING TIME: 20 MINUTES

INGREDIENTS

110 g / 4 oz / ½ cup self-raising flour, sifted
28 g / 1 oz / ¼ cup unsweetened cocoa powder, sifted
110 g / 4 oz / ½ cup caster (superfine) sugar
110 g / 4 oz / ½ cup butter, softened
2 large eggs
225 g / 8 oz / 1 cup dark chocolate, minimum 60% cocoa solids

TO DECORATE

225 ml / 8 fl. oz / 1 cup double (heavy) cream
2 tbsp icing (confectioners') sugar
Mixed summer berries

- Preheat the oven to 190°C (170° fan) / 375 F / gas 5 and oil 12 small mugs.
- Combine the flour, cocoa, sugar, butter and eggs in a bowl and whisk together for 2 minutes.
- Divide half the mixture between the mugs.
- Break the chocolate into squares and divide between the mugs, then spoon the rest of the cake mixture on top.
- Sit the mugs on a baking tray and bake in the oven for 15 – 20 minutes.
- Test with a wooden toothpick, if it comes out clean, the cakes are done.
- While the cakes are cooking, make the topping. Whisk the cream with the icing sugar until thick and spoon into a piping bag fitted with a large star nozzle.
- When the cakes are ready, pipe a swirl of cream on top and scatter over a few summer berries.

Marshmallow Hot Chocolate Cupcakes

56

For an extra indulgent treat, replace the berries with marshmallows and finish with a dusting of cocoa powder.

57

MAKES 12

Bacon Cupcakes

PREPARATION TIME: 25 MINUTES

COOKING TIME: 25 MINUTES

INGREDIENTS

12 rashers of bacon
2 large eggs
120 ml / 4 fl. oz / ½ cup sunflower oil
180 ml / 6 fl. oz / ¾ cup Greek yogurt
110 g / 4 oz / 1 cup Parmesan, grated
225 g / 8 oz / 1 ½ cups plain (all purpose) flour
2 tsp baking powder
½ tsp bicarbonate of (baking) soda
½ tsp salt

TO DECORATE

225 g / 8 oz / 1 cup cream cheese
12 little gem lettuce leaves
4 rashers of bacon, chopped and fried
1 tbsp balsamic glaze

- Preheat the oven to 180°C (160° fan) / 350 F / gas 4 and oil a 12-hole silicone muffin mould.
- Cut a long strip down one side of each bacon rasher and use them to line the inside of the cupcakes moulds.
- Chop the rest of the bacon.
- Beat the egg in a jug with the oil, yoghurt, cheese and chopped bacon until well mixed.
- Mix the flour, raising agents and salt in a bowl, then pour in the egg mixture and stir to combine.
- Divide the mixture between the moulds, then bake in the oven for 20 – 25 minutes.
- Transfer the cupcakes to a wire rack and leave to cool.
- Spoon the cream cheese into a piping bag fitted with a large star nozzle and pipe a swirl on top of each muffin.
- Top with a little gem leaf, fill with bacon pieces and drizzle with balsamic glaze.

Sour Cream and Bacon Cupcakes

58

Add a spoonful of soured cream to the top of each cupcake and sprinkle with chopped pistachios.

59

MAKES 12

Colourful Cupcakes

- Preheat the oven to 190°C (170° fan) / 375 F / gas 5 and line a 12-hole cupcake tin with paper cases.
- Combine the flour, sugar, butter, eggs and vanilla extract in a bowl and whisk together for 2 minutes.
- Divide the mixture between the paper cases, then transfer to the oven and bake for 15 – 20 minutes.
- Test with a wooden toothpick, if it comes out clean, the cakes are done.
- Transfer the cakes to a wire rack and leave to cool.
- Sift the icing sugar into a bowl, then slowly stir in the boiling water a few drops at a time until you have a thick icing.
- Divide the icing into 3 bowls and colour each with a different food colouring.
- Ice 4 cakes with each of the coloured icings, then sprinkle with your choice of toppings.

PREPARATION TIME: 45 MINUTES

COOKING TIME: 20 MINUTES

INGREDIENTS

110 g / 4 oz / ½ cup self-raising flour, sifted
110 g / 4 oz / ½ cup caster (superfine) sugar
110 g / 4 oz / ½ cup butter, softened
2 large eggs
1 tsp vanilla extract

TO DECORATE

225 g / 8 oz / 2 cups icing (confectioners') sugar
boiling water, to mix
yellow, pink and green food colouring
coloured sprinkles
small sweets

Rainbow Cupcakes

60

To make these cakes even more colourful, divide the cake mixture before it is cooked into 3 bowls and colour each one with a different food colouring.

61

MAKES 24

Sun-dried Tomato and Brie Mini Cupcakes

- Preheat the oven to 180°C (160° fan) / 350 F / gas 4 and oil a 24-hole silicone muffin tin.
- Beat the egg in a jug with the oil, yoghurt, tomatoes and cheese until well mixed.
- Mix the flour, raising agents, salt and herbs in a bowl, then pour in the egg mixture and stir just enough to combine.
- Divide the mixture between the moulds, then bake in the oven for 10 – 15 minutes.
- Test with a wooden toothpick, if it comes out clean, the cupcakes are done.
- Serve warm.

PREPARATION TIME: 25 MINUTES

COOKING TIME: 15 MINUTES

INGREDIENTS

2 large eggs
120 ml / 4 fl. oz / ½ cup sunflower oil
180 ml / 6 fl. oz / ¾ cup Greek yogurt
75 g / 2 ½ oz / ½ cup sundried tomatoes, chopped
110 g / 4 oz / 1 cup Brie, cubed
225 g / 8 oz / 1 ½ cups plain (all purpose) flour
2 tsp baking powder
½ tsp bicarbonate of (baking) soda
½ tsp salt
2 tsp dried herbs de Provence

Tomato, Brie and Pesto Cupcakes

62

Marble 4 tbsp of pesto through the muffin mix before filling the moulds.

63

MAKES 12

Chocolate Drizzle Cupcakes

Almond and Chocolate Drizzle Cupcakes

 64

Add 55 g / 2 oz of chopped almonds to the cupcake batter.

Walnut and Chocolate Drizzle Cupcakes

65

Add 55 g / 2 oz of chopped walnuts to the cupcake batter.

Raisin and Chocolate Drizzle Cupcakes

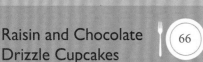 **66**

Add 75 g / 3 oz of raisins to the cupcake batter.

PREPARATION TIME: 25 MINUTES

COOKING TIME: 25 MINUTES

INGREDIENTS

1 large egg
120 ml / 4 fl. oz / ½ cup sunflower oil
120 ml / 4 fl. oz / ½ cup milk
375 g / 12 ½ oz / 2 ½ cups self-raising flour, sifted
55 g / 2 oz / ½ cup cocoa powder, sifted
1 tsp baking powder
200 g / 7 oz / ¾ cup caster (superfine) sugar
110 g / 4 oz / ½ cup dark chocolate, chopped

TO DECORATE

225 g / 8 oz / 2 cups icing (confectioners') sugar
28 g / 1 oz / ¼ cup unsweetened cocoa powder, sifted
boiling water, to mix

- Preheat the oven to 180°C (160° fan) / 350 F / gas 4 and line a 12-hole muffin tin with paper cases.
- Beat the egg in a jug with the oil and milk until well mixed.
- Mix the flour, cocoa, baking powder, sugar and chocolate in a bowl, then pour in the egg mixture and stir just enough to combine.
- Divide the mixture between the paper cases, then bake in the oven for 20 – 25 minutes.
- Test with a wooden toothpick, if it comes out clean, the cakes are done.
- Transfer the cakes to a wire rack and leave to cool.
- Sift the icing sugar and cocoa into a bowl, then slowly stir in the boiling water a few drops at a time until you have a thin icing.
- Drizzle the icing over the cupcakes.

67

MAKES 24

Mini Pumpkin Cupcakes

- Preheat the oven to 180°C (160° fan) / 350 F / gas 4 and line a 24-hole muffin tin with paper cases.
- Beat the egg in a jug with the oil, yoghurt, pumpkin and cheese until well mixed.
- Mix the flour, raising agents and salt in a bowl, then pour in the egg mixture and stir just enough to combine.
- Divide the mixture between the paper cases and sprinkle with pumpkin seeds, then bake in the oven for 10 – 15 minutes.
- Test with a wooden toothpick, if it comes out clean, the cupcakes are done.
- Serve warm.

PREPARATION TIME: 25 MINUTES

COOKING TIME: 15 MINUTES

INGREDIENTS

2 large eggs
120ml / 4 fl. oz / ½ cup sunflower oil
180ml / 6 fl. oz / ¾ cup Greek yogurt
150 g / 5 oz pumpkin, coarsely grated
110 g / 4 oz / 1 cup Parmesan, grated
225 g / 8 oz / 1 ½ cups plain (all purpose) flour
2 tsp baking powder
½ tsp bicarbonate of (baking) soda
½ tsp salt
2 tbsp pumpkin seeds

Pumpkin and Sage Mini Cupcakes

 68

Add 2 tbsp of chopped fresh sage to the mixture before baking.

69

MAKES 24

Ginger Cupcakes

- Preheat the oven to 190°C (170° fan) / 375 F / gas 5 and oil 24 small dariole moulds.
- Sieve the flour, bicarbonate of soda and ground ginger together into a bowl.
- Put the golden syrup, butter, brown sugar and stem ginger in a small saucepan and boil gently for 2 minutes, stirring to dissolve the sugar.
- Pour the butter and sugar mixture onto the flour with the eggs and milk and fold it all together until smooth.
- Divide the mixture between the dariole moulds, then sit them on a baking tray and bake in the oven for 20 – 25 minutes.
- Transfer the cakes to a wire rack and leave to cool.
- Top each cake with a piece of crystallised ginger.

PREPARATION TIME: 20 MINUTES

COOKING TIME: 20 MINUTES

INGREDIENTS

250 g / 9 oz / 1 ¼ cups self-raising flour
1 tsp bicarbonate of (baking) soda
2 tsp ground ginger
200 g / 8 ½ oz / ½ cup golden syrup
125 g / 4 ½ oz / ½ cup butter
125 g / 4 ½ oz / ¾ cup light brown sugar
4 pieces stem ginger, chopped
2 large eggs, beaten
240 ml / 8 fl. oz / 1 cup milk
24 pieces crystallised ginger

Extra Spicy Cupcakes

 70

Add 1 tsp mixed spice and 1 tsp ground cinnamon to the cake mixture with the ground ginger.

71

MAKES 12

Baby Boy Cupcakes

- Preheat the oven to 190°C (170° fan) / 375 F / gas 5 and line a 12-hole cupcake tin with blue paper cases.
- Combine the flour, sugar, butter, eggs and vanilla extract in a bowl and whisk together for 2 minutes.
- Divide the mixture between the paper cases, then bake for 15 – 20 minutes. Transfer to a wire rack to cool.
- Beat the butter with a wooden spoon until light and fluffy then beat in the icing sugar. Use a whisk to incorporate the milk and vanilla extract, then whisk for 2 minutes.
- Spoon the buttercream into a piping bag fitted with a star nozzle and pipe a swirl on top of each cake.
- Sprinkle with edible glitter. To make the blue baby feet, knead the fondant icing with a little blue food colouring until pliable and evenly coloured.
- Make a flattened pear shape for each foot and 5 little balls to make the toes. Assemble two feet on the top of each cake, attaching the toes with a little water.

PREPARATION TIME: 45 MINUTES

COOKING TIME: 20 MINUTES

INGREDIENTS

110 g / 4 oz / 1 cup self-raising flour
110 g / 4 oz / ½ cup caster sugar
110 g / 4 oz / ½ cup butter, softened
2 large eggs
1 tsp vanilla extract

TO DECORATE

110 g / 4 oz / ½ cup butter, softened
225 g / 8 oz / 2 cups icing sugar
2 tbsp milk
1 tsp vanilla extract
edible glitter
110 g / 4 oz / ½ cup ready-to-roll fondant icing
blue food colouring

Honey and Almond Cupcakes

72

MAKES 12

PREPARATION TIME: 25 MINUTES

COOKING TIME: 20 MINUTES

INGREDIENTS

55 g / 2 oz / ½ cup self-raising flour
55 g / 2 oz / ½ cup ground almonds
55 g / 2 oz / ¼ cup caster sugar
110 g / 4 oz / ½ cup honey
110 g / 4 oz / ½ cup butter, softened

2 large eggs
1 tsp almond essence

TO DECORATE

Icing sugar for dusting
6 strawberries, halved
12 raspberries

- Preheat the oven to 190°C (170° fan) / 375 F / gas 5 and line a 12-hole cupcake tin with paper cases.
- Combine the flour, ground almonds, sugar, honey, butter, eggs and almond essence in a bowl and whisk together for 2 minutes.
- Divide the mixture between the paper cases, then transfer to the oven and bake for 15 – 20 minutes.
- Test with a wooden toothpick, if it comes out clean, the cakes are done.
- Transfer the cakes to a wire rack to cool.
- Dust the cakes with icing sugar then top each one with half a strawberry and a raspberry.

Purple Party Cupcakes

73

MAKES 12

PREPARATION TIME: 30 MINUTES

COOKING TIME: 20 MINUTES

INGREDIENTS

110 g / 4 oz / ½ cup self-raising flour
110 g / 4 oz / ½ cup caster sugar
110 g / 4 oz / ½ cup butter, softened
2 large eggs
1 tsp vanilla extract

175 g / 6 oz fresh blueberries

TO DECORATE

110 g / 4 oz / ½ cup butter, softened
225 g / 8 oz / 2 cups icing sugar
2 tbsp milk
5 drops purple food colouring
edible glitter
silver balls

- Preheat the oven to 190°C (170° fan) / 375 F / gas 5 and line a 12-hole cupcake tin with paper cases.
- Combine the flour, sugar, butter, eggs and vanilla extract in a bowl and whisk together for 2 minutes.
- Fold in the blueberries and divide the mixture between the paper cases.
- Transfer the tin to the oven and bake for 15 – 20 minutes.
- Transfer the cakes to a wire rack and leave to cool.
- Beat the butter with a wooden spoon until light and fluffy then beat in the icing sugar.
- Use a whisk to incorporate the milk and food colouring, then whisk for 2 minutes.
- Spoon the buttercream into a piping bag fitted with a star nozzle and pipe a swirl on top of each cake.
- Sprinkle with edible glitter and silver balls and top with plastic cake novelties of your choice.

74

MAKES 12

Pink Iced Vanilla Cupcakes

- Preheat the oven to 190°C (170° fan) / 375 F / gas 5 and line a 12-hole cupcake tin with paper cases.
- Combine the flour, sugar, butter, eggs and vanilla extract in a bowl and whisk together for 2 minutes.
- Divide the mixture between the paper cases, then transfer to the oven and bake for 15 – 20 minutes.
- Transfer the cakes to a wire rack and leave to cool.
- Sieve the icing sugar into a bowl, then slowly stir in the boiling water a few drops at a time until you have a thick icing.
- Stir in the food colouring a drop at a time until you reach your desired colour.
- Spoon the icing onto the cakes and swirl with the back of the spoon.
- Scatter over the cake sprinkles.

PREPARATION TIME: 25 MINUTES

COOKING TIME: 20 MINUTES

INGREDIENTS

110 g / 4 oz / ½ cup self-raising flour, sifted
110 g / 4 oz / ½ cup caster (superfine) sugar
110 g / 4 oz / ½ cup butter, softened
2 large eggs
1 tsp vanilla extract

TO DECORATE
225 g / 8 oz / 2 cups icing (confectioners') sugar
boiling water, to mix
pink food colouring
pink heart-shaped cake sprinkles

Pink Iced Almond Cupcakes

 75

Replace the vanilla extract with almond extract and top with flaked almonds instead of heart-shaped sprinkles.

76

MAKES 12

Sugar Nib Cupcakes

- Preheat the oven to 190°C (170° fan) / 375 F / gas 5 and line a 12-hole cupcake tin with paper cases.
- Combine the flour, sugar, butter, eggs and vanilla extract in a bowl and whisk together for 2 minutes.
- Divide the mixture between the paper cases.
- Sprinkle with sugar nibs.
- Transfer the tin to the oven and bake for 15 – 20 minutes.
- Test with a wooden toothpick, if it comes out clean, the cakes are done.
- Transfer the cakes to a wire rack and leave to cool.

PREPARATION TIME: 25 MINUTES

COOKING TIME: 20 MINUTES

INGREDIENTS

110 g / 4 oz / 1 cup self-raising flour, sifted
110 g / 4 oz / ½ cup caster (superfine) sugar
110 g / 4 oz / ½ cup butter, softened
2 large eggs
1 tsp vanilla extract
55 g / 2 oz sugar nibs

Sugar Nib and Fruit Cupcakes

 77

Add 75 g / 3 oz of dried fruit to the cupcake batter, before baking.

78

MAKES 12

Almond and Rose Cupcakes

PREPARATION TIME: 20 MINUTES

COOKING TIME: 20 MINUTES

INGREDIENTS

55 g / 2 oz / ½ cup self-raising flour, sifted
55 g / 2 oz / ½ cup ground almonds
110 g / 4 oz / ½ cup caster (superfine) sugar
110 g / 4 oz / ½ cup butter, softened
2 large eggs
1 tsp rose water
1 tsp almond essence

TO DECORATE

225 g / 8 oz / 2 cups icing (confectioners') sugar
1 – 2 tsp rose water
3 drops pink food colouring
12 Icing roses
Pink silver balls

- Preheat the oven to 190°C (170° fan) / 375 F / gas 5 and line a 12-hole cupcake tin with paper cases.
- Combine the flour, ground almonds, sugar, butter, eggs, rose water and almond essence in a bowl and whisk together for 2 minutes.
- Divide the mixture between the paper cases, then transfer to the oven and bake for 15 – 20 minutes.
- Test with a wooden toothpick, if it comes out clean, the cakes are done.
- Transfer the cakes to a wire rack and leave to cool.
- Sieve the icing sugar into a bowl, then slowly stir in the rose water a few drops until you have a thick icing.
- Spoon the icing onto the cakes and decorate with icing roses and silver balls.

Orange Flower Water Cupcakes 79

These cakes work really well with orange flower water instead of rose water.

80

MAKES 12

Parmesan and Poppy Seed Cupcakes

PREPARATION TIME: 25 MINUTES

COOKING TIME: 25 MINUTES

INGREDIENTS

2 large eggs
120 ml / 4 fl. oz / ½ cup sunflower oil
180 ml / 6 fl. oz / ¾ cup Greek yogurt
110 g / 4 oz / 1 cup Parmesan, grated
225 g / 8 oz / 1 ½ cups plain (all purpose) flour
2 tsp baking powder
½ tsp bicarbonate of (baking) soda
½ tsp salt
2 tbsp poppy seeds

- Preheat the oven to 180°C (160° fan) / 350 F / gas 4 and line a 12-hole muffin tin with paper cases.
- Beat the egg in a jug with the oil, yoghurt and cheese until well mixed.
- Mix the flour, raising agents, salt and poppy seeds in a bowl, then pour in the egg mixture and stir just enough to combine.
- Divide the mixture between the paper cases, then bake in the oven for 20 – 25 minutes.
- Test with a wooden toothpick, if it comes out clean, the cupcakes are done.
- Serve warm.

Mixed Seed Cupcakes 81

Add 2 tbsp of pumpkin seeds and 2 tbsp of sunflower seeds for savoury mixed seed cupcakes.

82

MAKES 36

Chocolate Coffee Bean Mini Cupcakes

White Chocolate Coffee Bean Cupcakes

83

Replace the chocolate coated coffee beans with white chocolate coated coffee beans.

PREPARATION TIME: 20 MINUTES

COOKING TIME: 15 MINUTES

....

INGREDIENTS

110 g / 4 oz / ½ cup self-raising flour, sifted
110 g / 4 oz / ½ cup caster (superfine) sugar
110 g / 4 oz / ½ cup butter, softened
2 large eggs
1 tsp vanilla extract
150 g / 5 oz / 1 cup chocolate coated coffee beans, chopped

TO DECORATE
36 chocolate coated coffee beans

- Preheat the oven to 190°C (170° fan) / 375 F / gas 5 and line a 36-hole mini cupcake tin with paper cases.
- Combine the flour, sugar, butter and eggs in a bowl and whisk together for 2 minutes.
- Fold in the chopped coffee beans then divide the mixture between the cases.
- Transfer the tin to the oven and bake for 15 – 20 minutes.
- Test with a wooden toothpick, if it comes out clean, the cakes are done.
- Transfer the cakes to a wire rack and leave to cool completely before topping each cake with a whole coffee bean.

84

MAKES 18

Chocolate Orange Caramel Cupcakes

Chocolate and Fruit Caramel Cupcakes

85

Add 75 g / 3 oz of raisins to the cupcake batter.

Chocolate and Nut Caramel Cupcakes

86

Add 55 g / 2 oz of flaked almonds to the cupcake batter.

PREPARATION TIME: 40 MINUTE

COOKING TIME: 20 MINUTES

INGREDIENTS

110 g / 4 oz / ½ cup self-raising flour, sifted
28 g / 1 oz / ¼ cup unsweetened cocoa powder, sifted
110 g / 4 oz / ½ cup caster (superfine) sugar
110 g / 4 oz / ½ cup butter, softened
2 large eggs
1 orange, zest finely grated
Icing (confectioners') sugar, to dust

TO DECORATE

85 g / 3 oz / ½ cup butter
85 ml / 3 fl. oz / ⅓ cup double (heavy) cream
85 g / 3 oz / ¼ cup golden syrup
85 g / 3 oz / ½ cup dark brown sugar
2 chocolate flakes

- Preheat the oven to 190°C (170° fan) / 375 F / gas 5 and oil a 12-hole silicone cupcake mould.
- Combine the flour, cocoa, sugar, butter, eggs and orange zest in a bowl and whisk together for 2 minutes.
- Divide the mixture between the moulds, then transfer to the oven and bake for 15 – 20 minutes.
- Test with a wooden toothpick, if it comes out clean, the cakes are done.
- Transfer the cakes to a wire rack and leave to cool completely before dusting with icing sugar.
- Put the butter, cream, golden syrup and brown sugar in a small saucepan and boil for 2 minutes, stirring to dissolve the sugar.
- Leave to cool to room temperature, then spoon over the cupcakes and crumble over the chocolate flakes.

87

MAKES 12

Marmalade Cupcakes

Marmalade and Dark Chocolate Cupcakes

88

Add 110g / 4oz / ½ cup of dark chocolate chunks to the cupcake mixture for a chocolate orange taste.

Lime Marmalade Cupcakes

89

Replace the orange marmalade with lime marmalade for an extra citrus twist.

PREPARATION TIME: 25 MINUTES

COOKING TIME: 25 MINUTES

INGREDIENTS

1 large egg
120 ml / 4 fl. oz / ½ cup sunflower oil
120 ml / 4 fl. oz / ½ cup milk
375 g / 12 ½ oz / 2 ½ cups self-raising flour, sifted
1 tsp baking powder
200 g / 7 oz / ¾ cup caster (superfine) sugar
110 g / 4 oz / ½ cup marmalade

- Preheat the oven to 180°C (160° fan) / 350 F / gas 4 and oil a 12-hole silicone muffin tin.
- Beat the egg in a jug with the oil and milk until well mixed.
- Mix the flour, baking powder and sugar in a bowl, then pour in the egg mixture and stir just enough to combine.
- Divide half the mixture between the paper cases and add a big spoonful of marmalade on top.
- Top with the rest of the muffin mixture then bake in the oven for 20 – 25 minutes.
- Test with a wooden toothpick, if it comes out clean, the cakes are done.
- Transfer the cakes to a wire rack and leave to cool.

90
MAKES 12

Lavender Cupcakes

PREPARATION TIME: 25 MINUTES

COOKING TIME: 20 MINUTES

....

INGREDIENTS

110 g / 4 oz / ½ cup self-raising flour, sifted
110 g / 4 oz / ½ cup caster (superfine) sugar
110 g / 4 oz / ½ cup butter, softened
2 large eggs
5 drops lavender oil

TO DECORATE
225 g / 8 oz / 2 cups icing (confectioners') sugar
boiling water, to mix
purple and white ready to roll fondant icing

- Preheat the oven to 190°C (170° fan) / 375 F / gas 5 and line a 12-hole cupcake tin with paper cases.
- Combine the flour, sugar, butter, eggs and lavender oil in a bowl and whisk together for 2 minutes.
- Divide the mixture between the paper cases, then transfer to the oven and bake for 15 – 20 minutes.
- Transfer the cakes to a wire rack and leave to cool.
- Sieve the icing sugar into a bowl, then slowly stir in the boiling water a few drops at a time until you have a thick icing.
- Spoon the icing onto the cakes and tap the on the work surface to level the icing.
- Roll out the purple icing and cut out tiny petal shapes.
- Assemble the flowers on top of the cakes and make the centres from the white fondant icing.

Lavender and Chocolate Chip Cupcakes   91

Add 100 g / 4 oz of chocolate chips to the cupcake batter.

92
MAKES 12

Cheese and Chive Cupcakes

PREPARATION TIME: 25 MINUTES

COOKING TIME: 25 MINUTES

....

INGREDIENTS

2 large eggs
120 ml / 4 fl. oz / ½ cup sunflower oil
180 ml / 6 fl. oz / ¾ cup Greek yogurt
225 g / 8 oz / 2 cups Morbier cheese, cubed
225 g / 8 oz / 1 ½ cups plain (all purpose) flour
2 tsp baking powder
½ tsp bicarbonate of (baking) soda
½ tsp salt
2 tbsp chives, chopped

- Preheat the oven to 180°C (160° fan) / 350 F / gas 4 and oil 12 silicone muffin moulds.
- Beat the eggs in a jug with the oil, yogurt and half of the cheese until well mixed.
- Mix the flour, raising agents, salt and chives in a bowl, then pour in the egg mixture and stir just enough to combine.
- Divide the mixture between the moulds and top with the rest of the cheese, then bake in the oven for 20 – 25 minutes.
- Test with a wooden toothpick, if it comes out clean, the cupcakes are done.
- Serve warm.

Cheese, Chive and Shallot Cupcakes 93

Add a finely sliced shallot to the cupcake batter before baking.

94

MAKES 12

Sprinkle Cupcakes

- Preheat the oven to 190°C (170° fan) / 375 F / gas 5 and line a 12-hole cupcake tin with paper cases.
- Combine the flour, sugar, butter, eggs and lemon zest in a bowl and whisk together for 2 minutes.
- Divide the mixture between the paper cases, then transfer to the oven and bake for 15 – 20 minutes.
- Test with a wooden toothpick, if it comes out clean, the cakes are done.
- Transfer the cakes to a wire rack and leave to cool.
- Sift the icing sugar into a bowl, then slowly stir in the boiling water a few drops at a time until you have a thick icing.
- Divide the icing into 3 bowls and colour each with a different food colouring.
- Dip the top of 4 cakes in each of the coloured icings, then sprinkle with your choice of toppings.

Buttercream Sprinkle Cupcakes 〔95〕

To add height to your cupcakes, replace the icing with buttercream and apply a thick layer with a palette knife before dipping the tops in the cake sprinkles.

PREPARATION TIME: 45 MINUTES

COOKING TIME: 20 MINUTES

INGREDIENTS

110 g / 4 oz / ½ cup self-raising flour, sifted
110 g / 4 oz / ½ cup caster (superfine) sugar
110 g / 4 oz / ½ cup butter, softened
2 large eggs
1 lemon, zest finely grated

TO DECORATE
225 g / 8 oz / 2 cups icing (confectioners') sugar
boiling water, to mix
blue, pink and green food colouring
coloured sprinkles
heart-shaped cake sprinkles

96

MAKES 12

Orange and Hazelnut Cupcakes

- Preheat the oven to 190°C (170° fan) / 375 F / gas 5.
- Oil 12 small cups and divide the chopped hazelnuts between them.
- Shake to coat the inside of the cups with nuts and tip the excess into a mixing bowl.
- Combine the flour, sugar, butter, eggs and orange zest in the bowl and whisk together for 2 minutes.
- Divide the mixture between the cups and bake for 15 – 20 minutes.
- Test with a wooden toothpick, if it comes out clean, the cakes are done.
- Transfer the cakes to a wire rack to cool completely.
- Whip the cream with the icing sugar until thick.
- Spoon the cream into a piping bag fitted with a large star nozzle and pipe a small swirl on top of each cake.

Orange and Coconut Cupcakes 〔97〕

Replace the hazelnuts with 2 tbsp of desiccated coconut.

PREPARATION TIME: 30 MINUTES

COOKING TIME: 20 MINUTES

INGREDIENTS

75 g / 2 ½ oz / ½ cup hazelnuts, finely chopped
110 g / 4 oz / 1 cup self-raising flour, sifted
110 g / 4 oz / ½ cup caster (superfine) sugar
110 g / 4 oz / ½ cup butter, softened
2 large eggs
1 orange, zest finely grated

TO DECORATE
225 ml / 8 fl. oz / 1 cup double (heavy) cream
2 tbsp icing (confectioners') sugar

98

MAKES 12

Green Cardamom Cupcakes

Fragrant Cardamom Cupcakes

99

Add ½ tsp of orange flower water and ½ tsp rose water to the soaking syrup for extra fragrant cakes.

PREPARATION TIME: I HOUR

COOKING TIME: 20 MINUTES

INGREDIENTS

110 g / 4 oz / ½ cup self-raising flour, sifted
110 g / 4 oz / ½ cup caster (superfine) sugar
110 g / 4 oz / ½ cup butter, softened
2 large eggs
1 tsp ground cardamom

FOR THE SOAKING SYRUP

2 lemons, juiced
2 tbsp caster (superfine) sugar
3 green cardamom pods, crushed

- Preheat the oven to 190°C (170° fan) / 375 F / gas 5 and line a 12-hole cupcake tin with paper cases.
- Combine the flour, sugar, butter, eggs and ground cardamom in a bowl and whisk together for 2 minutes.
- Divide the mixture between the paper cases, then transfer to the oven and bake for 15 – 20 minutes.
- Test with a wooden toothpick, if it comes out clean, the cakes are done.
- While the cakes are cooking, make the soaking syrup. Put the lemon juice, caster sugar and crushed cardamom pods in a small saucepan and boil for 2 minutes, then strain through a sieve to remove the cardamom.
- When the cakes are ready, spoon over the soaking syrup and leave them to cool in their tin.

100
MAKES 12

Lemon and Nigella Seed Cupcakes

- Preheat the oven to 190°C (170° fan) / 375 F / gas 5 and line a 12-hole cupcake tin with paper cases.
- Combine the flour, sugar, butter, eggs and lemon zest in a bowl and whisk together for 2 minutes.
- Divide the mixture between the paper cases, then transfer to the oven and bake for 15 – 20 minutes.
- Test with a wooden toothpick, if it comes out clean, the cakes are done.
- Transfer the cakes to a wire rack and leave to cool.
- To make the icing, sieve the icing sugar into a bowl and stir in the lemon juice a little at a time until you have a thick pouring consistency.
- Stir in the lemon zest and nigella seeds then spoon the icing onto the cakes.

PREPARATION TIME: I HOUR

COOKING TIME: 20 MINUTES

INGREDIENTS

110 g / 4 oz / ½ cup self-raising flour, sifted
110 g / 4 oz / ½ cup caster (superfine) sugar
110 g / 4 oz / ½ cup butter, softened
2 large eggs
1 lemon, zest finely grated

TO DECORATE
225 g / 8 oz / 2 cups icing (confectioners') sugar
4 tsp lemon juice
1 tbsp lemon, zest finely grated
1 tsp nigella seeds

Crunchy Lemon Cupcakes

101

Add 2 tsp nigella seeds to the cake mixture before baking to add an extra crunch to the finished cakes.

102
MAKES 12

Chocolate and Raspberry Cupcakes

- Preheat the oven to 190°C (170° fan) / 375 F / gas 5 and line a 12-hole cupcake tin with paper cases.
- Combine the flour, cocoa, sugar, butter, eggs and raspberry syrup in a bowl and whisk together for 2 minutes.
- Divide the mixture between the paper cases, then transfer to the oven and bake for 15 – 20 minutes.
- Test with a wooden toothpick, if it comes out clean, the cakes are done.
- Transfer the cakes to a wire rack and leave to cool.
- To make the raspberry cream, whisk the cream with the raspberry syrup until thick.
- Spoon the cream into a piping bag fitted with a large star nozzle and pipe a generous swirl on top of each cake.
- Sprinkle with hundreds and thousands.

PREPARATION TIME: 30 MINUTES

COOKING TIME: 20 MINUTES

INGREDIENTS

110 g / 4 oz / ½ cup self-raising flour, sifted
28 g / 1 oz / ¼ cup unsweetened cocoa powder, sifted
110 g / 4 oz / ½ cup caster (superfine) sugar
110 g / 4 oz / ½ cup butter, softened
2 large eggs
2 tbsp raspberry syrup

TO DECORATE
225ml / 8 fl. oz / 1 cup double (heavy) cream
2 tbsp raspberry syrup
hundreds and thousands

Rose and Raspberry Cream Cupcakes

103

Replace the cocoa powder in the cake mixture with 1 tbsp rose water and add 2 tsp of rose water to the raspberry buttercream.

104

MAKES 12

Lemon Meringue Cupcakes

PREPARATION TIME:
I HOUR I5 MINUTES

COOKING TIME: 30 MINUTES

....

INGREDIENTS

110 g / 4 oz / ½ cup self-raising flour, sifted
110 g / 4 oz / ½ cup caster (superfine) sugar
110 g / 4 oz / ½ cup butter, softened
2 large eggs
1 lemon, zest finely grated
2 tsp ground cinnamon

TO DECORATE
225 g / 8 oz / 1 cup lemon curd
4 egg whites
110 g / 4 oz / 1 cup caster (superfine) sugar

- Preheat the oven to 190°C (170° fan) / 375 F / gas 5 and line a 12-hole cupcake tin with paper cases.
- Combine the flour, sugar, butter, eggs, lemon zest and cinnamon in a bowl and whisk together for 2 minutes.
- Divide the mixture between the paper cases, then transfer to the oven and bake for 15 – 20 minutes.
- Use a teaspoon to make a little hollow in the centre of each cake and fill with lemon curd.
- To make the meringue topping, whisk the egg whites until stiff, then gradually whisk in half the sugar until the mixture is very shiny. Fold in the remaining sugar then spoon the mixture into a large piping bag fitted with a plain nozzle.
- Pipe a swirl of meringue on top of each cake and return to the oven for 10 minutes or until the topping is golden brown. Serve warm.

Mini Queen of Puddings 105

Instead of filling the cakes with lemon curd, use raspberry jam (jelly) to make miniature Queen of Puddings.

106

MAKES 12

Mini Roquefort Frittata Cupcakes

PREPARATION TIME: 35 MINUTES

COOKING TIME: I0 MINUTES

....

INGREDIENTS

4 large eggs
110 g / 4 oz / 1 cup Roquefort, cubed
2 tbsp French tarragon, chopped

- Preheat the oven to 180°C (160° fan) / 350 F / gas 4 and oil a 12-hole silicone cupcake mould.
- Beat the eggs in a jug and stir in the cheese and tarragon.
- Season well with salt and black pepper.
- Pour the mixture into the prepared moulds then bake in the oven for 5 – 10 minutes or until set.

Mini Roquefort and Thyme Cupcakes 107

Replace the tarragon with fresh thyme leaves and sprinkle the tops with Parmesan.

108

MAKES 12

Cheese Cupcakes

Blue Cheese Cupcakes **109**

Replace the Cheddar cheese with blue cheese, such as Stilton.

Dutch Cheese Cupcakes **110**

Replace the Cheddar cheese with the same amount of Edam cheese.

Parmesan Cheese Cupcakes **111**

Replace the Cheddar cheese with the same amount of Parmesan cheese.

PREPARATION TIME: 25 MINUTES

COOKING TIME: 25 MINUTES

....

INGREDIENTS

2 large eggs
120 ml / 4 fl. oz / ½ cup sunflower oil
180 ml / 6 fl. oz / ¾ cup Greek yogurt
110 g / 4 oz / 1 cup Cheddar cheese, grated
225 g / 8 oz / 1 ½ cups plain (all purpose) flour
2 tsp baking powder
½ tsp bicarbonate of (baking) soda
½ tsp salt

- Preheat the oven to 180°C (160° fan) / 350 F / gas 4 and oil a 12-hole silicone muffin tin.
- Beat the egg in a jug with the oil, yogurt and cheese until well mixed.
- Mix the flour, raising agents and salt in a bowl, then pour in the egg mixture and stir just enough to combine.
- Divide the mixture between the moulds, then bake in the oven for 20 – 25 minutes.
- Test with a wooden toothpick, if it comes out clean, the cupcakes are done.
- Transfer the cupcakes to a wire rack and leave to cool.

112

MAKES 24

Feta, Olive and Rosemary Cupcakes

Garlic and Onion Cupcakes

113

Add 1 tsp of crushed garlic and 1 sliced onion that have been fried in a little olive oil to the muffin mixture.

Ricotta, Olive and Rosemary Cupcakes

114

Replace the feta cheese with the same amount of ricotta cheese.

Feta, Tomato and Rosemary Cupcakes

115

Replace the olives with 75 g of sun-dried tomatoes.

PREPARATION TIME: 25 MINUTES

COOKING TIME: 15 MINUTES

....

INGREDIENTS

2 large eggs
120 ml / 4 fl. oz / ½ cup sunflower oil
180 ml / 6 fl. oz / ¾ cup Greek yogurt
110 g / 4 oz / 1 cup feta cheese, cubed
225 g / 8 oz / 1 ½ cups plain (all purpose) flour
2 tsp baking powder
½ tsp bicarbonate of (baking) soda
½ tsp salt
75 g / 2 ½ oz / ½ cup black olives, stoned and chopped
2 tbsp fresh rosemary, chopped

- Preheat the oven to 180°C (160° fan) / 350 F / gas 4 and line a 24-hole mini muffin tin with paper cases.
- Beat the egg in a jug with the oil, yoghurt and cheese until well mixed.
- Mix the flour, raising agents, salt, olives and rosemary in a bowl, then pour in the egg mixture and stir just enough to combine.
- Divide the mixture between the paper cases, then bake in the oven for 10 – 15 minutes.
- Test with a wooden toothpick, if it comes out clean, the cupcakes are done.
- Serve warm.

116

MAKES 12

Blue Star Cupcakes

- Preheat the oven to 190°C (170° fan) / 375 F / gas 5 and line a 12-hole cupcake tin with blue paper cases.
- Combine the flour, sugar, butter and eggs in a bowl and whisk together for 2 minutes.
- Divide half of the mixture between the paper cases, then add 1 tsp of blueberry jam in the centre of each.
- Top with the rest of the cake mixture then transfer to the oven and bake for 15 – 20 minutes.
- Transfer the cakes to a wire rack and leave to cool.
- Beat the butter with a wooden spoon until light and fluffy then beat in the icing sugar a quarter at a time.
- Use a whisk to incorporate the rose water and food colouring, then whisk for 2 minutes.
- Spoon the buttercream into a piping bag fitted with a star nozzle and pipe a swirl on top of each cake.
- Sprinkle with star-shaped cake sprinkles.

PREPARATION TIME: 30 MINUTES

COOKING TIME: 20 MINUTES

INGREDIENTS

110 g / 4 oz / ½ cup self-raising flour, sifted
110 g / 4 oz / ½ cup caster (superfine) sugar
110 g / 4 oz / ½ cup butter, softened
2 large eggs
110 g / 4 oz / ½ cup blueberry jam (jelly)

TO DECORATE

110 g / 4 oz / ½ cup butter, softened
225 g / 8 oz / 2 cups icing (confectioners') sugar
2 tbsp milk
blue and white star-shaped cake sprinkles

Red Raspberry Cupcakes

 117

Fill half of the cakes with raspberry jam instead of blueberry and top the cakes with fresh raspberries.

118

MAKES 12

Banana and Blueberry Cupcakes

- Preheat the oven to 200°C (180° fan) / 400 F / gas 6 and line a 12-hole cupcake tin with paper cases.
- Mash the bananas with a fork then whisk in the sugar, eggs and oil.
- Sieve the flour and bicarbonate of soda into the bowl and add the blueberries and stir just enough to evenly mix all the ingredients together.
- Divide the mixture between the paper cases, then transfer to the oven and bake for 15 – 20 minutes.
- Test with a wooden toothpick, if it comes out clean, the cakes are done.
- Transfer the cakes to a wire rack and leave to cool.

PREPARATION TIME: 25 MINUTES

COOKING TIME: 25 MINUTES

INGREDIENTS

3 very ripe bananas
110 g / 4 oz / ⅔ cup soft light brown sugar
2 large eggs
120 ml / 4 fl. oz / ½ cup sunflower oil
225 g / 8 oz / 1 ½ cups plain (all purpose) flour
1 tsp bicarbonate of (baking) soda
150 g / 5 oz / 1 cup blueberries

Wholemeal Banana Cupcakes

 119

Replace the plain flour with wholemeal flour and double the quantity of bicarbonate of soda.

120

MAKES 12

Pink Confetti Cupcakes

PREPARATION TIME: 40 MINUTES

COOKING TIME: 20 MINUTES

INGREDIENTS

110 g / 4 oz / ½ cup self-raising flour, sifted
110 g / 4 oz / ½ cup caster (superfine) sugar
110 g / 4 oz / ½ cup butter, softened
2 large eggs
1 tsp vanilla extract

TO DECORATE

110 g / 4 oz / ½ cup butter, softened
225 g / 8 oz / 2 cups icing (confectioners') sugar
2 tbsp milk
pink food colouring
pink, red and white heart-shaped cake sprinkles

- Preheat the oven to 190°C (170° fan) / 375 F / gas 5 and line a 12-hole cupcake tin with paper cases.
- Combine the flour, sugar, butter, eggs and vanilla extract in a bowl and whisk together for 2 minutes.
- Divide the mixture between the paper cases then transfer to the oven and bake for 15 – 20 minutes.
- Transfer the cakes to a wire rack and leave to cool.
- To make the buttercream, beat the butter with a wooden spoon until light and fluffy then beat in the icing sugar a quarter at a time.
- Use a whisk to incorporate the milk and food colouring, then whisk for 2 minutes.
- Spoon the icing into a piping bag fitted with a large star nozzle and pipe a big swirl of icing on top of each cake.
- Scatter over the heart-shaped cake sprinkles to finish.

Purple Confetti Cupcakes

121

Replace the pink food colouring with purple food colouring and use purple, blue and white cake sprinkles to finish.

122

MAKES 12

Flower Cupcakes

PREPARATION TIME: 30 MINUTES

COOKING TIME: 20 MINUTES

INGREDIENTS

110 g / 4 oz / ½ cup self-raising flour, sifted
110 g / 4 oz / ½ cup caster (superfine) sugar
110 g / 4 oz / ½ cup butter, softened
2 large eggs
1 tsp vanilla extract

TO DECORATE

450 g / 1 lb / 2 cups ready-to-roll fondant icing
icing (confectioners') sugar

- Preheat the oven to 190°C (170° fan) / 375 F / gas 5 and line a 12-hole cupcake tin with paper cases.
- Combine the flour, sugar, butter, eggs and vanilla extract in a bowl and whisk together for 2 minutes.
- Divide the mixture between the paper cases, then transfer to the oven and bake for 15 – 20 minutes.
- Transfer the cakes to a wire rack and leave to cool completely, then remove the cases.
- Knead the fondant icing until pliable. Dust a work surface with icing sugar and roll out the fondant icing.
- Use a small flower-shaped cutter to cut out flowers for half of the cakes.
- Use a round scallop-edged cutter to cut tops for the other half of the cakes and press a pattern into the top using a sugar craft mould. Alternatively you can score in your own design with the end of a knitting needle.
- Transfer the flowers carefully to the top of the cakes.

Petal Cupcakes

123

Cut large individual petals out of fondant icing and attach them to the top of the cakes with a little buttercream for a 3D effect.

124

MAKES 12

Almond Cupcakes

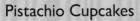

Hazelnut Cupcakes

 125

These cakes work really well with ground hazelnuts instead of almonds and a whole hazelnut pressed into the top.

Pistachio Cupcakes

126

Replace the ground almonds with pistachios and press a whole pistachio nut on top.

Walnut Cupcakes

 127

Replace the ground almonds with walnuts and press a whole walnut on top.

PREPARATION TIME: 20 MINUTES

COOKING TIME: 20 MINUTES

INGREDIENTS

55 g / 2 oz / ½ cup self-raising flour, sifted
2 tsp baking powder
55 g / 2 oz / ½ cup ground almonds
110 g / 4 oz / ½ cup caster (superfine) sugar
110 g / 4 oz / ½ cup butter, softened
2 large eggs
1 tsp almond essence
12 blanched almonds

- Preheat the oven to 190°C (170° fan) / 375 F / gas 5 and line a 12-hole cupcake tin with paper cases.
- Combine the flour, baking powder, ground almonds, sugar, butter, eggs and almond essence in a bowl and whisk together for 2 minutes.
- Divide the mixture between the paper cases and press a blanched almond into the top of each, then transfer to the oven and bake for 15 – 20 minutes.
- Test with a wooden toothpick, if it comes out clean, the cakes are done.
- Transfer the cakes to a wire rack and leave to cool.

Chocolate Star Cupcakes

Chocolate Caramel Cupcakes

129

Replace the chocolate stars with 110g / 4 oz / ½ cup chocolate caramel sweets.

Chocolate Star Coconut Cupcakes

130

Add 3 tbsp of desiccated coconut to the cupcake batter, before baking.

Chocolate Star and Fruit Cupcakes

131

Add 75 g / 3 oz of dried fruit to the cupcake batter, before baking.

PREPARATION TIME: 25 MINUTES

COOKING TIME: 25 MINUTES

INGREDIENTS

1 large egg
120 ml / 4 fl. oz / ½ cup sunflower oil
120 ml / 4 fl. oz / ½ cup milk
375 g / 12 ½ oz / 2 ½ cups self-raising flour, sifted
1 tsp baking powder
200 g / 7 oz / ¾ cup caster (superfine) sugar
110 g / 4 oz milk chocolate stars

- Preheat the oven to 180°C (160° fan) / 350 F / gas 4 and line a 12-hole muffin tin with paper cases.
- Beat the egg in a jug with the oil and milk until well mixed.
- Mix the flour, baking powder, sugar and ¾ of the chocolate stars in a bowl, then pour in the egg mixture and stir just enough to combine.
- Divide the mixture between the paper cases and stud the tops with the rest of the chocolate stars, then bake in the oven for 20 – 25 minutes.
- Test with a wooden toothpick, if it comes out clean, the cakes are done.
- Transfer the cakes to a wire rack and leave to cool.

132

MAKES 12

Wholemeal Chocolate Cupcakes

- Preheat the oven to 180°C (160° fan) / 350 F / gas 4 and line a 12-hole muffin tin with paper cases.
- Beat the egg in a jug with the oil and oat milk until well mixed.
- Mix the flour, cocoa, baking powder, sugar and chocolate in a bowl, then pour in the egg mixture and stir just enough to combine.
- Divide the mixture between the paper cases, then bake in the oven for 20 – 25 minutes.
- Test with a wooden toothpick, if it comes out clean, the cakes are done.
- Transfer the cakes to a wire rack and leave to cool.

PREPARATION TIME: 25 MINUTES

COOKING TIME: 25 MINUTES

INGREDIENTS

1 large egg
120 ml / 4 fl. oz / ½ cup sunflower oil
120 ml / 4 fl. oz / ½ cup oat milk
375 g / 12 ½ oz / 2 ½ cups wholemeal flour, sifted
55 g / 2 oz / ½ cup unsweetened cocoa powder, sifted
2 tsp baking powder
200 g / 7 oz / ¾ cup caster (superfine) sugar
110 g / 4 oz / ½ cup dark chocolate, chopped

Apple and Chocolate Cupcakes

133

Add 1 grated apple to the mixture to make them extra moist.

134

MAKES 12

Chocolate Chip Cupcakes

- Preheat the oven to 190°C (170° fan) / 375 F / gas 5 and oil a 12-hole silicone cupcake mould.
- Combine the flour, sugar, butter and eggs in a bowl and whisk together for 2 minutes.
- Fold in ¾ of the chocolate chips then divide the mixture between the paper cases.
- Sprinkle the rest of the chocolate chips on top then transfer to the oven and bake for 15 – 20 minutes.
- Test with a wooden toothpick, if it comes out clean, the cakes are done.
- Transfer the cakes to a wire rack and leave to cool.

PREPARATION TIME: 20 MINUTES

COOKING TIME: 20 MINUTES

INGREDIENTS

110 g / 4 oz / ½ cup self-raising flour, sifted
110 g / 4 oz / ½ cup caster (superfine) sugar
110 g / 4 oz / ½ cup butter, softened
2 large eggs
1 tsp vanilla extract
150 g / 5 oz / 1 cup chocolate chips

White and Dark Chocolate Cupcakes

135

Try using a mixture of white and dark chocolate chips.

136

MAKES 12

Strawberry Cupcakes

PREPARATION TIME: 25 MINUTES

COOKING TIME: 25 MINUTES

INGREDIENTS

1 large egg
120 ml / 4 fl. oz / ½ cup sunflower oil
120 ml / 4 fl. oz / ½ cup milk
225 g / 7 ½ oz / 1 ½ cups self-raising flour, sifted
1 tsp baking powder
200 g / 7 oz / ¾ cup caster (superfine) sugar
150 g / 5 oz / 1 cup strawberries, chopped

- Preheat the oven to 180°C (160° fan) / 350 F / gas 4 and line a 12-hole muffin tin with paper cases.
- Beat the egg in a jug with the oil and milk until well mixed.
- Mix the flour, baking powder, sugar and chopped strawberries in a bowl, then pour in the egg mixture and stir just enough to combine.
- Divide the mixture between the paper cases and bake in the oven for 20 – 25 minutes.
- Test with a wooden toothpick, if it comes out clean, the cakes are done.
- Transfer the cakes to a wire rack and leave to cool.

Strawberry and Orange Cupcakes

137

Try adding the grated zest of 1 orange to the muffin mixture.

138

MAKES 12

Honey and Calendula Cupcakes

PREPARATION TIME: 25 MINUTES

COOKING TIME: 20 MINUTES

INGREDIENTS

110 g / 4 oz / ½ cup self-raising flour, sifted
55 g / 2 oz / ¼ cup caster (superfine) sugar
110 g / 4 oz / ½ cup honey
110 g / 4 oz / ½ cup butter, softened
2 large eggs
1 tbsp dried calendula petals

TO DECORATE

1 tbsp cater (superfine) sugar
1 tbsp dried calendula petals

- Preheat the oven to 190°C (170° fan) / 375 F / gas 5 and oil a 12-hole silicone flower cupcake mould.
- Combine the flour, sugar, honey, butter, eggs and calendula petals in a bowl and whisk together for 2 minutes.
- Divide the mixture between the moulds, then transfer to the oven and bake for 15 – 20 minutes.
- Test with a wooden toothpick, if it comes out clean, the cakes are done.
- Transfer the cakes to a wire rack to cool, then turn out to reveal the flower impressions.
- Sprinkle the cakes with a little caster sugar and scatter with dried calendula petals.

Honey and Lavender Cupcakes

139

These cakes work really well with dried lavender flowers too, but reduce the quantity to 2 tsp in the cake mixture.

140

MAKES 12

Orange and Cinnamon Cupcakes

- Preheat the oven to 190°C (170° fan) / 375 F / gas 5 and line a 12-hole cupcake tin with paper cases.
- Combine the flour, sugar, butter, eggs, orange zest and cinnamon in a bowl and whisk together for 2 minutes, then fold in ¾ of the chocolate chips.
- Divide the mixture between the paper cases and sprinkle the rest of the chocolate chips on top, then transfer to the oven and bake for 15 – 20 minutes.
- Test with a wooden toothpick, if it comes out clean, the cakes are done.
- Transfer the cakes to a wire rack and leave to cool.
- To make the glaze, combine the ingredients in a small saucepan and boil for 2 minutes or until syrupy.
- Remove the cinnamon stick and leave to cool then spoon on top of the cakes.

PREPARATION TIME: 20 MINUTES

COOKING TIME: 20 MINUTES

INGREDIENTS

110 g / 4 oz / 1 cup self-raising flour, sifted
110 g / 4 oz / ½ cup caster (superfine) sugar
110 g / 4 oz / ½ cup butter, softened
2 large eggs
1 orange, zest finely grated
2 tsp ground cinnamon
150 g / 5 oz / 1 cup chocolate chips

FOR THE GLAZE
½ orange, juiced
60 ml / 2 fl. oz / ¼ cup honey
1 cinnamon stick

Orange, Cinnamon and Fruit Cupcakes

141

Replace the chocolate chips with 110g / 4 oz / ½ cup raisins that have been soaked in the juice of 1 orange for 1 hour.

142

MAKES 12

Coconut and Orange Cupcakes

- Preheat the oven to 190°C (170° fan) / 375 F / gas 5 and line a 12-hole cupcake tin with paper cases.
- Pour the orange juice over the coconut and leave to soak for 10 minutes.
- Combine the flour, sugar, butter, eggs and coconut mixture in a bowl and whisk together for 2 minutes.
- Divide the mixture between the paper cases, then transfer to the oven and bake for 15 – 20 minutes.
- Transfer the cakes to a wire rack and leave to cool.
- To make the topping, whisk the cream with the icing sugar until it forms soft peaks.
- Spoon the whipped cream into a piping bag fitted with a large star nozzle and pipe a swirl on top of each cake.
- Sprinkle each cake with shredded coconut and orange zest.

PREPARATION TIME: 30 MINUTES

COOKING TIME: 20 MINUTES

INGREDIENTS

1 orange, juiced
28 g / 1 oz / ⅛ cup desiccated coconut
110 g / 4 oz / ½ cup self-raising flour, sifted
110 g / 4 oz / ½ cup caster (superfine) sugar
110 g / 4 oz / ½ cup butter, softened
2 large eggs

TO DECORATE
225 ml / 8 fl. oz / 1 cup double (heavy) cream
2 tbsp icing (confectioners') sugar
2 tbsp sweetened shredded coconut
1 orange, zest finely pared

Coconut and Lemon Cupcakes

143

Replace the orange juice with lemon juice and decorate the cakes with finely pared lemon and lime zest for a bright combination.

144

MAKES 12

St. Clements Cupcakes

PREPARATION TIME: 1 HOUR

COOKING TIME: 20 MINUTES

·······························

INGREDIENTS

110 g / 4 oz / ½ cup self-raising flour, sifted
110 g / 4 oz / ½ cup caster (superfine) sugar
110 g / 4 oz / ½ cup butter, softened
2 large eggs
1 orange, zest finely grated
1 lemon, zest finely grated

TO DECORATE

110 g / 4 oz / ½ cup butter, softened
225 g / 8 oz / 2 cups icing (confectioners') sugar
2 tbsp lemon juice
110 g / 4 oz / ½ cup marmalade

- Preheat the oven to 190°C (170° fan) / 375 F / gas 5 and line a 12-hole cupcake tin with paper cases.
- Combine the flour, sugar, butter, eggs, orange and lemon zest in a bowl and whisk together for 2 minutes.
- Divide the mixture between the paper cases, then transfer to the oven and bake for 15 – 20 minutes.
- Transfer the cakes to a wire rack and leave to cool.
- To make the buttercream, beat the butter with a wooden spoon until light and fluffy then beat in the icing sugar a quarter at a time.
- Use a whisk to incorporate the lemon juice, then whisk for 2 minutes.
- Use a palate knife to spread each cake generously with the icing.
- Top each cake with a spoonful of marmalade.

Grapefruit Cupcakes

145

Replace the orange and lemon zest with the finely grated zest of a grapefruit and replace the lemon juice in the icing with grapefruit juice. Top the cakes with grapefruit marmalade.

146

MAKES 12

Chocolate Flower Cupcakes

PREPARATION TIME: 30 MINUTES

COOKING TIME: 20 MINUTES

·······························

INGREDIENTS

110 g / 4 oz / ½ cup self-raising flour, sifted
28 g / 1 oz / ¼ cup unsweetened cocoa powder, sifted
110 g / 4 oz / ½ cup caster (superfine) sugar
110 g / 4 oz / ½ cup butter, softened
2 large eggs
1 tsp vanilla extract

TO DECORATE

225 ml / 8 fl. oz / 1 cup double (heavy) cream
225 g / 8 oz / 1 cup dark chocolate, minimum 60% cocoa solids, chopped
pink ready to roll fondant icing
12 silver balls
edible glitter

- Preheat the oven to 190°C (170° fan) / 375 F / gas 5 and line a 12-hole cupcake tin with paper cases.
- Combine the flour, cocoa, sugar, butter, eggs and vanilla extract in a bowl and whisk for 2 minutes.
- Divide the mixture between the paper cases then transfer to the oven and bake for 15 – 20 minutes.
- Transfer the cakes to a wire rack and leave to cool.
- Heat the cream until it starts to simmer, then pour it over the chopped chocolate.
- Stir the ganache until the mixture has cooled and thickened, then refrigerate until thick enough to pipe.
- Spoon the ganache into a piping bag fitted with a large star nozzle and pipe a spiral on top of each cake.
- Roll out the fondant icing and cut out 12 flower shapes.
- Top each cake with a fondant flower and fix a silver ball in the middle of each one with a dab of water.
- Sprinkle with edible glitter.

White Chocolate Flower Cupcakes

147

Replace the dark chocolate in the ganache with chopped white chocolate.

148

MAKES 12

White Chocolate Cupcakes

Double White Chocolate Cupcakes

149

Stir 110 g of melted white chocolate through the muffin mixture before baking. Top the cakes with whipped cream and white chocolate curls.

Dark Chocolate Cupcakes

150

Stir 110 g of melted dark chocolate through the cupcake mixture before baking. Top the cakes with whipped cream and dark chocolate curls.

PREPARATION TIME: 25 MINUTES

COOKING TIME:
20 – 25 MINUTES

INGREDIENTS

1 large egg
120 ml / 4 fl. oz / ½ cup sunflower oil
120 ml / 4 fl. oz / ½ cup milk
375 g / 12 ½ oz / 2 ½ cups self-raising flour, sifted
1 tsp baking powder
200 g / 7 oz / ¾ cup caster (superfine) sugar
110 g / 4 oz white chocolate, chopped

TO DECORATE

110 g / 4 oz white chocolate, chopped
mixed sweets

- Preheat the oven to 180°°C (160° fan) / 350 F / gas 4 and oil 12 silicone muffin moulds.
- Beat the egg in a jug with the oil and milk until well mixed.
- Mix the flour, baking powder, sugar and chocolate in a bowl, then pour in the egg mixture and stir just enough to combine.
- Divide the mixture between the moulds, then bake in the oven for 20 – 25 minutes.
- Test with a wooden toothpick, if it comes out clean, the cakes are done.
- Transfer the cakes to a wire rack and leave to cool.
- Melt the chocolate in a microwave or bain marie and spoon on top of the cakes.
- Top with a selection of multicoloured sweets.

Chocolate and Pistachio Cupcakes

PREPARATION TIME: 30 MINUTES

COOKING TIME: 20 MINUTES

INGREDIENTS

55 g / 2 oz / ½ cup self-raising flour
55 g / 2 oz / ½ cup ground pistachios
28 g / 1 oz / ¼ cup cocoa powder
110 g / 4 oz / ½ cup caster sugar
110 g / 4 oz / ½ cup butter, softened
2 large eggs
75 g / 2 ½ oz / ½ cup pistachio nuts, chopped
110 g / 4 oz / ½ cup dark chocolate, chopped

TO DECORATE

110 g / 4 oz / ½ cup butter, softened
225 g / 8 oz / 2 cups icing sugar
2 tbsp milk
1 tsp almond essence
2 tbsp ground pistachios
75 g / 2 ½ oz / ½ cup pistachio nuts, finely chopped

- Preheat the oven to 190°C (170° fan) / 375 F / gas 5 and line a 12-hole cupcake tin with paper cases.
- Combine the flour, ground pistachios, cocoa, sugar, butter and eggs in a bowl and whisk together for 2 minutes.
- Fold in the chopped pistachios and chocolate and divide the mixture between the paper cases. Transfer the tin to the oven and bake for 15 – 20 minutes.
- Transfer the cakes to a wire rack and leave to cool.
- To make the topping, beat the butter with a wooden spoon until light and fluffy then beat in the icing sugar a quarter at a time.
- Use a whisk to incorporate the milk, almond essence and ground pistachios then whisk for 2 minutes.
- Spread each cake with the buttercream and sprinkle liberally with the chopped pistachios.
- Top with woodland animal figurines.

Pistachio Cupcakes with Pistachio Ice Cream

152

Serve these cakes warm from the oven, un-iced, with a scoop of pistachio ice cream.

Chocolate and Peppermint Cupcakes

PREPARATION TIME: 45 MINUTES

COOKING TIME: 20 MINUTES

INGREDIENTS

110 g / 4 oz / ½ cup self-raising flour, sifted
28 g / 1 oz / ¼ cup unsweetened cocoa powder, sifted
110 g / 4 oz / ½ cup caster (superfine) sugar
110 g / 4 oz / ½ cup butter, softened
2 large eggs
5 drops peppermint essence

TO DECORATE

55 g / 2 oz / ¼ cup butter, softened
110 g / 4 oz / 1 cup icing (confectioners') sugar
1 tbsp milk
5 drops peppermint essence
7 drops blue food colouring
blue edible glitter

- Preheat the oven to 190°C (170° fan) / 375 F / gas 5 and line a 12-hole cupcake tin with paper cases.
- Combine the flour, cocoa, sugar, butter, eggs and peppermint essence in a bowl and whisk for 2 minutes.
- Divide the mixture between the paper cases, then transfer to the oven and bake for 15 – 20 minutes.
- Transfer the cakes to a wire rack and leave to cool.
- To make the peppermint buttercream, beat the butter with a wooden spoon until light and fluffy then beat in the icing sugar a quarter at a time.
- Use a whisk to incorporate the milk, peppermint essence and food colouring, then whisk for 2 minutes.
- Use a palette knife to apply the icing, then sprinkle with edible glitter.

Coconut and Peppermint Cupcakes

154

Instead of the glitter, top the cakes with desiccated coconut.

Chocolate and Coconut Cupcakes

155
MAKES 12

- Preheat the oven to 190°C (170° fan) / 375 F / gas 5 and line a 12-hole cupcake tin with paper cases.
- Combine the flour, cocoa, sugar, butter, eggs and coconut in a bowl and whisk together for 2 minutes.
- Divide the mixture between the paper cases, then transfer to the oven and bake for 15 – 20 minutes.
- Test with a wooden toothpick, if it comes out clean, the cakes are done.
- Transfer the cakes to a wire rack and leave to cool.
- Beat the butter with a wooden spoon until light and fluffy then beat in the icing sugar a quarter at a time.
- Use a whisk to incorporate the coconut cream, then whisk for 2 minutes.
- Pile the buttercream on top of the cakes with a spoon and sprinkle with desiccated coconut.

PREPARATION TIME: 1 HOUR

COOKING TIME: 30 MINUTES

INGREDIENTS

110 g / 4 oz / ½ cup self-raising flour
28 g / 1 oz / ¼ cup cocoa powder
110 g / 4 oz / ½ cup caster sugar
110 g / 4 oz / ½ cup butter, softened
2 large eggs
28 g / 1 oz / ⅛ cup desiccated coconut

TO DECORATE

110 g / 4 oz / ½ cup butter, softened
225 g / 8 oz / 2 cups icing sugar
2 – 4 tbsp coconut cream
28 g / 1 oz / ⅛ cup desiccated coconut

Milk Chocolate Cupcakes

156
MAKES 12

PREPARATION TIME: 15 MINUTES

COOKING TIME: 20 MINUTES

INGREDIENTS

110 g / 4 oz / ½ cup self-raising flour, sifted
28 g / 1 oz / ¼ cup unsweetened cocoa powder, sifted
110 g / 4 oz / ½ cup caster (superfine) sugar
110 g / 4 oz / ½ cup butter, softened
110 g / 4 oz milk chocolate, chopped
2 large eggs

TO DECORATE

225 g / 8 oz / 1 cup milk chocolate
225 ml / 8 fl. oz / 1 cup double (heavy) cream

- Preheat the oven to 190°C (170° fan) / 375 F / gas 5 and line a 12-hole cupcake tin with paper cases.
- Combine the flour, cocoa, sugar, butter and eggs in a bowl and whisk together for 2 minutes.
- Fold in the chopped chocolate and divide the mixture between the paper cases.
- Transfer the tin to the oven and bake for 15 – 20 minutes.
- Test with a wooden toothpick, if it comes out clean, the cakes are done.
- Transfer the cakes to a wire rack and leave to cool.
- To make the milk chocolate ganache, chop the chocolate and transfer to a mixing bowl.
- Heat the cream until it starts to simmer, then pour over the chopped chocolate and stir until the mixture has cooled and thickened.
- Pile the ganache on top of the cakes with a spoon.

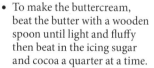

Valentine Cupcakes

157
MAKES 12

PREPARATION TIME: 1 HOUR

COOKING TIME: 20 MINUTES

INGREDIENTS

110 g / 4 oz / ½ cup self-raising flour
28 g / 1 oz / ¼ cup cocoa powde,
110 g / 4 oz / ½ cup caster sugar
110 g / 4 oz / ½ cup butter, softened
2 large eggs

TO DECORATE

110 g / 4 oz / ½ cup butter, softened
225 g / 8 oz / 2 cups icing (confectioners') sugar
28 g / 1 oz / ¼ cup unsweetened cocoa powder, sifted
2 tbsp milk
12 fruit jelly hearts

- Preheat the oven to 190°C (170° fan) / 375 F / gas 5 and line a 12-hole cupcake tin with paper cases.
- Combine the flour, cocoa, sugar, butter and eggs in a bowl and whisk together for 2 minutes.
- Divide the mixture between the paper cases, then transfer to the oven and bake for 15 – 20 minutes.
- Transfer the cakes to a wire rack and leave to cool.
- To make the buttercream, beat the butter with a wooden spoon until light and fluffy then beat in the icing sugar and cocoa a quarter at a time.
- Use a whisk to incorporate the milk, then whisk for 2 minutes.
- Spoon the buttercream into a piping bag fitted with a large plain nozzle and pipe a generous swirl on top of each cake.
- Top with a fruit jelly heart.

158

MAKES 12

Butterfly Cupcakes

Lemon Butterfly Cupcakes

159

Add the finely grated zest of 1 lemon to the cake mixture and replace the strawberry jam with lemon curd.

Blackberry Butterfly Cupcakes

160

Replace the strawberry jam with blackberry jam.

Strawberry and Lime Butterfly Cupcakes

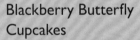
161

Replace the milk in the buttercream with lime juice.

PREPARATION TIME: 40 MINUTES

COOKING TIME: 20 MINUTES

INGREDIENTS

110 g / 4 oz / ½ cup self-raising flour, sifted
110 g / 4 oz / ½ cup caster (superfine) sugar
110 g / 4 oz / ½ cup butter, softened
2 large eggs
1 tsp vanilla extract

TO DECORATE

110 g / 4 oz / ½ cup butter, softened
225 g / 8 oz / 2 cups icing (confectioners') sugar
2 tbsp milk
1 tsp vanilla extract
110 g / 4 oz / ½ cup strawberry jam (jelly)

- Preheat the oven to 190°C (170° fan) / 375 F / gas 5 and line a 12-hole cupcake tin with paper cases.
- Combine the flour, sugar, butter, eggs and vanilla extract in a bowl and whisk together for 2 minutes.
- Divide the mixture between the cake cases then transfer to the oven and bake for 15 – 20 minutes.
- Test with a wooden toothpick, if it comes out clean, the cakes are done.
- Transfer the cakes to a wire rack and leave to cool.
- To make the buttercream, beat the butter with a wooden spoon until light and fluffy then beat in the icing sugar a quarter at a time.
- Use a whisk to incorporate the milk and vanilla extract, then whisk for 2 minutes.
- Spoon the icing into a piping bag fitted with a large star nozzle.
- Using a sharp knife, cut a shallow cone out of the centre of each cake and reserve.
- Pipe a swirl of buttercream into the centre of each cake.
- Take the reserved cake pieces and cut each one in half to make the butterfly wings.
- Press the wings into the icing then spoon on a line of jam to form the bodies.

162

MAKES 12

Chocolate, Pistachio and Cherry Cupcakes

- Preheat the oven to 190°C (170° fan) / 375 F / gas 5 and line a 12-hole cupcake tin with paper cases.
- Combine the flour, ground pistachios, sugar, butter and eggs in a bowl and whisk together for 2 minutes.
- Fold in the chopped chocolate, pistachios and cherries and divide the mixture between the paper cases.
- Transfer the tin to the oven and bake for 15 – 20 minutes.
- Transfer the cakes to a wire rack and leave to cool.
- To make the topping, beat the butter with a wooden spoon until light and fluffy then beat in the icing sugar a quarter at a time.
- Add the milk and whisk for 2 minutes.
- Spread each cake with the buttercream and sprinkle liberally with chopped pistachios and chocolate curls.
- Top each cake with a cocktail cherry.

Fresh Cherry Cupcakes

163

Replace the cocktail cherries in the mixture with fresh cherries and top the cakes with a fresh cherry with the stalk attached.

PREPARATION TIME: 30 MINUTES

COOKING TIME: 20 MINUTES

....

INGREDIENTS

55 g / 2 oz / ½ cup self-raising flour
55 g / 2 oz / ½ cup ground pistachios
110 g / 4 oz / ½ cup caster sugar
110 g / 4 oz / ½ cup butter, softened
2 large eggs
110 g / 4 oz white chocolate, chopped
75 g / 2 ½ oz / ½ cup pistachio nuts, chopped
75 g / 2 ½ oz / ½ cup cocktail cherries, drained and quartered

TO DECORATE

110 g / 4 oz / ½ cup butter, softened
225 g / 8 oz / 2 cups icing (confectioners') sugar
2 tbsp milk
75 g / 2 ½ oz / ½ cup pistachio nuts, finely chopped
white chocolate curls
12 cocktail cherries

164

MAKES 24

Bacon and Prune Mini Cupcakes

- Preheat the oven to 180⁰°C (160⁰ fan) / 350 F / gas 4 and line a 24-hole muffin tin with paper cases.
- Fry the bacon in the olive oil until crisp.
- Beat the egg in a jug with the oil, yoghurt, cheese and crispy bacon until well mixed.
- Mix the flour, raising agents and salt in a bowl, then pour in the egg mixture and stir just enough to combine.
- Divide the mixture between the paper cases and top each one with half a prune, then bake in the oven for 10 – 15 minutes.
- Test with a wooden toothpick, if it comes out clean, the cupcakes are done.
- Serve warm.

Bacon and Fig Mini Cupcakes

165

Replace the prune halves with quarters of fresh fig.

PREPARATION TIME: 25 MINUTES

**COOKING TIME:
10 – 15 MINUTES**

....

INGREDIENTS

2 rashers of bacon, chopped
1 tbsp olive oil
2 large eggs
120 ml / 4 fl. oz / ½ cup sunflower oil
180 ml / 6 fl. oz / ¾ cup Greek yoghurt
110 g / 4 oz / 1 cup parmesan, grated
225 g / 8 oz / 1 ½ cups plain flour
2 tsp baking powder
½ tsp bicarbonate of (baking) soda
½ tsp salt
12 prunes, halved and stoned

166

MAKES 12

Matcha Mini Loaf Cakes

PREPARATION TIME: 25 MINUTES

COOKING TIME: 25 MINUTES

INGREDIENTS

1 large egg
120 ml / 4 fl. oz / ½ cup sunflower oil
120 ml / 4 fl. oz / ½ cup milk
375 g / 12 ½ oz / 2 ½ cups wholemeal flour
2 tsp baking powder
200 g / 7 oz / ¾ cup caster (superfine) sugar
1 tbsp matcha green tea powder

- Preheat the oven to 180°C (160° fan) / 350 F / gas 4 and oil a 12-hole silicone mini loaf cake mould.
- Beat the egg in a jug with the oil and milk until well mixed.
- Mix the flour, baking powder, sugar and matcha in a bowl, then pour in the egg mixture and stir just enough to combine.
- Divide the mixture between the paper cases, then bake in the oven for 20 – 25 minutes.
- Test with a wooden toothpick, if it comes out clean, the cakes are done.
- Transfer the cakes to a wire rack and leave to cool.

Rose Petal Tea Flavour Loaf Cake

167

Substitute the matcha powder for 1 tbsp dried rose petals.

168

MAKES 12

Pink Iced Strawberry Cupcakes

PREPARATION TIME: 25 MINUTES

COOKING TIME: 25 MINUTES

INGREDIENTS

1 large egg
120 ml / 4 fl. oz / ½ cup sunflower oil
120 ml / 4 fl. oz / ½ cup milk
225 g / 7 ½ oz / 1 ½ cups self-raising flour, sifted
1 tsp baking powder
200 g / 7 oz / ¾ cup caster (superfine) sugar
150 g / 5 oz / 1 cup strawberries, chopped

TO DECORATE

110 g / 4 oz / ½ cup butter, softened
225 g / 8 oz / 2 cups icing (confectioners') sugar
2 tbsp strawberry syrup
2 tbsp hundreds and thousands
2 tbsp heart-shaped cake sprinkles

- Preheat the oven to 180°C (160° fan) / 350 F / gas 4 and line a 12-hole muffin tin with paper cases.
- Beat the egg in a jug with the oil and milk until well mixed.
- Mix the flour, baking powder, sugar and chopped strawberries in a bowl, then pour in the egg mixture and stir just enough to combine.
- Divide the mixture between the paper cases and bake in the oven for 20 – 25 minutes.
- Transfer the cakes to a wire rack and leave to cool.
- Beat the butter with a wooden spoon until light and fluffy then beat in the icing sugar a quarter at a time.
- Use a whisk to incorporate the strawberry syrup, then whisk for 2 minutes. Use a palette knife to cover the top of the cupcakes in icing.
- Mix the hundreds and thousands and cake sprinkles in a bowl and dip the top of the cupcakes in to coat.

Purple Iced Blueberry Cupcakes

169

Replace the strawberries with blueberries and replace the strawberry syrup in the buttercream with blueberry syrup.

170

MAKES 36

Chocolate Iced Mini Cupcakes

- Preheat the oven to 190°C (170° fan) / 375 F / gas 5 and line a 36 hole mini cupcake tin with paper cases.
- Combine the flour, cocoa, sugar, butter and eggs in a bowl and whisk together for 2 minutes.
- Divide the mixture between the paper cases, then transfer to the oven and bake for 10 – 15 minutes.
- Transfer the cakes to a wire rack and leave to cool.
- Beat the butter with a wooden spoon until light and fluffy then beat in the icing sugar and cocoa a quarter at a time.
- Use a whisk to incorporate the milk, then whisk for 2 minutes.
- Use a palette knife to apply the icing then sprinkle the cakes with sugar strands.

PREPARATION TIME: 1 HOUR

COOKING TIME: 15 MINUTES

....

INGREDIENTS

110 g / 4 oz / ½ cup self-raising flour, sifted
28 g / 1 oz / ¼ cup unsweetened cocoa powder, sifted
110 g / 4 oz / ½ cup caster (superfine) sugar
110 g / 4 oz / ½ cup butter, softened
2 large eggs

TO DECORATE

110 g / 4 oz / ½ cup butter, softened
225 g / 8 oz / 2 cups icing (confectioners') sugar
28 g / 1 oz / ¼ cup unsweetened cocoa powder, sifted
2 tbsp milk
4 tbsp sugar strands

Double Chocolate Iced Mini Cupcakes

 171

Add white chocolate chips to the cake mixture and top the cake with white and dark chocolate chips instead of the sugar strands.

172

MAKES 12

Mint Chocolate Cupcakes

- Preheat the oven to 180°C (160° fan) / 350 F / gas 4 and line a 12-hole muffin tin with paper cases.
- Beat the egg in a jug with the oil and milk until well mixed.
- Mix the flour, cocoa, baking powder, sugar, chocolate and peppermint essence in a bowl, then pour in the egg mixture and stir just enough to combine.
- Divide the mixture between the paper cases, then bake in the oven for 20 – 25 minutes.
- Test with a wooden toothpick, if it comes out clean, the cakes are done.
- Transfer the cakes to a wire rack and leave to cool before dusting with icing sugar.

PREPARATION TIME: 25 MINUTES

COOKING TIME: 25 MINUTES

....

INGREDIENTS

1 large egg
120 ml / 4 fl. oz / ½ cup sunflower oil
120 ml / 4 fl. oz / ½ cup milk
375 g / 12 ½ oz / 2 ½ cups self-raising flour, sifted
55 g / 2 oz / ½ cup unsweetened cocoa powder, sifted
1 tsp baking powder
200 g / 7 oz / ¾ cup caster (superfine) sugar
110 g / 4 oz / ½ cup dark chocolate, minimum 60% cocoa solids, chopped
1 tsp peppermint essence
icing (confectioners') sugar to dust

Fresh Mint Chocolate Cupcakes

 173

Replace the peppermint essence with 1 tbsp chopped fresh mint leaves. Top the cupcakes with whipped cream and a fresh mint leaf.

174
MAKES 12

Cashew and Maple Syrup Cupcakes

PREPARATION TIME: I HOUR

COOKING TIME: 20 MINUTES

INGREDIENTS

110 g / 4 oz / ½ cup self-raising flour, sifted
110 g / 4 oz / ½ cup caster (superfine) sugar
110 g / 4 oz / ½ cup butter, softened
2 large eggs
75 g / 2 ½ oz / ½ cup cashew nuts, chopped
120 ml / 4 fl. oz / ½ cup maple syrup

- Preheat the oven to 190°C (170° fan) / 375 F / gas 5 and line a 12-hole cupcake tin with paper cases.
- Combine the flour, sugar, butter, eggs and cashew nuts in a bowl and whisk together for 2 minutes.
- Divide the mixture between the paper cases, then transfer to the oven and bake for 15 – 20 minutes.
- Test with a wooden toothpick, if it comes out clean, the cakes are done.
- As soon as the cakes have come out of the oven, spoon over the maple syrup and let it soak in as they cool.

Pecan and Bourbon Cupcakes 175

Try this recipe with chopped pecans instead of the cashews and drizzle a tsp of bourbon over each cake after the maple syrup.

176
MAKES 12

Blackcurrant Buttercream Cupcakes

PREPARATION TIME: I HOUR

COOKING TIME: 20 MINUTES

INGREDIENTS

110 g / 4 oz / ½ cup self-raising flour, sifted
110 g / 4 oz / ½ cup caster (superfine) sugar
110 g / 4 oz / ½ cup butter, softened
2 large eggs
75 g / 2 ½ oz / ½ cup blackcurrants

TO DECORATE

110 g / 4 oz / ½ cup butter, softened
225 g / 8 oz / 2 cups icing (confectioners') sugar
2 tbsp blackcurrant syrup
white cake sprinkles

- Preheat the oven to 190°C (170° fan) / 375 F / gas 5 and line a 12-hole cupcake tin with paper cases.
- Combine the flour, sugar, butter and eggs in a bowl and whisk together for 2 minutes.
- Fold in the blackcurrants and divide the mixture between the paper cases. Transfer the tin to the oven and bake for 15 – 20 minutes.
- Transfer the cakes to a wire rack and leave to cool.
- To make the buttercream, beat the butter with a wooden spoon until light and fluffy then beat in the icing sugar a quarter at a time.
- Use a whisk to incorporate the blackcurrant syrup, then whisk for 2 minutes.
- Spoon the buttercream into a piping bag fitted with a star nozzle and pipe a rosette on top of each cake.
- Finish with a scattering of cake sprinkles.

Fresh Blackcurrant Cupcakes 177

Try topping the finished cakes with a handful of fresh blackcurrants.

178

MAKES 12

Pineapple Cupcakes

Pineapple and Chilli Cupcakes

179

Add 1 small finely chopped red chilli to the muffin mixture.

Spiced Pineapple Muffins

180

Add ½ teaspoon of cinnamon and ½ teaspoon of ground nutmeg to the mixture.

Pina Colada Muffins

181

Add 1 tsp of coconut rum to the cake mixture. Decorate with coconut frosting, made with butter, icing sugar and coconut cream.

PREPARATION TIME: 25 MINUTES

COOKING TIME: 25 MINUTES

....

INGREDIENTS

1 large egg
120ml / 4 fl. oz / ½ cup sunflower oil
120ml / 4 fl. oz / ½ cup milk
375 g / 12 ½ oz / 2 ½ cups self-raising flour, sifted
1 tsp baking powder
200 g / 7 oz / ¾ cup caster (superfine) sugar
150 g / 5 oz / 1 cup canned pineapple pieces, drained

- Preheat the oven to 180°C (160° fan) / 350 F / gas 4 and line a 12-hole muffin tin with paper cases.
- Beat the egg in a jug with the oil and milk until well mixed.
- Mix the flour, baking powder, sugar and pineapple in a bowl, then pour in the egg mixture and stir just enough to combine.
- Divide the mixture between the paper cases, then bake in the oven for 20 – 25 minutes.
- Test with a wooden toothpick, if it comes out clean, the cakes are done.
- Transfer the cakes to a wire rack and leave to cool.

182

MAKES 12

Vanilla Cupcakes with Cheese Icing

- Preheat the oven to 190°C (170° fan) / 375 F / gas 5 and line a 12-hole cupcake tin with paper cases.
- Combine the flour, sugar, butter, eggs and vanilla extract in a bowl and whisk together for 2 minutes.
- Divide the mixture between the paper cases, then transfer to the oven and bake for 15 – 20 minutes.
- Transfer the cakes to a wire rack and leave to cool.
- To make the icing, beat the cream cheese and butter together with a wooden spoon until light and fluffy then beat in the icing sugar a quarter at a time.
- Add the vanilla extract then use a whisk to whip the mixture for 2 minutes until light.
- Spoon the icing into a piping bag fitted with a large plain nozzle and pipe a swirl on top of each cake.

PREPARATION TIME: 1 HOUR

COOKING TIME: 20 MINUTES

INGREDIENTS

110 g / 4 oz / ½ cup self-raising flour
110 g / 4 oz / ½ cup caster sugar
110 g / 4 oz / ½ cup butter, softened
2 large eggs
1 tsp vanilla extract

TO DECORATE

225 g / 8 oz / 1 cup cream cheese
110 g / 4 oz / ½ cup butter, softened
225 g / 8 oz / 2 cups icing (confectioners') sugar
1 tsp vanilla extract

Marshmallow Cupcakes

183

MAKES 12

PREPARATION TIME: 1 HOUR

COOKING TIME: 20 MINUTES

INGREDIENTS

110 g / 4 oz / 1 cup self-raising flour, sifted
110 g / 4 oz / ½ cup caster (superfine) sugar

110 g / 4 oz / ½ cup butter, softened
2 large eggs
1 tsp vanilla extract
110 g / 4 oz mini marshmallows

TO DECORATE

1 jar strawberry flavour marshmallow fluff (creme)
Multicoloured sugar strands

- Preheat the oven to 190°C (170° fan) / 375 F / gas 5 and line a 12-hole cupcake tin with paper cases.
- Combine the flour, sugar, butter, eggs and vanilla extract in a bowl and whisk together for 2 minutes.
- Fold in the mini marshmallows, then divide the mixture between the paper cases.
- Transfer the tin to the oven and bake for 15 – 20 minutes.
- Test with a wooden toothpick, if it comes out clean, the cakes are done.
- Transfer the cakes to a wire rack and leave to cool.
- Use a palette knife to spread the cakes with the marshmallow fluff, then sprinkle with the sugar strands.

Mini Strawberry Cupcakes

184

MAKES 36

PREPARATION TIME: 20 MINUTES

COOKING TIME: 15 MINUTES

INGREDIENTS

110 g / 4 oz / ½ cup self-raising flour, sifted
110 g / 4 oz / ½ cup caster (superfine) sugar

110 g / 4 oz / ½ cup butter, softened
2 large eggs
2 tbsp strawberry syrup

TO DECORATE

225 g / 8 oz / 2 cups icing (confectioners') sugar
Boiling water, to mix
36 Red icing flowers to decorate

- Preheat the oven to 190°C (170° fan) / 375 F / gas 5 and line a 36 hole mini cupcake tin with paper cases.
- Combine the flour, sugar, butter, eggs and strawberry syrup in a bowl and whisk together for 2 minutes.
- Divide the mixture between the paper cases, then transfer to the oven and bake for 10 – 15 minutes.
- Test with a wooden toothpick, if it comes out clean, the cakes are done.
- Transfer the cakes to a wire rack and leave to cool.
- Sift the icing sugar into a bowl, then slowly stir in the boiling water a few drops at a time until you have a thick icing.
- Spoon the icing on top of the cakes and top each one with an icing flower.

185
MAKES 12

Honey and Red Berry Cupcakes

- Preheat the oven to 190°C (170° fan) / 375 F / gas 5 and line a 12-hole cupcake tin with paper cases.
- Combine the flour, sugar, honey, butter and eggs in a bowl and whisk together for 2 minutes.
- Fold in the berries and divide the mixture between the paper cases.
- Transfer the tin to the oven and bake for 15 – 20 minutes.
- While the cakes are cooking, make the soaking syrup. Put the lemon juice and honey in a small saucepan and boil for 2 minutes.
- Test the cakes with a wooden toothpick, if it comes out clean, the cakes are done.
- As soon as the cakes come out of the oven, spoon over the soaking syrup.

Orange Syrup Cupcakes 186

Add the zest of 1 orange to the cake mixture and use orange juice instead of lemon juice in the soaking syrup.

PREPARATION TIME: 25 MINUTES

COOKING TIME: 20 MINUTES

INGREDIENTS

110 g / 4 oz / ½ cup self-raising flour, sifted
55 g / 2 oz / ¼ cup caster (superfine) sugar
110 g / 4 oz / ½ cup honey
110 g / 4 oz / ½ cup butter, softened
2 large eggs
175 g / 6 oz mixed berries

FOR THE SOAKING SYRUP
1 lemon, juiced
110 g / 4 oz / ½ cup honey

TO DECORATE
mixed berries

187
MAKES 12

Cranberry and Almond Cupcakes

- Preheat the oven to 190°C (170° fan) / 375 F / gas 5 and line a 12-hole cupcake tin with paper cases.
- Combine the flour, sugar, butter, eggs and vanilla extract in a bowl and whisk together for 2 minutes.
- Fold in the cranberries and divide the mixture between the paper cases, then sprinkle over the flaked almonds.
- Transfer the tin to the oven and bake for 15 – 20 minutes.
- Test with a wooden toothpick, if it comes out clean, the cakes are done.
- Transfer the cakes to a wire rack and leave to cool.

Iced Cranberry and Almond Cupcakes 188

Stir 2 tsp of lemon juice into 150g / 5 oz / ⅔ cup icing sugar until runny and smooth, then drizzle over the cupcakes.

PREPARATION TIME 20 MINUTES

COOKING TIME 20 MINUTES

INGREDIENTS

110 g / 4 oz / ½ cup self-raising flour, sifted
110 g / 4 oz / ½ cup caster (superfine) sugar
110 g / 4 oz / ½ cup butter, softened
2 large eggs
1 tsp vanilla extract
175 g / 6 oz / ¾ cup fresh cranberries
75 g / 2 ½ oz / ½ cup flaked (slivered) almonds

189

MAKES 12

Kiwi and Citrus Cupcakes

PREPARATION TIME: 45 MINUTES

COOKING TIME: 20 MINUTES

INGREDIENTS

110 g / 4 oz / ½ cup self-raising flour, sifted

110 g / 4 oz / ½ cup caster (superfine) sugar

110 g / 4 oz / ½ cup butter, softened

2 large eggs

1 lemon, zest finely grated

1 orange, zest finely grated

3 kiwi fruit, sliced

- Preheat the oven to 190°C (170° fan) / 375 F / gas 5 and oil a 12-hole silicone cupcake mould.
- Combine the flour, sugar, butter, eggs, lemon zest and orange zest in a bowl and whisk together for 2 minutes.
- Put a slice of kiwi in the bottom of each hole in the mould and spoon the cake mixture on top.
- Transfer the mould to the oven and bake for 15 – 20 minutes.
- Test with a wooden toothpick, if it comes out clean, the cakes are done.
- Turn the cakes out onto a wire rack and leave to cool completely.

Apricot Upside-down Cupcakes

190

Use this recipe to make any kind of mini upside-down cake – try it with tinned apricot halves or pieces of pineapple too.

191

MAKES 12

Bubblegum Buttercream Cupcakes

PREPARATION TIME: 1 HOUR

COOKING TIME: 20 MINUTES

INGREDIENTS

110 g / 4 oz / ½ cup self-raising flour, sifted

110 g / 4 oz / ½ cup caster (superfine) sugar

110 g / 4 oz / ½ cup butter, softened

2 large eggs

1 tsp vanilla extract

TO DECORATE

110 g / 4 oz / ½ cup butter, softened

225 g / 8 oz / 2 cups icing (confectioners') sugar

2 tbsp bubblegum syrup

5 drops blue food colouring

2 tbsp hundreds and thousands

- Preheat the oven to 190°C (170° fan) / 375 F / gas 5 and line a 12-hole cupcake tin with paper cases.
- Combine the flour, sugar, butter, eggs and vanilla extract in a bowl and whisk together for 2 minutes.
- Divide the mixture between the paper cases, then transfer to the oven and bake for 15 – 20 minutes.
- Transfer the cakes to a wire rack and leave to cool.
- To make the buttercream, beat the butter with a wooden spoon until light and fluffy then beat in the icing sugar a quarter at a time.
- Use a whisk to incorporate the bubblegum syrup and blue food colouring, then whisk for 2 minutes.
- Spoon the buttercream into a piping bag fitted with a star nozzle and pipe a swirl on top of each cake.
- Sprinkle with hundreds and thousands.

Bubblegum Ball Cupcakes

 192

For an eye catching finish, top each cake with a different coloured bubblegum ball.

Chocolate and Raspberry Mini Cupcakes

193

MAKES 36

Chocolate and Cherry Mini Cupcakes

194

Add a stoned cherry to the top of each cake instead of the raspberries before baking.

Vanilla and Raspberry Cupcakes

195

Substitute the cocoa powder with a teaspoon of vanilla extract.

Raspberry Cream Cupcakes

196

Instead of whole raspberries, decorate these cakes with raspberry cream frosting.

PREPARATION TIME: 45 MINUTES

COOKING TIME: 15 MINUTES

INGREDIENTS

110 g / 4 oz / ½ cup self-raising flour, sifted
28 g / 1 oz / ¼ cup unsweetened cocoa powder, sifted
110 g / 4 oz / ½ cup caster (superfine) sugar
110 g / 4 oz / ½ cup butter, softened
2 large eggs
225 g / 8 oz / 1 cup raspberries

TO DECORATE
2 tbsp honey

- Preheat the oven to 190°C (170° fan) / 375 F / gas 5 and line a 36 hole mini cupcake tin with paper cases.
- Combine the flour, cocoa, sugar, butter and eggs in a bowl and whisk together for 2 minutes.
- Divide the mixture between the paper cases, and press a few raspberries into the top of each.
- Transfer the tin to the oven and bake for 10 – 15 minutes.
- Test with a wooden toothpick, if it comes out clean, the cakes are done.
- Warm the honey in the microwave for a few seconds then brush it over the cakes to glaze.
- Transfer the cakes to a wire rack and leave to cool.

197

MAKES 12

Lemon Porridge Breakfast Cupcakes

Lemon Marmalade Breakfast Cupcakes

198

Glaze these cupcakes with warm lemon marmalade when they come out of the oven.

Fruit and Porridge Muffins

199

Add a handful of raisins and sultanas to the mixture before baking.

Orange Porridge Breakfast Muffins

200

Substitute the lemon juice and zest for orange.

PREPARATION TIME: 25 MINUTES

COOKING TIME: 25 MINUTES

....

INGREDIENTS

1 large egg
120 ml / 4 fl. oz / ½ cup sunflower oil
120 ml / 4 fl. oz / ½ cup milk
1 lemon, juiced
375 g / 12 ½ oz / 2 ½ cups self-raising flour, sifted
1 tsp baking powder
200 g / 7 oz / ¾ cup caster (superfine) sugar
1 tbsp lemon zest, finely grated
75 g / 2 ½ oz / ½ cup porridge oats

- Preheat the oven to 180°C (160° fan) / 350 F / gas 4 and oil a 12-hole silicone muffin tin.
- Beat the egg in a jug with the oil, milk and lemon juice until well mixed.
- Mix the flour, baking powder, sugar, lemon zest and oats in a bowl, then pour in the egg mixture and stir just enough to combine.
- Divide the mixture between the moulds, then bake in the oven for 20 – 25 minutes.
- Test with a wooden toothpick, if it comes out clean, the cakes are done.
- Transfer the cakes to a wire rack and leave to cool.

201

MAKES 12

Chocolate Caramac cupcakes

- Preheat the oven to 190°C (170° fan) / 375 F / gas 5 and line a 12-hole cupcake tin with paper cases.
- Combine the flour, cocoa, sugar, butter, eggs and vanilla extract in a bowl and whisk together for 2 minutes.
- Fold in the chopped Caramac then divide the mixture between the paper cases and bake for 15 – 20 minutes.
- Transfer the cakes to a wire rack and leave to cool.
- Heat the cream until it starts to simmer, then pour it over the chopped chocolate.
- Stir the ganache until the mixture has cooled and thickened, then refrigerate until thick enough to pipe.
- Spoon the ganache into a piping bag fitted with a large star nozzle and pipe a spiral on top of each cake.
- Use a vegetable peeler to make small curls of Caramac and scatter over the cakes.
- Sprinkle with edible glitter.

Caramac Cupcakes

202

Leave the cocoa powder out of the cake mixture and top the cakes with melted Caramac instead of the dark chocolate ganache.

PREPARATION TIME 10 MINUTES

COOKING TIME 45 MINUTES

INGREDIENTS

110 g / 4 oz / ½ cup self-raising flour, sifted
28 g / 1 oz / ¼ cup unsweetened cocoa powder, sifted
110 g / 4 oz / ½ cup caster (superfine) sugar
110 g / 4 oz / ½ cup butter, softened
2 large eggs
1 tsp vanilla extract
110 g / 4 oz Caramac

TO DECORATE

225 ml / 8 fl. oz / 1 cup double (heavy) cream
225 g / 8 oz / 1 cup dark chocolate, minimum 60% cocoa solids, chopped
55 g / 2 oz Caramac
edible glitter

203

MAKES 24

Goat's Cheese and Thyme Mini Cupcakes

- Preheat the oven to 180°C (160° fan) / 350 F / gas 4 and line a 24-hole muffin tin with paper cases.
- Beat the egg in a jug with the oil, yoghurt and cheese until well mixed.
- Mix the flour, raising agents, salt and thyme in a bowl, then pour in the egg mixture and stir just enough to combine.
- Divide the mixture between the paper cases, then bake in the oven for 10 – 15 minutes.
- Test with a wooden toothpick, if it comes out clean, the cupcakes are done.
- Serve warm.

PREPARATION TIME: 25 MINUTES

COOKING TIME: 15 MINUTES

INGREDIENTS

2 large eggs
120 ml / 4 fl. oz / ½ cup sunflower oil
180 ml / 6 fl. oz / ¾ cup Greek yogurt
110 g / 4 oz / 1 cup goat's cheese, cubed
225 g / 8 oz / 1 ½ cups plain (all purpose) flour
2 tsp baking powder
½ tsp bicarbonate of (baking) soda
½ tsp salt
2 tbsp fresh thyme leaves

Cheese, Onion and Thyme Mini Cupcakes

204

Try adding 1 sliced onion that has been fried in a little olive oil to the cupcake mixture.

205

MAKES 12

Iced Almond Cupcakes

PREPARATION TIME: 35 MINUTES

COOKING TIME: 20 MINUTES

INGREDIENTS

55 g / 2 oz / ½ cup self-raising flour, sifted
55 g / 2 oz / ½ cup ground almonds
110 g / 4 oz / ½ cup caster (superfine) sugar
110 g / 4 oz / ½ cup butter, softened
2 large eggs
1 tsp almond essence

TO DECORATE

225 g / 8 oz / 2 cups icing (confectioners') sugar
3 drops of almond essence
boiling water, to mix
12 small pink sweets

- Preheat the oven to 190°C (170° fan) / 375 F / gas 5 and line a 12-hole cupcake tin with paper cases.
- Combine the flour, ground almonds, sugar, butter, eggs and almond essence in a bowl and whisk together for 2 minutes.
- Divide the cake mixture between the paper cases, then transfer to the oven and bake for 15 – 20 minutes.
- Test with a wooden toothpick, if it comes out clean, the cakes are done.
- Transfer the cakes to a wire rack to cool completely.
- Sift the icing sugar into a bowl and add the almond essence, then slowly stir in the boiling water a few drops at a time until you have a thick icing.
- Spoon the icing on top of the cakes and decorate with the sweets.

Double Almond Cupcakes

206

These little cakes look great scattered with flaked (slivered) almonds instead of the sweets too.

207

MAKES 12

Apple, Almond and Cinnamon Cupcakes

PREPARATION TIME: 25 MINUTES

COOKING TIME: 25 MINUTES

INGREDIENTS

1 large egg
120 ml / 4 fl. oz / ½ cup sunflower oil
120 ml / 4 fl. oz / ½ cup milk
225 g / 7 ½ oz / 1 ½ cups self-raising flour, sifted
1 tsp baking powder
150 g / 5 oz / 1 ¼ cups ground almonds
200 g / 7 oz / ¾ cup caster (superfine) sugar
1 tsp ground cinnamon
1 apple, peeled, cored and sliced

- Preheat the oven to 180°C (160° fan) / 350 F / gas 4 and line a 12-hole muffin tin with paper cases.
- Beat the egg in a jug with the oil and milk until well mixed.
- Mix the flour, baking powder, ground almonds, sugar, cinnamon and apple slices in a bowl, then pour in the egg mixture and stir just enough to combine.
- Divide the mixture between the paper cases and bake in the oven for 20 – 25 minutes.
- Test with a wooden toothpick, if it comes out clean, the cakes are done.
- Transfer the cakes to a wire rack and leave to cool.

Pear, Almond and Cinnamon Cupcakes

208

This recipe is lovely with sliced pears instead of the apple.

209
MAKES 12

White and Dark Chocolate Cupcakes

- Preheat the oven to 190°C (170° fan) / 375 F / gas 5 and line a 12-hole cupcake tin with paper cases.
- Combine the flour, sugar, butter, eggs and vanilla extract in a bowl and whisk together for 2 minutes.
- Use half of the mixture to fill 6 of the paper cases.
- Mix the cocoa with the milk then fold it into the rest of the mixture and use it to fill the remaining cake cases.
- Bake for 15 – 20 minutes. Transfer the cakes to a wire rack and leave to cool.
- Chop the 2 chocolates and transfer to 2 separate mixing bowls. Heat the cream until it starts to simmer, then divide between the 2 chocolate bowls.
- Stir the ganache until the mixture has cooled and thickened. Use the white chocolate ganache to top the chocolate cupcakes and the dark chocolate ganache to top the vanilla cupcakes.

PREPARATION TIME:
1 HOUR 15 MINUTES

COOKING TIME: 20 MINUTES

INGREDIENTS

110 g / 4 oz / 1 cup self-raising flour, sifted
110 g / 4 oz / ½ cup caster (superfine) sugar
110 g / 4 oz / ½ cup butter, softened
2 large eggs
1 tsp vanilla extract
28 g / 1 oz / ¼ cup unsweetened cocoa powder, sifted
1 tbsp milk

TO DECORATE
110 g / 4 oz / ½ cup white chocolate
110 g / 4 oz / ½ cup dark chocolate, minimum 60% cocoa solids
225 ml / 8 fl. oz / 1 cup double (heavy) cream

Mix and Match Cupcakes
210
Stir 5 tbsp white chocolate chips into the chocolate cake mixture and stir 5 tbsp dark chocolate chips into the vanilla cake mixture.

211
MAKES 12

Wholemeal Cranberry Cupcakes

- Preheat the oven to 180°C (160° fan) / 350 F / gas 4 and oil a 12-hole silicone muffin tin.
- Beat the egg in a jug with the oil and milk until well mixed.
- Mix the flour, baking powder, sugar and cranberries in a bowl, then pour in the egg mixture and stir just enough to combine.
- Divide the mixture between the moulds, then bake in the oven for 20 – 25 minutes.
- Test with a wooden toothpick, if it comes out clean, the cakes are done.
- Transfer the cakes to a wire rack and leave to cool.

PREPARATION TIME: 25 MINUTES

COOKING TIME: 25 MINUTES

INGREDIENTS

1 large egg
120 ml / 4 fl. oz / ½ cup sunflower oil
120 ml / 4 fl. oz / ½ cup milk
375 g / 12 ½ oz / 2 ½ cups wholemeal flour
2 tsp baking powder
200 g / 7 oz / ¾ cup caster (superfine) sugar
150 g / 5 oz / 1 cup cranberries

Cranberry Cupcakes with Orange Butter
212

Mix 110g / 4 oz softened butter with the finely grated zest of 1 orange then refrigerate until firm. Form into small pats and serve with the cupcakes.

213

MAKES 12

Banana Cupcakes with Chocolate Ganache

PREPARATION TIME: 25 MINUTES

COOKING TIME: 25 MINUTES

....

INGREDIENTS

3 very ripe bananas
110 g / 4 oz / ⅔ cup soft light brown sugar
2 large eggs
120 ml / 4 fl. oz / ½ cup sunflower oil
225 g / 8 oz / 1 ½ cups plain (all purpose) flour
1 tsp bicarbonate of (baking) soda

TO DECORATE

225 g / 8 oz / ½ cup dark chocolate, minimum 60% cocoa solids
225 ml / 8 fl. oz / 1 cup double (heavy) cream
2 tbsp flaked (slivered) almonds

- Preheat the oven to 200°C (180° fan) / 400 F / gas 6 and line a 12-hole cupcake tin with paper cases.
- Mash the bananas with a fork then whisk in the sugar, eggs and oil.
- Sieve the flour and bicarbonate of soda into the bowl and stir to evenly mix all the ingredients together.
- Divide the mixture between the paper cases, then transfer to the oven and bake for 15 – 20 minutes.
- Transfer the cakes to a wire rack and leave to cool.
- To make the ganache, chop the chocolate and transfer to a mixing bowl.
- Heat the cream until it starts to simmer, then pour over the chopped chocolate and stir until the mixture has cooled and thickened.
- Apply the ganache with a palette knife and sprinkle the cakes with flaked almonds.

Chocolate and Banana Cupcakes

214

Try adding 110g / 4oz / ½ cup chopped dark chocolate to the cake mixture for chocolate and banana cupcakes.

215

MAKES 12

Fairy Ring Cupcakes

PREPARATION TIME: 1 HOUR

COOKING TIME: 20 MINUTES

....

INGREDIENTS

110 g / 4 oz / ½ cup self-raising flour, sifted
110 g / 4 oz / ½ cup caster (superfine) sugar
110 g / 4 oz / ½ cup butter, softened
2 large eggs
75 g / 2 ½ oz / ½ cup mixed forest fruits, chopped if large

TO DECORATE

110 g / 4 oz / ½ cup butter, softened
225 g / 8 oz / 2 cups icing (confectioners') sugar
2 tbsp milk
5 drops of blue, green and red food colouring
55 g / 2 oz ready to roll fondant icing

- Preheat the oven to 190°C (170° fan) / 375 F / gas 5 and line a 12-hole cupcake tin with foil cases.
- Combine the flour, sugar, butter and eggs in a bowl and whisk together for 2 minutes.
- Fold in the forest fruits and divide the mixture between the paper cases. Bake for 15 – 20 minutes.
- Transfer the cakes to a wire rack and leave to cool.
- Beat the butter with a wooden spoon until light and fluffy then beat in the icing sugar. Add the milk, then whisk for 2 minutes.
- Spoon 1 tbsp of the buttercream into a small piping bag fitted with a small plain nozzle and set aside.
- Stir the green food colouring into the rest of the buttercream until evenly coloured, then stir the blue food colouring in just enough to create a marbled effect.
- Spoon the buttercream into a piping bag fitted with a large star nozzle and pipe a swirl on top of each cake.
- Divide the fondant icing in 2 and colour one half red. Use the white icing to make the toadstool stalks and the red to make the caps and attach with a drop of water.
- Assemble the toadstools on top of the cakes and pipe the spots on with the reserved white buttercream.

216

MAKES 12

Orange and Ginger Cupcakes

Orange and Nutmeg Cupcakes

217

Replace the ground ginger with 1 tsp of freshly grated nutmeg.

Orange and Cinnamon Cupcakes

218

Replace the ground ginger with 1 tsp of cinnamon.

Lemon and Ginger Cupcakes

219

Replace the orange with a lemon.

PREPARATION TIME: 25 MINUTES

COOKING TIME: 20 MINUTES

INGREDIENTS

110 g / 4 oz / ½ cup self-raising flour, sifted
110 g / 4 oz / ½ cup caster (superfine) sugar
110 g / 4 oz / ½ cup butter, softened
2 large eggs
2 tsp ground ginger
1 orange, zest finely grated
Icing (confectioners') sugar to dust

- Preheat the oven to 190°C (170° fan) / 375 F / gas 5 and line a 12-hole cupcake tin with paper cases.
- Combine the flour, sugar, butter, eggs, ground ginger and orange zest in a bowl and whisk together for 2 minutes.
- Divide the mixture between the paper cases, then transfer to the oven and bake for 15 – 20 minutes.
- Test with a wooden toothpick, if it comes out clean, the cakes are done.
- Transfer the cakes to a wire rack and leave to cool completely before dusting with icing sugar.

220

MAKES 12

Banana, Almond and Rum Cupcakes

Rum and Raisin Cupcakes

221

Try soaking 2 tbsp sultanas in 2 tbsp of rum overnight and adding them to the cake mixture.

Rum, Raisin and Cinnamon Cupcakes

222

Ass 1 tsp of cinnamon to the cake mixture before cooking.

PREPARATION TIME: 20 MINUTES

COOKING TIME: 20 MINUTES

INGREDIENTS

55 g / 2 oz / ½ cup self-raising flour, sifted
2 tsp baking powder
55 g / 2 oz / ½ cup ground almonds
110 g / 4 oz / ½ cup caster (superfine) sugar
110 g / 4 oz / ½ cup butter, softened
2 large eggs
1 tsp almond essence
2 medium bananas, sliced
60 ml / 2 fl. oz / ¼ cup dark rum

- Preheat the oven to 190°C (170° fan) / 375 F / gas 5 and line a 12-hole cupcake tin with paper cases.
- Combine the flour, baking powder, ground almonds, sugar, butter, eggs and almond essence in a bowl and whisk together for 2 minutes.
- Divide the mixture between the paper cases and press a banana slice into the top of each, then transfer to the oven and bake for 15 – 20 minutes.
- Test with a wooden toothpick, if it comes out clean, the cakes are done.
- As soon as the cakes come out of the oven, spoon 1 tsp of rum over each one.
- Transfer the cakes to a wire rack and leave to cool.

223
MAKES 36 Chocolate Maraschino Mini Cupcakes

- Preheat the oven to 190°C (170° fan) / 375 F / gas 5 and line a 36 mini cupcake tin with paper cases.
- Combine the flour, cocoa, sugar, butter and eggs in a bowl and whisk together for 2 minutes.
- Divide the mixture between the paper cases. Press a square of chocolate into the top of each one and top with a cherry.
- Transfer the tin to the oven and bake for 10 – 15 minutes.
- Serve immediately while the chocolate is still molten inside.

PREPARATION TIME: 45 MINUTES

COOKING TIME: 15 MINUTES

INGREDIENTS

110 g / 4 oz / ½ cup self-raising flour, sifted
28 g / 1 oz / ¼ cup unsweetened cocoa powder, sifted
110 g / 4 oz / ½ cup caster (superfine) sugar
110 g / 4 oz / ½ cup butter, softened
2 large eggs
150 g / 5 oz / ⅔ cup dark chocolate, minimum 60% cocoa solids
36 maraschino cherries with stems

Double Cherry Cupcakes 224

Try adding a spoonful of cherry jam (jelly) before topping with the chocolate and cherries for an extra layer of cherry flavour.

225
MAKES 12 Coconut Cream Cupcakes

- Preheat the oven to 190°C (170° fan) / 375 F / gas 5 and line a 12-hole cupcake tin with paper cases.
- Combine the flour, sugar, butter, eggs and coconut in a bowl and whisk together for 2 minutes.
- Divide the mixture between the paper cases, then transfer to the oven and bake for 15 – 20 minutes.
- Transfer the cakes to a wire rack and leave to cool.
- Sprinkle the desiccated coconut onto a baking tray and lightly toast under a hot grill for 2 minutes. Leave to cool.
- Sieve the icing sugar into a bowl and stir in the coconut cream a little at a time until it forms a thick, spreadable icing.
- Use a palate knife to apply a thick layer of icing to each cake, then dip the tops in the toasted coconut.

PREPARATION TIME:
1 HOUR 15 MINUTES

COOKING TIME: 20 MINUTES

INGREDIENTS

28 g / 1 oz / ⅛ cup desiccated coconut
110 g / 4 oz / 1 cup self-raising flour, sifted
110 g / 4 oz / ½ cup caster (superfine) sugar
110 g / 4 oz / ½ cup butter, softened
2 large eggs
28 g / 1 oz / ⅛ cup desiccated coconut

TO DECORATE

225 g / 8 oz / 2 cups icing (confectioners') sugar
2 – 4 tbsp coconut cream

Coconut and Rum Cupcakes 226

Drizzle a tablespoon of white rum over each cupcake as they come out of the oven before cooling and icing.

227

MAKES 12

Chocolate and Almond Cupcakes

- Preheat the oven to 180°C (160° fan) / 350 F / gas 4 and line a 12-hole muffin tin with paper cases.
- Beat the egg in a jug with the oil and milk until well mixed.
- Mix the flour, baking powder, ground almonds and sugar in a bowl, then pour in the egg mixture and chopped chocolate and stir just enough to combine.
- Divide the mixture between the paper cases and sprinkle with flaked almonds, then bake in the oven for 20 – 25 minutes.
- Test with a wooden toothpick, if it comes out clean, the cakes are done.
- Transfer the cakes to a wire rack and leave to cool.

PREPARATION TIME: 25 MINUTES

COOKING TIME: 25 MINUTES

INGREDIENTS

1 large egg
120ml / 4 fl. oz / ½ cup sunflower oil
120ml / 4 fl. oz / ½ cup milk
375 g / 12 ½ oz / 2 ½ cups self-raising flour, sifted
1 tsp baking powder
55 g / 2 oz / ½ cup ground almonds
200 g / 7 oz / ¾ cup caster sugar
110 g / 4 oz / ½ cup dark chocolate, chopped
75 g / 2 ½ oz / ½ cup flaked (slivered) almonds

Blackcurrant Cupcakes

228

MAKES 12

PREPARATION TIME: 25 MINUTES

COOKING TIME: 25 MINUTES

INGREDIENTS

1 large egg
120 ml / 4 fl. oz / ½ cup sunflower oil
120 ml / 4 fl. oz / ½ cup milk
375 g / 12 ½ oz / 2 ½ cups self-raising flour, sifted
1 tsp baking powder
200 g / 7 oz / ¾ cup caster (superfine) sugar
150 g / 5 oz / 1 cup blackcurrants

- Preheat the oven to 180°C (160° fan) / 350 F / gas 4 and oil a 12-hole silicone muffin mould.
- Beat the egg in a jug with the oil and milk until well mixed.
- Mix the flour, baking powder, sugar and blackcurrants in a bowl, then pour in the egg mixture and stir just enough to combine.
- Divide the mixture between the moulds, then bake in the oven for 20 – 25 minutes.
- Test with a wooden toothpick, if it comes out clean, the cakes are done.
- Transfer the cakes to a wire rack and leave to cool.

Fruit Gum Cupcakes

229

MAKES 12

PREPARATION TIME: 1 HOUR

COOKING TIME: 20 MINUTES

INGREDIENTS

110 g / 4 oz / ½ cup self-raising flour
110 g / 4 oz / ½ cup caster sugar
110 g / 4 oz / ½ cup butter, softened
2 large eggs
75 g / 2 ½ oz / ½ cup small fruit gums

TO DECORATE

110 g / 4 oz / ½ cup butter, softened
225 g / 8 oz / 2 cups icing (confectioners') sugar
2 tbsp milk
75 g / 2 ½ oz / ½ cup small fruit gums

- Preheat the oven to 190°C (170° fan) / 375 F / gas 5 and line a 12-hole cupcake tin with paper cases.
- Combine the flour, sugar, butter and eggs in a bowl and whisk together for 2 minutes.
- Fold in the fruit gums and divide the mixture between the paper cases. Transfer the tin to the oven and bake for 15 – 20 minutes. Transfer the cakes to a wire rack and leave to cool.
- To make the buttercream, beat the butter with a wooden spoon until light and fluffy then beat in the icing sugar a quarter at a time.
- Use a whisk to incorporate the milk, then whisk for 2 minutes.
- Spoon the buttercream into a piping bag fitted with a large star nozzle and pipe a generous rosette on top of each cake.
- Finish with a scattering of fruit gums.

230

MAKES 12

Raspberry and Ginger Cupcakes

- Preheat the oven to 180°C (160° fan) / 350 F / gas 4 and line a 12-hole muffin tin with paper cases.
- Beat the egg in a jug with the oil and milk until well mixed.
- Mix the flour, baking powder, sugar, raspberries and ginger in a bowl, then pour in the egg mixture and stir just enough to combine.
- Divide the mixture between the moulds, then bake in the oven for 20 – 25 minutes.
- Test with a wooden toothpick, if it comes out clean, the cakes are done.
- Transfer the cakes to a wire rack and leave to cool.

PREPARATION TIME: 25 MINUTES

COOKING TIME: 25 MINUTES

INGREDIENTS

1 large egg
120 ml / 4 fl. oz / ½ cup sunflower oil
120 ml / 4 fl. oz / ½ cup milk
375 g / 12 ½ oz / 2 ½ cups self-raising flour, sifted
1 tsp baking powder
200 g / 7 oz / ¾ cup caster (superfine) sugar
150 g / 5 oz / 1 cup raspberries
75 g / 2 ½ oz / ½ cup crystallised ginger, chopped

Extra Ginger Cupcakes

231

For extra ginger flavour, add 2 tsp ground ginger to the dry ingredients before mixing.

232

MAKES 24

Wholemeal Apple and Cheddar Mini Cupcakes

- Preheat the oven to 180°C (160° fan) / 350 F / gas 4 and oil a 24-hole silicone muffin mould.
- Beat the egg in a jug with the oil, yoghurt, cheese and apple until well mixed.
- Mix the flour, raising agents and salt in a bowl, then pour in the egg mixture and stir just enough to combine.
- Divide the mixture between the paper cases, then bake in the oven for 10 – 15 minutes.
- Test with a wooden toothpick, if it comes out clean, the cupcakes are done.
- Serve warm.

PREPARATION TIME: 25 MINUTES

COOKING TIME: 15 MINUTES

INGREDIENTS

2 large eggs
120 ml / 4 fl. oz / ½ cup sunflower oil
180 ml / 6 fl. oz / ¾ cup Greek yogurt
110 g / 4 oz / 1 cup Cheddar, grated
1 apple, peeled, cored and grated
225 g / 8 oz / 1 ½ cups wholemeal flour
2 tsp baking powder
½ tsp bicarbonate of (baking) soda
½ tsp salt

Pear and Cheddar Mini Cupcakes

233

Replace the apple with a pear.

234

MAKES 12

Coconut Cupcakes

PREPARATION TIME: 1 HOUR

COOKING TIME: 20 MINUTES

INGREDIENTS

110 g / 4 oz / 1 cup self-raising flour, sifted

110 g / 4 oz / ½ cup caster (superfine) sugar

110 g / 4 oz / ½ cup butter, softened

2 large eggs

28 g / 1 oz / ⅛ cup desiccated coconut

TO DECORATE

28 g / 1 oz / ⅛ cup desiccated coconut

- Preheat the oven to 190°C (170° fan) / 375 F / gas 5 and line a 12-hole cupcake tin or 36 hole mini cupcake tin with paper cases.
- Combine the flour, sugar, butter, eggs and coconut in a bowl and whisk together for 2 minutes.
- Divide the mixture between the paper cases, then transfer to the oven and bake for 15 – 20 minutes for the normal sized cakes or 10 – 15 minutes for the mini ones.
- Test with a wooden toothpick, if it comes out clean, the cakes are done.
- Sprinkle the desiccated coconut onto a small plate and press the top of each cake in it whilst still warm.
- Transfer the cakes to a wire rack and leave to cool.

Sweet Chocolate Coconut Cupcakes

 235

Spread the top of the cakes with melted chocolate before dipping in the coconut.

236

MAKES 12

Lemon Cupcakes

PREPARATION TIME: 20 MINUTES

COOKING TIME: 20 MINUTES

INGREDIENTS

110 g / 4 oz / 1 cup self-raising flour, sifted

110 g / 4 oz / ½ cup caster (superfine) sugar

110 g / 4 oz / ½ cup butter, softened

2 large eggs

1 lemon, zest finely grated

- Preheat the oven to 190°C (170° fan) / 375 F / gas 5 and line 12 dariole moulds with greaseproof paper.
- Combine the flour, sugar, butter, eggs and lemon zest in a bowl and whisk together for 2 minutes.
- Divide the mixture between the paper cases, then transfer to the oven and bake for 15 – 20 minutes.
- Test with a wooden toothpick, if it comes out clean, the cakes are done.
- Transfer the cakes to a wire rack and leave to cool.

Lemon Curd Cupcakes

 237

Slice a circle out of the cupcake. Top each cupcake with a spoonful of lemon curd and replace the top.

238

MAKES 12

Walnut and Coffee Cupcakes

Cupcakes with Coffee Icing 239

Sieve 150g / 5 oz / ⅔ cup icing sugar and 2 tsp instant coffee powder into a bowl and add enough boiling water to make a pourable icing. Drizzle over the cakes before topping with the walnut halves.

Pistachio and Coffee Cupcakes 240

Replace the walnuts with pistachio nuts.

PREPARATION TIME: 20 MINUTES

COOKING TIME: 20 MINUTES

INGREDIENTS

110 g / 4 oz / 1 cup self-raising flour, sifted
110 g / 4 oz / ½ cup caster (superfine) sugar
110 g / 4 oz / ½ cup butter, softened
2 large eggs
2 tsp instant espresso powder
75 g / 2 ½ oz / ½ cup walnuts, chopped
12 walnut halves

- Preheat the oven to 190°C (170° fan) / 375 F / gas 5 and line a 12-hole cupcake tin with paper cases.
- Combine the flour, sugar, butter, eggs, espresso powder and chopped walnuts in a bowl and whisk together for 2 minutes.
- Divide the mixture between the paper cases, then transfer to the oven and bake for 15 – 20 minutes.
- Test with a wooden toothpick, if it comes out clean, the cakes are done.
- Transfer the cakes to a wire rack and leave to cool.
- Top each cake with a walnut half to finish.

241

MAKES 12

Raspberry and Almond Cupcakes

PREPARATION TIME: 20 MINUTES

COOKING TIME: 20 MINUTES

....

INGREDIENTS

55 g / 2 oz / ½ cup self-raising flour, sifted
55 g / 2 oz / ½ cup ground almonds
110 g / 4 oz / ½ cup caster (superfine) sugar
110 g / 4 oz / ½ cup butter, softened
2 large eggs
1 tsp almond essence
150 g / 5 oz / 1 cup raspberries

- Preheat the oven to 190°C (170° fan) / 375 F / gas 5 and line a 12-hole cupcake tin with paper cases.
- Combine the flour, ground almonds, sugar, butter, eggs and almond essence in a bowl and whisk together for 2 minutes.
- Fold in the raspberries, divide the mixture between the paper cases and transfer the tin to the oven to bake for 15 – 20 minutes.
- Test with a wooden toothpick, if it comes out clean, the cakes are done.
- Transfer the cakes to a wire rack and leave to cool.

Cupcakes with Almond Drizzle 242

Mix 225g / 8 oz / 1 cup icing sugar with ½ tsp almond essence and just enough boiling water to make a runny glaze.

243

MAKES 12

Saffron and Honey Cupcakes

PREPARATION TIME: 1 HOUR

COOKING TIME: 20 MINUTES

....

INGREDIENTS

110 g / 4 oz / 1 cup self-raising flour, sifted
110 g / 4 oz / ½ cup caster (superfine) sugar
110 g / 4 oz / ½ cup butter, softened
2 large eggs

FOR THE SOAKING SYRUP
1 lemon, juiced
110 g / 4 oz / ½ cup honey
pinch saffron

- Preheat the oven to 190°C (170° fan) / 375 F / gas 5 and 12-hole silicone cake mould with oil.
- Combine the flour, sugar, butter and eggs in a bowl and whisk together for 2 minutes.
- Divide the mixture between the moulds, then transfer them to the oven and bake for 15 – 20 minutes.
- Test with a wooden toothpick, if it comes out clean, the cakes are done.
- While the cakes are cooking, make the soaking syrup. Put the lemon juice and honey in a small saucepan and boil for 2 minutes.
- Turn off the heat, stir in the saffron and leave to infuse for 10 minutes.
- Strain the syrup through a sieve to remove the saffron.
- When the cakes are ready, spoon over the soaking syrup and leave them to cool in their moulds.

Calendula Cupcakes 244

To add extra sunshine to these cheerful cakes, garnish with fresh calendula petals.

245

MAKES 12

Hot Cherry and Amaretto Cupcakes

- Preheat the oven to 180°C (160° fan) / 350 F / gas 4 and oil a 12 ramekin dishes.
- Beat the egg in a jug with the oil, milk and Amaretto until well mixed.
- Mix the flour, baking powder, sugar and cherries in a bowl, then pour in the egg mixture and stir just enough to combine.
- Divide the mixture between the moulds, then bake in the oven for 20 – 25 minutes.
- Test with a wooden toothpick, if it comes out clean, the cakes are done.
- Transfer the cakes to a wire rack and leave to cool.

PREPARATION TIME: 25 MINUTES

COOKING TIME: 25 MINUTES

INGREDIENTS

1 large egg
120 ml / 4 fl. oz / ½ cup sunflower oil
120 ml / 4 fl. oz / ½ cup milk
2 tbsp Amaretto
375 g / 12 ½ oz / 2 ½ cups self-raising flour, sifted
1 tsp baking powder
200 g / 7 oz / ¾ cup caster (superfine) sugar
150 g / 5 oz / 1 cup cherries, stoned

Cupcakes with Amaretto Cream

246

Whip together 300ml / 10 fl. oz / 1 ⅓ cups double (heavy) cream with 2 tbsp Amaretto and 2 tbsp icing sugar until thick.

247

MAKES 12

Chestnut and Orange Cupcakes

- Preheat the oven to 190°C (170° fan) / 375 F / gas 5 and line a 12-hole cupcake tin with paper cases.
- Combine the flours, sugar, butter, eggs and marmalade in a bowl and whisk together for 2 minutes.
- Divide the mixture between the paper cases, then transfer to the oven and bake for 15 – 20 minutes.
- Test with a wooden toothpick, if it comes out clean, the cakes are done.
- Transfer the cakes to a wire rack and leave to cool.

PREPARATION TIME: 20 MINUTES

COOKING TIME: 20 MINUTES

INGREDIENTS

55 g / 2 oz / ½ cup self-raising flour, sifted
55 g / 2 oz / ½ cup chestnut flour, sifted
110 g / 4 oz / ½ cup caster (superfine) sugar
110 g / 4 oz / ½ cup butter, softened
2 large eggs
55 g / 2 oz / ¼ cup thick cut marmalade

Double Chestnut Cupcakes

248

For extra texture, try adding 6 chopped cooked chestnuts to the cake mixture.

249

MAKES 12

Strawberry Mint Cupcakes

PREPARATION TIME: 35 MINUTES

COOKING TIME: 20 MINUTES

INGREDIENTS

110 g / 4 oz / ½ cup self-raising flour, sifted
110 g / 4 oz / ½ cup caster (superfine) sugar
110 g / 4 oz / ½ cup butter, softened
2 large eggs
6 strawberries, chopped
2 tbsp fresh mint, shredded

- Preheat the oven to 190°C (170° fan) / 375 F / gas 5 and oil a 12-hole silicone cupcake mould.
- Combine the flour, baking powder, sugar, butter and eggs in a bowl and whisk together for 2 minutes.
- Fold in the strawberries and shredded mint.
- Divide the mixture between the paper cases then transfer to the oven and bake for 15 – 20 minutes.
- Test with a wooden toothpick, if it comes out clean, the cakes are done.
- Transfer the cakes to a wire rack and leave to cool.

Strawberry and Black Pepper Cupcakes

250

Replace the mint with ½ tsp freshly ground black pepper for a spicy kick.

251

MAKES 12

Ginger and Cinnamon Cupcakes

PREPARATION TIME: 20 MINUTES

COOKING TIME: 20 MINUTES

INGREDIENTS

250 g / 9 oz / 1 ¾ cups self-raising flour
1 tsp bicarbonate of (baking) soda
2 tsp ground ginger
2 tsp ground cinnamon
200 g / 8 ½ oz / ½ cup golden syrup
125 g / 4 ½ oz / ½ cup butter
125 g / 4 ½ oz / ¾ cup light brown sugar
4 pieces stem ginger, chopped
2 large eggs, beaten
240 ml / 8 fl. oz / 1 cup milk

- Preheat the oven to 190°C (170° fan) / 375 F / gas 5 and line a 12-hole muffin tin with paper cases.
- Sieve the flour, bicarbonate of soda and spices into a bowl.
- Put the golden syrup, butter, brown sugar and stem ginger in a small saucepan and boil gently for 2 minutes, stirring to dissolve the sugar.
- Pour the butter and sugar mixture onto the flour with the eggs and milk and fold it all together until smooth.
- Divide the mixture between the cases and bake in the oven for 20 – 25 minutes.
- Test with a wooden toothpick, if it comes out clean, the cakes are done.
- Transfer the cakes to a wire rack and leave to cool.

Ginger and Nutmeg Cupcakes

252

Replace the ground cinnamon with 1 tsp freshly grated nutmeg. Mix 1 tsp of freshly grated nutmeg with 2 tbsp caster sugar and sprinkle over the cupcakes, once cooked.

253

MAKES 12

Marbled Cupcakes

Marbled Chocolate Chunk Cupcakes

254

Add 110g / 4 oz / ½ cup of chopped white chocolate to the cupcake mixture. Top with melted dark and white chocolate, marbled together.

Nutty Marbled Cupcakes

255

Add 75g / 3 oz of chopped walnuts to the cupcake mixture and sprinkle the tops with chopped hazelnuts.

PREPARATION TIME: 25 MINUTES

COOKING TIME: 25 MINUTES

INGREDIENTS

1 large egg
120 ml / 4 fl. oz / ½ cup sunflower oil
120 ml / 4 fl. oz / ½ cup milk
375 g / 12 ½ oz / 2 ½ cups self-raising flour, sifted
1 tsp baking powder
200 g / 7 oz / ¾ cup caster (superfine) sugar
110 g / 4 oz / ½ cup dark chocolate, chopped

TO DECORATE

110 g / 4 oz / ½ cup dark chocolate, minimum 60% cocoa solids, chopped
2 tbsp grape-nuts

- Preheat the oven to 180°C (160° fan) / 350 F / gas 4 and line a 12-hole muffin tin with paper cases.
- Beat the egg in a jug with the oil and milk until well mixed.
- Mix the flour, baking powder and sugar in a bowl, then pour in the egg mixture and stir just enough to combine.
- Melt the chocolate in a microwave or bain marie and fold through the muffin mixture until it looks marbled.
- Divide the mixture between the paper cases, then bake in the oven for 20 – 25 minutes.
- Test with a wooden toothpick, if it comes out clean, the cakes are done.
- Transfer the cakes to a wire rack and leave to cool.
- Melt the chocolate in a bain marie and leave to cool until thick.
- Spoon the chocolate onto the cakes and top with a sprinkle of grape-nuts.

256

MAKES 12

Rhubarb and Vanilla Cupcakes

PREPARATION TIME: 35 MINUTES

COOKING TIME: 20 MINUTES

··

INGREDIENTS

1 stem of rhubarb
2 tbsp granulated sugar
110 g / 4 oz / 1 cup self-raising flour, sifted
110 g / 4 oz / ½ cup caster (superfine) sugar
110 g / 4 oz / ½ cup butter, softened
2 large eggs
1 vanilla pod, seeds only

- Preheat the oven to 190°C (170° fan) / 375 F / gas 5 and line a 12-hole cupcake tin with paper cases.
- Cut the rhubarb into small chunks and toss with the granulated sugar, then tip into a roasting tin and bake for 10 minutes.
- Combine the flour, sugar, butter, eggs and vanilla seeds in a bowl and whisk together for 2 minutes.
- Divide the mixture between the paper cases, and top with the cooked rhubarb pieces, then transfer to the oven and bake for 15 – 20 minutes.
- Test with a wooden toothpick, if it comes out clean, the cakes are done.
- Transfer the cakes to a wire rack and leave to cool.

Rhubarb and Ginger Cupcakes 257

Try replacing the vanilla seeds with 2 tbsp chopped stem ginger.

258

MAKES 12

Black Cherry and Marzipan Cupcakes

PREPARATION TIME: 25 MINUTES

COOKING TIME: 25 MINUTES

··

INGREDIENTS

1 large egg
120 ml / 4 fl. oz / ½ cup sunflower oil
120 ml / 4 fl. oz / ½ cup milk
375 g / 12 ½ oz / 2 ½ cups self-raising flour, sifted
1 tsp baking powder
200 g / 7 oz / ¾ cup caster (superfine) sugar
150 g / 5 oz / 1 cup black cherries in syrup, drained
150 g / 5 oz / 1 cup marzipan, cubed

- Preheat the oven to 180°C (160° fan) / 350 F / gas 4 and line a 12-hole muffin tin with paper cases.
- Beat the egg in a jug with the oil and milk until well mixed.
- Mix the flour, baking powder, sugar, cherries and marzipan in a bowl, then pour in the egg mixture and stir just enough to combine.
- Divide the mixture between the paper cases, then bake in the oven for 20 – 25 minutes.
- Test with a wooden toothpick, if it comes out clean, the cakes are done.
- Transfer the cakes to a wire rack and leave to cool.

Zesty Cherry and Marzipan Cupcakes 259

These cupcakes are even tastier with the addition of 2 tsp of finely grated orange zest.

260

MAKES 12

Pistachio and Black Cherry Cupcakes

- Preheat the oven to 190°C (170° fan) / 375 F / gas 5 and line a 12-hole cupcake tin with paper cases.
- Combine the flour, baking powder, ground pistachios, sugar, butter, eggs and almond essence in a bowl and whisk together for 2 minutes.
- Divide half the mixture between the paper cases and press 2 cherries into the top of each.
- Divide the rest of the mixture between the cases then transfer to the oven and bake for 15 – 20 minutes.
- Test with a wooden toothpick, if it comes out clean, the cakes are done.
- Transfer the cakes to a wire rack and leave to cool.
- Pull away the tops of the cupcakes to reveal the cherries within.

PREPARATION TIME: 20 MINUTES

COOKING TIME: 20 MINUTES

INGREDIENTS

55 g / 2 oz / ½ cup self-raising flour, sifted
2 tsp baking powder
55 g / 2 oz / ½ cup ground pistachios
110 g / 4 oz / ½ cup caster (superfine) sugar
110 g / 4 oz / ½ cup butter, softened
2 large eggs
1 tsp almond essence
24 black cherries in syrup, drained

Pistachio and Red Cherry Cupcakes

261

Replace the black cherries with red cherries.

262

MAKES 12

Spicy Raisin Cupcakes

- Preheat the oven to 190°C (170° fan) / 375 F / gas 5 and line a 12-hole cupcake tin with paper cases.
- Combine the flour, ground pecans, sugar, butter, eggs, raisins and spices in a bowl and whisk together for 2 minutes.
- Divide the mixture between the paper cases, then transfer to the oven and bake for 15 – 20 minutes.
- Test with a wooden toothpick, if it comes out clean, the cakes are done.
- Transfer the cakes to a wire rack to cool.

PREPARATION TIME: 35 MINUTES

COOKING TIME: 20 MINUTES

INGREDIENTS

110 g / 4 oz / ½ cup self-raising flour, sifted
110 g / 4 oz / ½ cup caster (superfine) sugar
110 g / 4 oz / ½ cup butter, softened
2 large eggs
75 g / 2 ½ oz / ½ cup raisins
1 tsp mixed spice
½ tsp freshly grated nutmeg

Spicy Sultana Cupcakes

263

Replace the raisins with sultanas.

264

MAKES 12

Chocolate Cupcakes

PREPARATION TIME: 25 MINUTES

COOKING TIME: 20 MINUTES

....

INGREDIENTS

110 g / 4 oz / 1 cup self-raising flour, sifted
28 g / 1 oz / ¼ cup unsweetened cocoa powder, sifted
110 g / 4 oz / ½ cup caster (superfine) sugar
110 g / 4 oz / ½ cup butter, softened
2 large eggs

TO DECORATE
icing (confectioners') sugar to dust

- Preheat the oven to 190°C (170° fan) / 375 F / gas 5 and line a 12-hole cupcake tin with paper cases.
- Combine the flour, cocoa, sugar, butter and eggs in a bowl and whisk together for 2 minutes.
- Divide the mixture between the paper cases, then transfer to the oven and bake for 15 – 20 minutes.
- Test with a wooden toothpick, if it comes out clean, the cakes are done.
- Transfer the cakes to a wire rack and leave to cool completely before dusting lightly with icing (confectioners') sugar.

Chocolate Lime Cupcakes 265

Top these cakes with a spoonful of lime marmalade for chocolate lime cupcakes.

266

MAKES 12

Almond and Pistachio Cupcakes

PREPARATION TIME: 25 MINUTES

COOKING TIME: 25 MINUTES

....

INGREDIENTS

250 g / 9 oz / 1 ¼ cups self-raising flour
1 tsp bicarbonate of (baking) soda
200 g / 8 ½ oz / ½ cup golden syrup
125 g / 4 ½ oz / ½ cup butter
125 g / 4 ½ oz / ¾ cup dark brown sugar
2 large eggs, beaten
240 ml / 8 fl. oz / 1 cup milk
1 tsp almond essence
75 g / 2 ½ oz / ½ cup flaked (slivered) almonds
75 g / 2 ½ oz / ½ cup pistachio nuts, shelled and chopped

- Preheat the oven to 190°C (170° fan) / 375 F / gas 5 and line a 12-hole mini loaf cake tin with paper cases.
- Sieve the flour and bicarbonate of soda together into a bowl.
- Put the golden syrup, butter and brown sugar in a small saucepan and boil gently for 2 minutes, stirring to dissolve the sugar.
- Pour the butter and sugar mixture onto the flour with the eggs, milk and almond essence and fold it all together until smooth.
- Divide the mixture between the paper cases, sprinkle with the flaked almonds and chopped pistachios, then transfer to the oven and bake for 20 – 25 minutes.
- Transfer the cakes to a wire rack and leave to cool.

Crunchy Cupcakes 267

For extra crunch, double the quantity of nuts and stir half of them through the cake mixture before spooning into the cases.

Pecan and Maple Syrup Cupcakes

Pecan and Honey Cupcakes

269

For a sweeter taste, add 1 tsp of honey to the syrup micture.

Almond and Honey Cupcakes

270

Replace the pecans with almonds.

PREPARATION TIME: 35 MINUTES

COOKING TIME: 20 MINUTES

....

INGREDIENTS

55 g / 2 oz / ½ cup self-raising flour, sifted

55 g / 2 oz / ½ cup ground pecan nuts

110 g / 4 oz / ½ cup caster (superfine) sugar

110 g / 4 oz / ½ cup butter, softened

2 large eggs

75 g / 2 ½ oz / ½ cup pecan nuts, chopped

120 ml / 4 fl. oz / ½ cup maple syrup

• Preheat the oven to 190°C (170° fan) / 375 F / gas 5 and line a 12-hole cupcake tin with paper cases.

• Combine the flour, ground pecans, sugar, butter, eggs and chopped pecans in a bowl and whisk together for 2 minutes.

• Divide the mixture between the paper cases, then transfer to the oven and bake for 15 – 20 minutes.

• Test with a wooden toothpick, if it comes out clean, the cakes are done.

• Leave the cakes to cool completely, then pour over the maple syrup.

MAKES 24

Smoked Haddock Mini Cupcakes

271

Smoked Haddock and Garlic Cupcakes

272

Try adding 1 tsp of crushed garlic to the egg mixture before stirring into the dry ingredients.

Smoked Salmon Cupcakes

273

Replace the smoked haddock with smoked salmon.

PREPARATION TIME: 25 MINUTES

COOKING TIME: 15 MINUTES

....

INGREDIENTS

150 g / 5 oz smoked haddock fillet
2 large eggs
120 ml / 4 fl. oz / ½ cup sunflower oil
180 ml / 6 fl. oz / ¾ cup Greek yogurt
110 g / 4 oz / 1 cup Emmental, grated
225 g / 8 oz / 1 ½ cups plain (all purpose) flour
2 tsp baking powder
½ tsp bicarbonate of (baking) soda
½ tsp salt
2 tbsp flat leaf parsley, chopped

- Put the smoked haddock fillet in a bowl and pour over enough boiling water to cover.
- Cover the bowl and leave to stand for 10 minutes, then drain.
- Remove any skin and bones from the fish and break it into flakes with your fingers.
- Preheat the oven to 180°C (160° fan) / 350 F / gas 4 and line a 24-hole muffin tin with paper cases.
- Beat the egg in a jug with the oil, yoghurt and cheese until well mixed.
- Mix the flour, raising agents, salt, parsley and flaked haddock in a bowl, then pour in the egg mixture and stir just enough to combine.
- Divide the mixture between the paper cases, then bake in the oven for 10 – 15 minutes.
- Test with a wooden toothpick, if it comes out clean, the cupcakes are done.
- Serve warm.

274

MAKES 12

Marbled Chocolate Cupcakes

- Preheat the oven to 190°C (170° fan) / 375 F / gas 5 and line a 12-hole cupcake tin with paper cases.
- Combine the flour, sugar, butter and eggs in a bowl and whisk together for 2 minutes.
- Divide the mixture in half and stir the cocoa powder into one half.
- Fill the paper cases with alternate teaspoons of each cake mixture until they are both used up.
- Use a tooth pick to swirl the mixtures together to create a marbled effect.
- Transfer the tin to the oven and bake for 15 – 20 minutes.
- Test with a wooden toothpick, if it comes out clean, the cakes are done.
- Transfer the cakes to a wire rack and leave to cool completely before dusting lightly with icing sugar.

PREPARATION TIME: 25 MINUTES

COOKING TIME: 20 MINUTES

INGREDIENTS

110 g / 4 oz / ½ cup self-raising flour, sifted
110 g / 4 oz / ½ cup caster (superfine) sugar
110 g / 4 oz / ½ cup butter, softened
2 large eggs
28 g / 1 oz / ¼ cup unsweetened cocoa powder, sifted

Marbled Chocolate Chip Cupcakes

275

Add 75g / 3 oz / ⅓ cup white chocolate chips to the plain cake mixture and 75g / 3 oz / ⅓ cup dark chocolate chips to the chocolate cake mixture.

276

MAKES 24

Parmesan and Rosemary Mini Cupcakes

- Preheat the oven to 180°C (160° fan) / 350 F / gas 4 and line a 24-hole muffin tin with paper cases.
- Beat the egg in a jug with the oil, yoghurt and cheese until well mixed.
- Mix the flour, raising agents, salt and rosemary in a bowl, then pour in the egg mixture and stir just enough to combine.
- Divide the mixture between the paper cases, then bake in the oven for 10 – 15 minutes.
- Test with a wooden toothpick, if it comes out clean, the cupcakes are done.
- Serve warm.

PREPARATION TIME: 25 MINUTES

COOKING TIME: 15 MINUTES

INGREDIENTS

2 large eggs
120 ml / 4 fl. oz / ½ cup sunflower oil
180 ml / 6 fl. oz / ¾ cup Greek yogurt
110 g / 4 oz / 1 cup Parmesan, grated
225 g / 8 oz / 1 ½ cups plain (all purpose) flour
2 tsp baking powder
½ tsp bicarbonate of (baking) soda
½ tsp salt
2 tbsp fresh rosemary, chopped

Parmesan and Pine Nut Cupcakes

277

Add 2 tbsp of pine nuts to the cupcake mixture.

278

MAKES 12

Milk Chocolate Ganache Cupcakes

PREPARATION TIME: 30 MINUTES

COOKING TIME: 20 MINUTES

....

INGREDIENTS

110 g / 4 oz / ½ cup self-raising flour, sifted
28 g / 1 oz / ¼ cup unsweetened cocoa powder, sifted
110 g / 4 oz / ½ cup caster (superfine) sugar
110 g / 4 oz / ½ cup butter, softened
2 large eggs
1 tsp vanilla extract

TO DECORATE

225 ml / 8 fl. oz / 1 cup double (heavy) cream
225 g / 8 oz milk chocolate, chopped
2 tbsp unsweetened cocoa powder

- Preheat the oven to 190°C (170° fan) / 375 F / gas 5 and line a 12-hole cupcake tin with paper cases.
- Combine the flour, cocoa, sugar, butter, eggs and vanilla extract in a bowl and whisk together for 2 minutes.
- Divide the mixture between the paper cases then transfer to the oven and bake for 15 – 20 minutes.
- Transfer the cakes to a wire rack and leave to cool.
- Heat the cream until it starts to simmer, then pour it over the chopped chocolate.
- Stir the ganache until the mixture has cooled and thickened, then refrigerate until thick enough to pipe.
- Spoon the ganache into a piping bag and pipe a generous swirl on top of each cake.
- Dust the cakes with cocoa powder.

White Chocolate Ganache Cupcakes

279

Replace the milk chocolate in the ganache with chopped white chocolate and decorate the cakes with dark chocolate curls.

280

MAKES 12

Little Bear Cupcakes

PREPARATION TIME: 1 HOUR

COOKING TIME: 20 MINUTES

....

INGREDIENTS

110 g / 4 oz / ½ cup self-raising flour, sifted
110 g / 4 oz / ½ cup caster (superfine) sugar
110 g / 4 oz / ½ cup butter, softened
2 large eggs
1 tsp vanilla extract

TO DECORATE

110 g / 4 oz / ½ cup butter, softened
225 g / 8 oz / 2 cups icing (confectioners') sugar
2 tbsp milk
1 tsp vanilla extract
pink ready to roll fondant icing
2 tbsp dark chocolate, melted

- Preheat the oven to 190°C (170° fan) / 375 F / gas 5 and line a 12-hole cupcake tin with pink paper cases.
- Combine the flour, sugar, butter, eggs and vanilla extract in a bowl and whisk together for 2 minutes.
- Divide the mixture between the paper cases, then transfer to the oven and bake for 15 – 20 minutes.
- Transfer the cakes to a wire rack and leave to cool.
- Beat the butter with a wooden spoon until light and fluffy then beat in the icing sugar. Use a whisk to add the milk and vanilla extract, then whisk for 2 minutes.
- Reserve 1 tbsp of the buttercream and spoon the rest into a piping bag fitted with a star nozzle and pipe a swirl on top of each cake.
- Model the bears out of fondant icing. Spoon the melted chocolate into a small piping bag.
- Colour the reserved buttercream with a little blue food colouring and spoon into a small piping bag.
- Sit a bear on top of each cupcake and pipe on the eyes and noses with the chocolate.
- Finally, pipe on the blue bows with the buttercream.

281

MAKES 12

Chocolate and Strawberry Cupcakes

- Preheat the oven to 190°C (170° fan) / 375 F / gas 5 and line a 12-hole cupcake tin with paper cases.
- Combine the flour, cocoa, sugar, butter, eggs and strawberry syrup in a bowl and whisk together for 2 minutes.
- Divide the mixture between the paper cases, then transfer to the oven and bake for 15 – 20 minutes.
- Transfer the cakes to a wire rack and leave to cool.
- To make the strawberry cream, whisk the cream with the strawberry syrup until thick.
- Spoon the cream into a piping bag fitted with a large star nozzle and pipe a generous swirl on top of each cake.
- Sprinkle with heart-shaped cake sprinkles.

Chocolate and Orange Cream Cupcakes

282

Replace the strawberry syrup in the cake mixture and cream with 2 tsp of finely grated orange zest and decorate the cupcakes with candied peel.

PREPARATION TIME: 35 MINUTES

COOKING TIME: 20 MINUTES

....

INGREDIENTS

110 g / 4 oz / ½ cup self-raising flour, sifted
28 g / 1 oz / ¼ cup unsweetened cocoa powder, sifted
110 g / 4 oz / ½ cup caster (superfine) sugar
110 g / 4 oz / ½ cup butter, softened
2 large eggs
2 tbsp strawberry syrup

TO DECORATE
225 ml / 8 fl. oz / 1 cup double (heavy) cream
2 tbsp strawberry syrup
Heart-shaped cake sprinkles

283

MAKES 36

Chocolate and Sesame Cupcakes

- Preheat the oven to 170°C (150° fan) / 325 F / gas 3 and line a 36-hole mini cupcake tin with paper cases.
- Melt the chocolate, cocoa and butter together in a saucepan, then leave to cool a little.
- Whisk the sugar and eggs together with an electric whisk for 3 minutes or until very light and creamy.
- Pour in the chocolate mixture and sieve over the flour, then fold everything together with the sesame seeds until evenly mixed.
- Spoon into the cake cases and bake for 10 – 15 minutes or until the outside is set, but the centres are still quite soft, as they will continue to cook as they cool.

Sesame and Coconut Cupcakes

284

Try adding 2 tbsp of desiccated coconut to the mixture with the sesame seeds.

PREPARATION TIME: 25 MINUTES

COOKING TIME: 15 MINUTES

....

INGREDIENTS

110 g / 4 oz / ½ cup dark chocolate, minimum 60% cocoa solids, chopped
85 g / 3 oz / ¾ cup unsweetened cocoa powder, sifted
225 g / 8 oz / 1 cup butter
450 g / 15 oz / 2 ½ cups light brown sugar
4 large eggs
110 g / 4 oz / 1 cup self-raising flour
2 tbsp sesame seeds

285
MAKES 24

Cheddar and Chive Mini Cupcakes

Sour Cream, Cheddar and Chive Cupcakes

286

Top the cupcakes with a spoonful of sour cream and a sprinkling of chopped chives.

PREPARATION TIME: 25 MINUTES

**COOKING TIME:
10 – 15 MINUTES**

....

INGREDIENTS

2 large eggs
120 ml / 4 fl. oz / ½ cup sunflower oil
180 ml / 6 fl. oz / ¾ cup Greek yoghurt
110 g / 4 oz / 1 cup cheddar, grated
225 g / 8 oz / 1 ½ cups plain flour
2 tsp baking powder
½ tsp bicarbonate of (baking) soda
½ tsp salt
2 tbsp fresh chives, chopped

- Preheat the oven to 180°°C (160° fan) / 350 F / gas 4 and oil a 24-hole muffin mould.
- Beat the egg in a jug with the oil, yoghurt and cheese until well mixed.
- Mix the flour, raising agents, salt and chives in a bowl, then pour in the egg mixture and stir just enough to combine.
- Divide the mixture between the paper cases, then bake in the oven for 10 – 15 minutes.
- Test with a wooden toothpick, if it comes out clean, the cupcakes are done.
- Serve warm.

287

MAKES 12

Sweet Potato Cupcakes

- Preheat the oven to 190C (170C fan) / 375F / gas 5 and line a 12-hole cupcake tin with paper cases.
- Combine the flour, sugar, butter, eggs and sweet potato puree in a bowl and whisk together for 2 minutes or until smooth.
- Divide the mixture between the paper cases, then transfer the tin to the oven and bake for 15 – 20 minutes.
- Test with a wooden toothpick, if it comes out clean, the cakes are done.
- Transfer the cakes to a wire rack and leave to cool completely.
- Melt the chocolate in a microwave or bain marie and spoon into a piping bag with a small star nozzle.
- Pipe the chocolate onto the cakes and finish with a couple of dried mango strips.

PREPARATION TIME 35 MINUTES

COOKING TIME 20 MINUTES

INGREDIENTS

110g / 4 oz / 1/2 cup self-raising flour, sifted
110g / 4 oz / ½ cup caster (superfine) sugar
110g / 4 oz / ½ cup butter, softened
2 large eggs
1 sweet potato (110g / 4oz / 1/2 cup) , peeled, cooked and pureed

TO DECORATE
110g / 4 oz / ½ cup milk chocolate, chopped
4 dried mango slices, cut into thin strips

288

MAKES 12

Pink Iced Wholemeal Cupcakes

- Preheat the oven to 190°C (170° fan) / 375 F / gas 5 and line a 12-hole cupcake tin with paper cases.
- Combine the flours, sugar, butter, eggs and vanilla extract in a bowl and whisk together for 2 minutes.
- Divide the mixture between the paper cases, then transfer to the oven and bake for 15 – 20 minutes.
- Test with a wooden toothpick, if it comes out clean, the cakes are done.
- Transfer the cakes to a wire rack and leave to cool completely before dusting with icing sugar.
- Beat the butter with a wooden spoon until light and fluffy then beat in the icing sugar a quarter at a time.
- Use a whisk to incorporate the milk and food colouring, then whisk for 2 minutes.
- Spoon the icing into a piping bag and pipe a small swirl on top of each cake.

PREPARATION TIME: 25 MINUTES

COOKING TIME: 20 MINUTES

INGREDIENTS

55 g / 2 oz / ½ cup self-raising flour, sifted
55 g / 2 oz / ½ cup wholemeal flour
1 tsp bicarbonate of (baking) soda
110 g / 4 oz / ½ cup caster (superfine) sugar
110 g / 4 oz / ½ cup butter, softened
2 large eggs
1 tsp vanilla extract
Icing (confectioners') sugar, to dust

TO DECORATE
110 g / 4 oz / ½ cup butter, softened
225 g / 8 oz / 2 cups icing (confectioners') sugar
2 tbsp milk
pink food colouring

Wholemeal Cupcakes with Orange Buttercream

289

Replace the milk in the buttercream with orange juice and replace the pink food colouring with 1 tsp finely grated orange zest.

290

MAKES 36

Elderflower Mini Cupcakes

PREPARATION TIME: 45 MINUTES

COOKING TIME: 15 MINUTES

INGREDIENTS

110 g / 4 oz / ½ cup self-raising flour, sifted
110 g / 4 oz / ½ cup caster (superfine) sugar
110 g / 4 oz / ½ cup butter, softened
2 large eggs
1 tbsp elderflower cordial

TO DECORATE

1 lemon, juiced
2 tbsp caster (superfine) sugar
2 tsp elderflower cordial
Handful fresh elderflowers

- Preheat the oven to 190°C (170 fan) / 375 F / gas 5 and line a 36 hole mini cupcake tin with paper cases.
- Combine the flour, sugar, butter, eggs and cordial in a bowl and whisk together for 2 minutes.
- Divide the mixture between the paper cases then transfer to the oven and bake for 10 – 15 minutes.
- Test with a wooden toothpick, if it comes out clean, the cakes are done.
- While the cakes are cooking, make the soaking syrup. Put the lemon juice and caster sugar in a small saucepan and boil for 2 minutes, then turn off the heat and stir in the elderflower cordial.
- When the cakes are ready, spoon over the soaking syrup and leave them to cool in their tin before topping with the fresh elderflowers.

Lemon Elderflower Cupcakes **291**

For lemon and elderflower cupcakes, just add the grated zest of 1 lemon to the cake mixture and continue as above.

292

MAKES 12

Moist Cherry Frangipane Cupcakes

PREPARATION TIME: 20 MINUTES

COOKING TIME: 25 MINUTES

INGREDIENTS

55 g / 2 oz / ½ cup self-raising flour, sifted
55 g / 2 oz / ½ cup ground almonds
110 g / 4 oz / ½ cup caster (superfine) sugar
110 g / 4 oz / ½ cup butter, softened
2 large eggs
1 tsp almond essence
350 g / 12 oz fresh cherries
2 tbsp icing (confectioners') sugar

- Preheat the oven to 190°C (170° fan) / 375 F / gas 5 and oil a 6-hole silicone tartlet mould or 6 individual tartlet tins.
- Combine the flour, ground almonds, sugar, butter, eggs and almond essence in a bowl and whisk together for 2 minutes.
- Divide the mixture between the moulds.
- Stone the cherries with a cherry pitter and press 6 or 7 into the top of each cake.
- Transfer the cakes to the oven and bake for 20 – 25 minutes.
- Test with a wooden toothpick, if it comes out clean, the cakes are done.
- Transfer the cakes to a wire rack to cool.
- Dust the top of the cakes with icing sugar just before serving.

Mirabelle Plum Frangipane Cupcakes **293**

For a seasonal change, try using small Mirabelle plums or greengages instead of the cherries.

294

MAKES 24

Courgette and Mint Mini Cupcakes

Courgette and Brie Cupcakes
295

Try adding 5 tbsp of chopped Brie to the mixture before baking.

Carrot and Parsley Mini Cupcakes
296

Replace the courgette with 2 grated carrots and the mint with fresh parsley.

PREPARATION TIME: 25 MINUTES

COOKING TIME: 15 MINUTES

....

INGREDIENTS

2 large eggs
120 ml / 4 fl. oz / ½ cup sunflower oil
180 ml / 6 fl. oz / ¾ cup Greek yogurt
2 courgettes (zucchini), coarsely grated
110 g / 4 oz / 1 cup Parmesan, grated
225 g / 8 oz / 1 ½ cups plain (all purpose) flour
2 tsp baking powder
½ tsp bicarbonate of (baking) soda
½ tsp salt
2 tbsp fresh mint, chopped

- Preheat the oven to 180°C (160° fan) / 350 F / gas 4 and line a 24-hole muffin tin with paper cases.
- Beat the egg in a jug with the oil, yoghurt, courgette and cheese until well mixed.
- Mix the flour, raising agents, salt and mint in a bowl, then pour in the egg mixture and stir just enough to combine.
- Divide the mixture between the paper cases, then bake in the oven for 10 – 15 minutes.
- Test with a wooden toothpick, if it comes out clean, the cupcakes are done.
- Serve warm.

MUFFINS AND MACAROONS

297

MAKES 12

Gremolata Muffins

PREPARATION TIME: 10 MINUTES

COOKING TIME: 45 MINUTES

INGREDIENTS

2 large eggs
120 ml / 4 fl. oz / ½ cup sunflower oil
180 ml / 6 fl. oz / ¾ cup Greek yogurt
110 g / 4 oz / 1 cup Parmesan, grated
225 g / 8 oz / 1 ½ cups plain (all purpose) flour
2 tsp baking powder
½ tsp bicarbonate of (baking) soda
½ tsp salt
½ tbsp chopped garlic
½ tbsp lemon zest, finely grated
2 tbsp flat leaf parsley, finely chopped

- Preheat the oven to 180°C (160° fan) / 350 F / gas 4 and oil a 12-hole silicone muffin tin.
- Beat the egg in a jug with the oil, yogurt and cheese until well mixed.
- Mix the flour, raising agents, salt garlic, lemon zest and parsley in a bowl, then pour in the egg mixture and stir just enough to combine.
- Divide the mixture between the moulds, then bake in the oven for 20 – 25 minutes.
- Test with a wooden toothpick, if it comes out clean, the muffins are done.
- Transfer the muffins to a wire rack and leave to cool.

Gremolata and Mozzarella Muffins

298

Add a cube of fresh mozzarella to the centre of each muffin before baking.

299

MAKES 12

Chocolate Orange Muffins

PREPARATION TIME: 25 MINUTES

COOKING TIME: 25 MINUTES

INGREDIENTS

1 large egg
120ml / 4 fl oz / ½ cup sunflower oil
120ml / 4 fl oz / ½ cup milk
375g / 12 ½ oz / 2 ½ cups self-raising flour, sifted
55g / 2 oz / ½ cup unsweetened cocoa powder, sifted
1 tsp baking powder
200g / 7 oz / ¾ cup caster (superfine) sugar
110g / 4 oz / ½ cup orange flavoured chocolate, chopped
1 orange, zest finely grated

- Preheat the oven to 180C (160C fan) / 350F / gas 4 and line a 12-hole muffin tin with paper cases.
- Beat the egg in a jug with the oil and milk until well mixed.
- Mix the flour, cocoa, baking powder, sugar, chocolate and orange zest in a bowl, then pour in the egg mixture and stir just enough to combine.
- Divide the mixture between the paper cases, then bake in the oven for 20 – 25 minutes.
- Test with a wooden toothpick, if it comes out clean, the muffins are done.
- Transfer the muffins to a wire rack and leave to cool completely.

Hot Orange Sauce

300

Make a hot chocolate orange sauce to accompany the muffins: heat 225ml / 8 fl. oz / 1 cup double cream until boiling then pour over 225g / 8 oz / 1 cup chopped orange flavoured chocolate and stir until smooth.

301

MAKES 12

Summer Fruit and Almond Muffins

Almond Drizzle Icing

302

Make an almond drizzle icing by mixing 225g / 8 oz icing sugar with ½ tsp almond essence and just enough boiling water to make a spoonable icing.

Summer Fruit and Walnut Muffins

303

Replace the almonds with walnuts.

PREPARATION TIME: 25 MINUTES

COOKING TIME:
20 – 25 MINUTES

....

INGREDIENTS

1 large egg
120 ml / 4 fl. oz / ½ cup sunflower oil
120 ml / 4 fl. oz / ½ cup milk
375 g / 12 ½ oz / 2 ½ cups self-raising flour, sifted
1 tsp baking powder
200 g / 7 oz / ¾ cup caster (superfine) sugar
150 g / 5 oz / 1 cup mixed summer fruits
75 g / 2 ½ oz / ½ cup flaked (slivered) almonds

- Preheat the oven to 180°C (160° fan) / 350 F / gas 4 and line a 12-hole muffin tin with paper cases.
- Beat the egg in a jug with the oil and milk until well mixed.
- Mix the flour, baking powder, sugar, fruit and almonds in a bowl, then pour in the egg mixture and stir just enough to combine.
- Divide the mixture between the paper cases, then bake in the oven for 20 – 25 minutes.
- Test with a wooden toothpick, if it comes out clean, the muffins are done.
- Transfer the muffins to a wire rack and leave to cool completely.

MAKES 12 304

Almond Muffins

Fruit and Nut Muffins 305

Use this as a base recipe and add your choice of dried fruit and nuts.

Marzipan Covered Muffins 306

Roll out 200 g / 7 oz of marzipan and cut out 12 circles. Lay a circle of marzipan on top of each muffin before baking for a golden bubbly crust.

PREPARATION TIME: 25 MINUTES

COOKING TIME:
20 – 25 MINUTES
....

INGREDIENTS

1 large egg
120 ml / 4 fl. oz / ½ cup sunflower oil
120 ml / 4 fl. oz / ½ cup milk
375 g / 12 ½ oz / 2 ½ cups self-raising flour, sifted
1 tsp baking powder
200 g / 7 oz / ¾ cup caster (superfine) sugar
75 g / 2 ½ oz / ½ cup ground almonds
75 g / 2 ½ oz / ½ cup flaked (slivered) almonds

- Preheat the oven to 180°°C (160° fan) / 350 F / gas 4 and oil a 12-hole silicone muffin mould.
- Beat the egg in a jug with the oil and milk until well mixed.
- Mix the flour, baking powder, sugar and almonds in a bowl, then pour in the egg mixture and stir just enough to combine.
- Divide the mixture between the paper cases and sprinkle with flaked almonds, then bake in the oven for 20 – 25 minutes.
- Test with a wooden toothpick, if it comes out clean, the muffins are done.
- Transfer the muffins to a wire rack and leave to cool completely.

307

MAKES 12

Almond and Raspberry Muffins

- Preheat the oven to 180°C (160° fan) / 350 F / gas 4 and line a 12-hole muffin tin with paper cases.
- Beat the egg in a jug with the oil and milk until well mixed.
- Mix the flour, baking powder, sugar, ground almonds and raspberries in a bowl, then pour in the egg mixture and stir just enough to combine.
- Divide the mixture between the paper cases and bake in the oven for 20 – 25 minutes.
- Test with a wooden toothpick, if it comes out clean, the muffins are done.
- Transfer the muffins to a wire rack and leave to cool before dusting with icing sugar.

PREPARATION TIME: 25 MINUTES

COOKING TIME: 25 MINUTES

INGREDIENTS

1 large egg
120 ml / 4 fl. oz / ½ cup sunflower oil
120 ml / 4 fl. oz / ½ cup milk
375 g / 12 ½ oz / 2 ½ cups self-raising flour, sifted
1 tsp baking powder
200 g / 7 oz / ¾ cup caster (superfine) sugar
75 g / 2 ½ oz / ½ cup ground almonds
150 g / 5 oz / 1 cup raspberries
Icing (confectioners') sugar for dusting

Almond Muffins with Rosewater

308

Add 1 tbsp of rose water to the wet ingredients before mixing for an aromatic change.

309

MAKES 12

Spring Onion Muffins

- Preheat the oven to 180°C (160° fan) / 350 F / gas 4 and oil a 12-hole silicone muffin mould.
- Beat the egg in a jug with the oil, yogurt, cheese and spring onion until well mixed.
- Mix the flour, raising agents and salt in a bowl, then pour in the egg mixture and stir just enough to combine.
- Divide the mixture between the moulds, then bake in the oven for 20 – 25 minutes.
- Test with a wooden toothpick, if it comes out clean, the muffins are done.
- Serve warm.

PREPARATION TIME: 25 MINUTES

COOKING TIME: 25 MINUTES

INGREDIENTS

2 large eggs
120 ml / 4 fl. oz / ½ cup sunflower oil
180 ml / 6 fl. oz / ¾ cup Greek yogurt
110 g / 4 oz / 1 cup Comte cheese, grated
6 spring onions (scallions), chopped
225 g / 8 oz / 1 cup plain (all purpose) flour
2 tsp baking powder
½ tsp bicarbonate of (baking) soda
½ tsp salt

Spring Onion and Bacon Muffins

 310

Add 4 chopped rashers of smoked streaky bacon to the wet ingredients before folding everything together.

311

MAKES 24

Coconut and Almond Mini Muffins

PREPARATION TIME: 10 MINUTES

COOKING TIME: 45 MINUTES

INGREDIENTS

1 large egg
120 ml / 4 fl. oz / ½ cup sunflower oil
120 ml / 4 fl. oz / ½ cup milk
2 tbsp honey
375 g / 12 ½ oz / 2 ½ cups self-raising flour, sifted
1 tsp baking powder
200 g / 7 oz / ¾ cup caster (superfine) sugar
55 g / 2 oz / ½ cup ground almonds
55 g / 2 oz / ½ cup desiccated coconut

- Preheat the oven to 180°C (160° fan) / 350 F / gas 4 and oil a 24-hole silicone mini muffin mould.
- Beat the egg in a jug with the oil, milk and honey until well mixed.
- Mix the flour, baking powder, sugar, ground almonds and coconut in a bowl, then pour in the egg mixture and stir just enough to combine.
- Divide the mixture between the moulds, then bake in the oven for 15 – 20 minutes.
- Test with a wooden toothpick, if it comes out clean, the muffins are done.
- Transfer the muffins to a wire rack and leave to cool.

Coconut Topped Muffins

312

Try drizzling the muffins with a little plain white icing and topping with sweetened shredded coconut.

313

MAKES 12

Dried Fig and Stilton Muffins

PREPARATION TIME: 10 MINUTES

COOKING TIME: 45 MINUTES

INGREDIENTS

2 large eggs
120 ml / 4 fl. oz / ½ cup sunflower oil
180 ml / 6 fl. oz / ¾ cup Greek yogurt
110 g / 4 oz / 1 cup Stilton, crumbled
75 g / 2 ½ oz / ½ cup dried figs, chopped
225 g / 8 oz / 1 ½ cups plain (all purpose) flour
2 tsp baking powder
½ tsp bicarbonate of (baking) soda
½ tsp salt

- Preheat the oven to 180°C (160° fan) / 350 F / gas 4 and line a 12-hole muffin tin with paper cases.
- Beat the egg in a jug with the oil, yoghurt, cheese and figs until well mixed.
- Mix the flour, raising agents and salt in a bowl, then pour in the egg mixture and stir just enough to combine.
- Divide the mixture between the paper cases, then bake in the oven for 20 – 25 minutes.
- Test with a wooden toothpick, if it comes out clean, the muffins are done.
- Serve warm.

Dried Fig and Thyme Muffins

314

Try adding 2 tbsp of fresh thyme leaves to the muffin mixture.

315

MAKES 36

Vanilla Mini Muffins

- Preheat the oven to 190°C (170° fan) / 375 F / gas 5 and oil 36 mini silicone cupcake cases.
- Combine the flour, sugar, butter, eggs and vanilla extract in a bowl and whisk together for 2 minutes or until smooth.
- Divide the mixture between the paper cases and bake for 10 – 15 minutes.
- Test with a wooden toothpick, if it comes out clean, the muffins are done.
- Transfer the muffins to a wire rack and leave to cool completely.

PREPARATION TIME: 25 MINUTES

COOKING TIME: I5 MINUTES

INGREDIENTS

110 g / 4 oz / ½ cup self-raising flour, sifted

110 g / 4 oz / ½ cup caster (superfine) sugar

110 g / 4 oz / ½ cup butter, softened

2 large eggs

1 tsp vanilla extract

Hazelnut and Vanilla Muffins 316

Spread half a teaspoon of chocolate hazelnut spread on the top of the muffins and chill for 1 hour to set.

317

MAKES 12

Blackberry Muffins

- Preheat the oven to 190°C (170° fan) / 375 F / gas 5 and oil a 12-hole silicone cupcake mould.
- Combine the flour, sugar, butter and eggs in a bowl and whisk together for 2 minutes or until smooth.
- Fold in the blackberries then divide the mixture between the moulds.
- Transfer the mould to the oven and bake for 15 – 20 minutes.
- Test with a wooden toothpick, if it comes out clean, the muffins are done.
- Transfer the muffins to a wire rack and leave to cool.

PREPARATION TIME: 10 MINUTES

COOKING TIME: 45 MINUTES

INGREDIENTS

110 g / 4 oz / ½ cup self-raising flour, sifted

110 g / 4 oz / ½ cup caster (superfine) sugar

110 g / 4 oz / ½ cup butter, softened

2 large eggs

1 tsp vanilla extract

150 g / 5 oz / 1 cup blackberries

Blackberry and Cream Muffins 318

Try topping with a swirl of whipped cream and a few fresh blackberries.

319
MAKES 12

Pear and Chocolate Chunk Muffins

PREPARATION TIME: 25 MINUTES

COOKING TIME: 25 MINUTES

INGREDIENTS

1 large egg
120 ml / 4 fl. oz / ½ cup sunflower oil
120 ml / 4 fl. oz / ½ cup milk
375 g / 12 ½ oz / 2 ½ cups self-raising flour, sifted
1 tsp baking powder
200 g / 7 oz / ¾ cup caster (superfine) sugar
110 g / 4 oz / ½ cup dark chocolate, minimum 60% cocoa solids, chopped
6 canned pear halves, chopped
To decorate
2 canned pear halves, sliced

- Preheat the oven to 180°C (160° fan) / 350 F / gas 4 and oil a 12-hole silicone muffin tin.
- Beat the egg in a jug with the oil and milk until well mixed.
- Mix the flour, baking powder, sugar, chocolate and chopped pear in a bowl, then pour in the egg mixture and stir just enough to combine.
- Divide the mixture between the moulds, then bake in the oven for 20 – 25 minutes.
- Test with a wooden toothpick, if it comes out clean, the muffins are done.
- Transfer the muffins to a wire rack and leave to cool completely before topping the muffins with a slice of pear.

Pear Muffins with Chocolate Sauce

320

Heat 225ml / 8 fl. oz / 1 cup double cream until boiling then pour over 225g / 8 oz chopped dark chocolate and stir until smooth.

321
MAKES 12

Spinach and Pine Nut Muffins

PREPARATION TIME: 25 MINUTES

COOKING TIME: 25 MINUTES

INGREDIENTS

110 g / 4 oz / 4 cups fresh spinach
2 large eggs
120 ml / 4 fl. oz / ½ cup sunflower oil
180 ml / 6 fl. oz / ¾ cup Greek yogurt
110 g / 4 oz / 1 cup Parmesan, grated
75 g / 2 ½ oz / ½ cup pine nuts, chopped
225 g / 8 oz / 1 ½ cups plain (all purpose) flour
2 tsp baking powder
½ tsp bicarbonate of (baking) soda
½ tsp salt

- Preheat the oven to 180°C (160° fan) / 350 F / gas 4 and line a 12-hole muffin tin with paper cases.
- Put the spinach in a large saucepan with 2 tbsp of water.
- Cover the pan and put over a medium heat for 4 minutes or until the spinach has cooked right down.
- Squeeze out any excess moisture and puree in a food processor.
- Beat the egg in a jug with the oil, yoghurt, cheese and spinach puree until well mixed.
- Mix the pine nuts, flour, raising agents and salt in a bowl, then pour in the spinach mixture and stir just enough to combine.
- Divide the mixture between the paper cases, then bake in the oven for 20 – 25 minutes.
- Test with a wooden toothpick, if it comes out clean, the muffins are done.
- Serve warm.

Spinach and Smoked Salmon Muffins

322

Serve the warm muffins with a dollop of crème fraiche and some thinly sliced smoked salmon.

323

MAKES 12

Black Onion Seed Muffins

Black Onion and
Feta Muffins

324

Try adding 75g / 3 oz / ⅓ cup
cubed feta.

Black Onion and
Poppy Seed Muffins

325

Replace the black onion seeds
with poppy seeds.

PREPARATION TIME: 25 MINUTES

COOKING TIME: 25 MINUTES

....

INGREDIENTS

2 large eggs
120 ml / 4 fl. oz / ½ cup sunflower oil
180 ml / 6 fl. oz / ¾ cup Greek yogurt
110 g / 4 oz / 1 cup Parmesan, grated
225 g / 8 oz / 1 ½ cups plain (all
purpose) flour
2 tsp baking powder
½ tsp bicarbonate of (baking) soda
½ tsp salt
2 tbsp black onion seeds

- Preheat the oven to 180°C (160° fan) / 350 F / gas 4 and
  oil 12 muffin tins.
- Beat the egg in a jug with the oil, yoghurt and cheese
  until well mixed.
- Mix the flour, raising agents, salt and ¾ of the onion
  seeds in a bowl, then pour in the egg mixture and stir
  just enough to combine.
- Divide the mixture between the paper cases and
  sprinkle with the rest of the seeds, then bake in the oven
  for 20 – 25 minutes.
- Test with a wooden toothpick, if it comes out clean, the
  muffins are done.
- Serve warm.

326

MAKES 24

Mini Vanilla Muffins

PREPARATION TIME: 25 MINUTES

COOKING TIME: 15-20 MINUTES

INGREDIENTS

1 large egg
120 ml / 4 fl. oz / ½ cup sunflower oil
120 ml / 4 fl. oz / ½ cup milk
1 tsp vanilla extract
375 g / 12 ½ oz / 2 ½ cups self-raising
flour, sifted
1 tsp baking powder
200 g / 7 oz / ¾ cup caster (superfine)
sugar

- Preheat the oven to 180°°C (160° fan) / 350 F / gas 4 and oil a 24-hole heart-shaped mini muffin mould.
- Beat the egg in a jug with the oil, milk and vanilla extract until well mixed.
- Mix the flour, baking powder and sugar in a bowl, then pour in the egg mixture and stir just enough to combine.
- Divide the mixture between the moulds, then bake in the oven for 15 – 20 minutes.
- Test with a wooden toothpick, if it comes out clean, the muffins are done.
- Transfer the muffins to a wire rack and leave to cool completely.

Vanilla and Pear Mini Muffins
327

Add 1 chopped pear to the muffin mixture.

328

MAKES 12

Green Olive and Emmental Muffins

PREPARATION TIME: 25 MINUTES

COOKING TIME: 25 MINUTES

INGREDIENTS

2 large eggs
120 ml / 4 fl. oz / ½ cup sunflower oil
180 ml / 6 fl. oz / ¾ cup Greek yogurt
225 g / 8 oz / 2 cups Emmental,
grated
225 g / 8 oz / 1 ½ cups plain flour
2 tsp baking powder
½ tsp bicarbonate of (baking) soda
½ tsp salt
75 g / 2 ½ oz / ½ cup green olives,
pitted

- Preheat the oven to 180°C (160° fan) / 350 F / gas 4 and oil a 12-hole silicone muffin tin.
- Beat the egg in a jug with the oil, yogurt and half of the cheese until well mixed.
- Mix the flour, raising agents, salt and olives in a bowl, then pour in the egg mixture and stir just enough to combine.
- Divide the mixture between the moulds and sprinkle with the rest of the cheese, then bake in the oven for 20 – 25 minutes.
- Test with a wooden toothpick, if it comes out clean, the muffins are done.
- Serve warm.

Green Olive and Anchovy Muffins
329

Try adding 2 tbsp chopped anchovies to the muffin mixture.

330

MAKES 12

Halloween Pumpkin Muffins

- Preheat the oven to 180°C (160° fan) / 350 F / gas 4 and line a 12-hole muffin tin with paper cases.
- Beat the egg in a jug with the oil and milk until well mixed.
- Mix the flour, baking powder, sugar and grated pumpkin in a bowl, then pour in the egg mixture and stir just enough to combine.
- Divide the mixture between the cases and sprinkle with sugar nibs, then bake in the oven for 20 – 25 minutes.
- Test with a wooden toothpick, if it comes out clean, the muffins are done.
- Transfer the muffins to a wire rack and leave to cool.

PREPARATION TIME: 25 MINUTES

COOKING TIME: 25 MINUTES

INGREDIENTS

1 large egg
120 ml / 4 fl. oz / ½ cup sunflower oil
120 ml / 4 fl. oz / ½ cup milk
375 g / 12 ½ oz / 2 ½ cups self-raising flour, sifted
1 tsp baking powder
200 g / 7 oz / ¾ cup caster (superfine) sugar
150 g / 5 oz / 1 cup pumpkin, peeled and grated
2 tbsp sugar nibs

Pumpkin and Orange Muffins

331

Add 2 tbsp of orange juice and the zest of 1 orange to the muffin mixture before cooking.

332

MAKES 12

Porridge Muffins

- Soak all but 2 tbsp of the oats in the milk for 1 hour.
- Preheat the oven to 180°°C (160° fan) / 350 F / gas 4 and oil a 12-hole silicone muffin tin.
- Beat the egg in a jug with the oil and oat mixture until well mixed.
- Mix the flour, baking powder and sugar in a bowl, then pour in the egg mixture and stir just enough to combine.
- Divide the mixture between the paper cases and sprinkle with the reserved oats, then bake in the oven for 20 – 25 minutes.
- Test with a wooden toothpick, if it comes out clean, the muffins are done.
- Serve the muffins warm with butter.

PREPARATION TIME: 25 MINUTES

COOKING TIME: 20 – 25 MINUTES

INGREDIENTS

75 g / 2 ½ oz / ½ cup porridge oats
120 ml / 4 fl. oz / ½ cup milk
1 large egg
120 ml / 4 fl. oz / ½ cup sunflower oil
375 g / 12 ½ oz / 2 ½ cups self-raising flour, sifted
1 tsp baking powder
200 g / 7 oz / ¾ cup caster (superfine) sugar

Honey Porridge Muffins

333

Stir 75 g of honey into the wet ingredients before mixing together.

334

MAKES 12

Chocolate Egg Muffins

White Chocolate Egg Muffins

335

Replace the milk chocolate eggs with white chocolate eggs.

PREPARATION TIME: 25 MINUTES

COOKING TIME: 20 MINUTES

INGREDIENTS

110 g / 4 oz / ½ cup self-raising flour, sifted
28 g / 1 oz / ¼ cup unsweetened cocoa powder, sifted
110 g / 4 oz / ½ cup caster (superfine) sugar
110 g / 4 oz / ½ cup butter, softened
2 large eggs
To Decorate
Cocoa powder to dust
36 chocolate eggs

• Preheat the oven to 190°C (170° fan) / 375 F / gas 5 and oil a 12-hole silicone cupcake mould.
• Combine the flour, cocoa, sugar, butter and eggs in a bowl and whisk together for 2 minutes or until smooth.
• Divide the mixture between the paper cases, then transfer the tin to the oven and bake for 15 – 20 minutes.
• Test with a wooden toothpick, if it comes out clean, the cakes are done.
• Transfer the cakes to a wire rack and leave to cool completely before dusting lightly with cocoa powder.
• Arrange 3 chocolate eggs on top of each cake.

336

MAKES 12

White Chocolate and Poppy Seed Muffins

- Preheat the oven to 180°C (160° fan) / 350 F / gas 4 and line a 12-hole muffin tin with paper cases.
- Beat the egg in a jug with the oil and milk until well mixed.
- Mix the flour, baking powder, sugar, white chocolate and poppy seeds in a bowl, then pour in the egg mixture and stir just enough to combine.
- Divide the mixture between the moulds, then bake in the oven for 20 – 25 minutes.
- Test with a wooden toothpick, if it comes out clean, the muffins are done.
- Transfer the muffins to a wire rack and leave to cool completely.
- To decorate, melt the white chocolate in a microwave or bain marie and spoon over the muffins.
- Sprinkle with poppy seeds then leave the chocolate to set.

PREPARATION TIME: 25 MINUTES

COOKING TIME: 25 MINUTES

INGREDIENTS

1 large egg
120 ml / 4 fl. oz / ½ cup sunflower oil
120 ml / 4 fl. oz / ½ cup milk
375 g / 12 ½ oz / 2 ½ cups self-raising flour, sifted
1 tsp baking powder
200 g / 7 oz / ¾ cup caster (superfine) sugar
110 g / 4 oz white chocolate, chopped
1 tbsp poppy seeds

TO DECORATE

110 g / 4 oz / ½ cup white chocolate, chopped
1 tbsp poppy seeds

Dark Chocolate and Poppy Seed Muffins

337

Replace the white chocolate with dark chocolate.

338

MAKES 12

Blueberry and White Chocolate Muffins

- Preheat the oven to 180°C (160° fan) / 350 F / gas 4 and line a 12-hole muffin tin with paper cases.
- Beat the egg in a jug with the oil and milk until well mixed.
- Mix the flour, baking powder, sugar, chocolate buttons and blueberries in a bowl, then pour in the egg mixture and stir just enough to combine.
- Divide the mixture between the moulds, then bake in the oven for 20 – 25 minutes.
- Test with a wooden toothpick, if it comes out clean, the muffins are done.
- Transfer the muffins to a wire rack and leave to cool completely.

PREPARATION TIME: 25 MINUTES

COOKING TIME: 25 MINUTES

INGREDIENTS

1 large egg
120 ml / 4 fl. oz / ½ cup sunflower oil
120 ml / 4 fl. oz / ½ cup milk
375 g / 12 ½ oz / 2 ½ cups self-raising flour, sifted
1 tsp baking powder
200 g / 7 oz / ¾ cup caster (superfine) sugar
110 g / 4 oz / ½ cup white chocolate buttons
150 g / 5 oz / 1 cup blueberries

Raspberry and White Chocolate Muffins

339

Replace the blueberries with raspberries.

340
MAKES 12

Orange and Blackcurrant Muffins

PREPARATION TIME: 25 MINUTES

COOKING TIME: 25 MINUTES

INGREDIENTS

1 large egg
120 ml / 4 fl. oz / ½ cup sunflower oil
2 tbsp orange juice
120 ml / 4 fl. oz / ½ cup milk
375 g / 12 ½ oz / 2 ½ cups self-raising flour, sifted
1 tsp baking powder
200 g / 7 oz / ¾ cup caster (superfine) sugar
150 g / 5 oz / 1 cup blackcurrants
1 orange, zest finely grated

- Preheat the oven to 180°C (160° fan) / 350 F / gas 4 and line a 12-hole muffin tin with paper cases.
- Beat the egg in a jug with the oil, orange juice and milk until well mixed.
- Mix the flour, baking powder, sugar, blackcurrants and orange zest in a bowl, then pour in the egg mixture and stir just enough to combine.
- Divide the mixture between the moulds, then bake in the oven for 20 – 25 minutes.
- Test with a wooden toothpick, if it comes out clean, the muffins are done.
- Transfer the muffins to a wire rack and leave to cool completely.

Apple and Blackcurrant Muffins | 341

Replace the orange zest and juice with 150g / 5 oz / ⅔ cup chopped apple and 1 tsp of ground cinnamon.

342
MAKES 12

Wholemeal Brie and Sesame Muffins

PREPARATION TIME: 25 MINUTES

COOKING TIME: 25 MINUTES

INGREDIENTS

2 large eggs
120 ml / 4 fl. oz / ½ cup sunflower oil
180 ml / 6 fl. oz / ¾ cup Greek yogurt
110 g / 4 oz / 1 cup Brie, cubed
2 tbsp sesame seeds
225 g / 8 oz / 1 ½ cups wholemeal flour
2 tsp baking powder
½ tsp bicarbonate of (baking) soda
½ tsp salt

- Preheat the oven to 180°C (160° fan) / 350 F / gas 4 and oil a 12-hole silicone muffin tin.
- Beat the egg in a jug with the oil, yogurt and cheese until well mixed.
- Mix the sesame seeds, flour, raising agents and salt in a bowl, then pour in the egg mixture and stir just enough to combine.
- Divide the mixture between the paper cases, then bake in the oven for 20 – 25 minutes.
- Test with a wooden toothpick, if it comes out clean, the muffins are done.
- Serve warm.

Brie and Bacon Muffins | 343

Try adding 4 chopped rashers of fried bacon to the mixture.

344

MAKES 24

Smoked Salmon and Dill Mini Muffins

Salmon Filled Muffins

345

Try splitting the muffins in half and filling with cream cheese and extra smoked salmon and chopped dill.

Salmon and Capers Muffins

346

Add 1 tbsp of capers and 4 chopped spring onions to the muffin mixture before baking.

PREPARATION TIME: 10 MINUTES

COOKING TIME: 45 MINUTES

INGREDIENTS

2 large eggs
120 ml / 4 fl. oz / ½ cup sunflower oil
180 ml / 6 fl. oz / ¾ cup Greek yogurt
110 g / 4 oz / 1 cup smoked salmon, chopped
225 g / 8 oz / 1 ½ cups plain (all purpose) flour
2 tsp baking powder
½ tsp bicarbonate of (baking) soda
½ tsp salt
2 tbsp fresh dill, chopped

- Preheat the oven to 180°C (160° fan) / 350 F / gas 4 and oil a 24-hole silicone muffin mould.
- Beat the egg in a jug with the oil, yogurt and salmon until well mixed.
- Mix the flour, raising agents, salt and dill in a bowl, then pour in the egg mixture and stir just enough to combine.
- Divide the mixture between the paper cases, then bake in the oven for 10 – 15 minutes.
- Test with a wooden toothpick, if it comes out clean, the muffins are done.
- Serve warm.

347

MAKES 12

Cherry Tomato and Pecorino Muffins

Cherry Tomato, Pesto and Mozzarella Muffins

348

Replace the Pecorino with cubed mozzarella and replace the basil with 100 g of pesto marbled through the mixture.

Sun-dried Tomato and Pecorino Muffins

349

Replace the cherry tomatoes with sun-dried tomatoes for a mediterranean twist.

PREPARATION TIME: 20 MINUTES

COOKING TIME: 20-25 MINUTES

INGREDIENTS

2 large eggs
120 ml / 4 fl. oz / ½ cup sunflower oil
180 ml / 6 fl. oz / ¾ cup Greek yoghurt
110 g / 4 oz / 1 cup Pecorino, cubed
150 g / 5 oz / 1 cup cherry tomatoes, halved
2 tbsp basil leaves, shredded
225 g / 8 oz / 1 ½ cups plain flour
2 tsp baking powder
½ tsp bicarbonate of (baking) soda
½ tsp salt

- Preheat the oven to 180°°C (160° fan) / 350 F / gas 4 and line a 12-hole muffin tin with paper cases.
- Beat the egg in a jug with the oil, yoghurt and cheese until well mixed.
- Mix the tomatoes, basil, flour, raising agents and salt in a bowl, then pour in the egg mixture and stir just enough to combine.
- Divide the mixture between the paper cases, then bake in the oven for 20 – 25 minutes.
- Test with a wooden toothpick, if it comes out clean, the muffins are done.
- Serve warm.

350

MAKES 12

Apple and Clove Muffins

- Preheat the oven to 180°C (160° fan) / 350 F / gas 4 and line a 12-hole muffin tin with paper cases.
- Beat the egg in a jug with the oil and milk until well mixed.
- Mix the flour, baking powder, sugar and cloves in a bowl, then pour in the egg mixture and stir just enough to combine.
- Divide the mixture between the paper cases and top with the sliced apple.
- Brush the apples with honey and bake in the oven for 20 – 25 minutes.
- Test with a wooden toothpick, if it comes out clean, the muffins are done.
- Transfer the muffins to a wire rack and leave to cool.

PREPARATION TIME: 25 MINUTES

COOKING TIME: 25 MINUTES

INGREDIENTS

1 large egg
120 ml / 4 fl. oz / ½ cup sunflower oil
120 ml / 4 fl. oz / ½ cup milk
225 g / 7 ½ oz / 1 ½ cups self-raising flour, sifted
1 tsp baking powder
200 g / 7 oz / ¾ cup caster (superfine) sugar
1 tsp ground cloves
2 apples, peeled, cored and sliced
2 tbsp honey

Spicy Apple and Clove Muffins

351

This recipe is lovely with sliced pears or plums instead of the apple. Alternatively, replace the ground cloves with ground allspice berries.

352

MAKES 12

Banana and Orange Muffins

- Preheat the oven to 190°C (170° fan) / 375 F / gas 5 and line a 12-hole cupcake tin with paper cases.
- Combine the flour, sugar, butter, eggs and orange zest in a bowl and whisk together for 2 minutes or until smooth.
- Divide the mixture between the paper cases.
- Cut each banana into 12 pieces and press 2 pieces of banana into the top of each cake.
- Transfer the tin to the oven and bake for 15 – 20 minutes.
- Test with a wooden toothpick, if it comes out clean, the muffins are done.
- Transfer the muffins to a wire rack and leave to cool completely.

PREPARATION TIME: 35 MINUTES

COOKING TIME: 20 MINUTES

INGREDIENTS

110 g / 4 oz / ½ cup self-raising flour, sifted
110 g / 4 oz / ½ cup caster (superfine) sugar
110 g / 4 oz / ½ cup butter, softened
2 large eggs
1 orange, zest finely grated
2 bananas
Icing (confectioners') sugar, to dust

Banana and Lime Muffins

353

Try making the muffins with lime zest instead of orange zest and make lime drizzle icing to go with them: sieve 110g / 4 oz / ½ cup icing sugar into a bowl and add just enough lime juice to make a runny icing.

Chocolate, Banana and Hazelnut Muffins

Chocolate
Glazed Muffins

355

Mix 100g / 4oz / ½ cup icing sugar with 1 tbsp cocoa and enough boiling water to make a runny icing. Drizzle over the warm muffins.

Honey
Glazed Muffins

356

Mix 100g / 4oz / ½ cup icing sugar with 1 tbsp honey and enough boiling water to make a runny icing. Drizzle over the warm muffins.

PREPARATION TIME: 10 MINUTES

COOKING TIME: 25 MINUTES

INGREDIENTS

1 large egg
120 ml / 4 fl. oz / ½ cup sunflower oil
120 ml / 4 fl. oz / ½ cup milk
375 g / 12 ½ oz / 2 ½ cups self-raising flour, sifted
55 g / 2 oz / ½ cup unsweetened cocoa powder, sifted
1 tsp baking powder
200 g / 7 oz / ¾ cup caster (superfine) sugar
110 g / 4 oz / ½ cup dark chocolate, minimum 60% cocoa solids, chopped
2 bananas, sliced
5 tbsp hazelnuts (cob nuts), chopped

- Preheat the oven to 180°C (160° fan) / 350 F / gas 4 and line a 12-hole muffin tin with paper cases.
- Beat the egg in a jug with the oil and milk until well mixed.
- Mix the flour, cocoa, baking powder, sugar, chocolate, banana and chopped hazelnuts in a bowl, then pour in the egg mixture and stir just enough to combine.
- Divide the mixture between the paper cases, then bake in the oven for 20 – 25 minutes.
- Test with a wooden toothpick, if it comes out clean, the muffins are done.
- Transfer the muffins to a wire rack and leave to cool completely.

357

MAKES 6

White Chocolate Muffins

- Oil 6 mini pudding basins and dust the insides with icing sugar.
- Melt the chocolate, butter and sugar together in a saucepan, stirring to dissolve the sugar.
- Leave to cool a little then beat in the eggs and egg yolks and fold in the flour.
- Divide the mixture between the pudding basins, then chill them for 30 minutes.
- Preheat the oven to 180°C (160° fan) / 350 F / gas 4 and put a baking tray in to heat.
- Transfer the fondants to the heated baking tray and bake in the oven for 8 minutes.
- Leave the fondants to cool for 2 minutes, then turn them out of their moulds and serve immediately.

PREPARATION TIME: 10 MINUTES

COOKING TIME: 45 MINUTES

INGREDIENTS

2 tbsp icing (confectioners') sugar
150 g / 6 oz / ⅔ cup white chocolate, chopped
150 g / 6 oz / ⅔ cup butter, chopped
85 g / 3 oz / ⅓ cup caster (superfine) sugar
3 large eggs
3 egg yolks
1 tbsp plain (all purpose) flour

Pistachio Buttercream Muffins

358

Beat together 110g / 4 0z / ½ cup butter, 110g / 4 0z / ½ cup icing sugar, 2 tbsp ground pistachios and 2 tbsp milk until smooth. Pipe a rosette on top of each fondant.

359

MAKES 12

Chocolate and Vanilla Cream Muffins

- Preheat the oven to 180°C (160° fan) / 350 F / gas 4 and line a 12-hole muffin tin with paper cases.
- Beat the egg in a jug with the oil and milk until well mixed.
- Mix the flour, baking powder and sugar in a bowl, then pour in the egg mixture and chopped chocolate and stir just enough to combine.
- Divide the mixture between the paper cases, then bake in the oven for 20 – 25 minutes.
- Transfer the muffins to a wire rack and leave to cool completely. Whip the cream with the icing sugar and vanilla extract until thick.
- Spoon the vanilla cream into a piping bag fitted with a large star nozzle and pipe a big swirl on top of each cake.
- Melt the chocolate in a microwave or bain marie and leave to cool a little before spooning over the cakes.

PREPARATION TIME: 15 MINUTES

COOKING TIME: 25 MINUTES

INGREDIENTS

1 large egg
120 ml / 4 fl. oz / ½ cup sunflower oil
120 ml / 4 fl. oz / ½ cup milk
375 g / 12 ½ oz / 2 ½ cups self-raising flour, sifted
1 tsp baking powder
200 g / 7 oz / ¾ cup caster (superfine) sugar
110 g / 4 oz milk chocolate, chopped
To decorate
225 ml / 8 fl. oz / 1 cup double (heavy) cream
2 tbsp icing (confectioners') sugar
1 tsp vanilla extract
55 g / 2 oz / ¼ cup dark chocolate, minimum 60% cocoa solids

Chocolate and Mint Cream Muffins

360

Replace the vanilla extract with a few drops of peppermint essence. Top the muffins with a mint thin after drizzling with dark chocolate.

361

MAKES 12

Apricot and Sultana Muffins

PREPARATION TIME: 15 MINUTES

COOKING TIME: 25 MINUTES

INGREDIENTS

1 large egg
120 ml / 4 fl. oz / ½ cup sunflower oil
120 ml / 4 fl. oz / ½ cup milk
375 g / 12 ½ oz / 2 ½ cups self-raising flour, sifted
1 tsp baking powder
200 g / 7 oz / ¾ cup caster (superfine) sugar
75 g / 2 ½ oz / ½ cup dried apricots, chopped
75 g / 2 ½ oz / ½ cup sultanas

- Preheat the oven to 180°C (160° fan) / 350 F / gas 4 and oil a 12-hole silicone muffin tin.
- Beat the egg in a jug with the oil and milk until well mixed.
- Mix the flour, baking powder, sugar, apricots and sultanas in a bowl, then pour in the egg mixture and stir just enough to combine.
- Divide the mixture between the moulds, then bake in the oven for 20 – 25 minutes.
- Test with a wooden toothpick, if it comes out clean, the muffins are done.
- Transfer the muffins to a wire rack and leave to cool completely.

Apricot, Sultana and Oat Muffins

362

Add 2 tbsp rolled oats to the mixture to boost the fibre content.

363

MAKES 12

Bacon and Chive Muffins

PREPARATION TIME: 15 MINUTES

COOKING TIME: 25 MINUTES

INGREDIENTS

2 large eggs
120 ml / 4 fl. oz / ½ cup sunflower oil
180 ml / 6 fl. oz / ¾ cup Greek yogurt
110 g / 4 oz / 1 cup Parmesan, grated
75 g / 2 ½ oz / ½ cup streaky bacon, chopped
2 tbsp fresh chives, chopped
225 g / 8 oz / 1 ½ cups plain (all purpose) flour
2 tsp baking powder
½ tsp bicarbonate of (baking) soda
½ tsp salt

- Preheat the oven to 180°C (160° fan) / 350 F / gas 4 and line a 12-hole muffin tin with paper cases.
- Beat the egg in a jug with the oil, yoghurt and cheese until well mixed.
- Mix the bacon, chives, flour, raising agents and salt in a bowl, then pour in the egg mixture and stir just enough to combine.
- Divide the mixture between the paper cases, then bake in the oven for 20 – 25 minutes.
- Test with a wooden toothpick, if it comes out clean, the muffins are done.
- Transfer the muffins to a wire rack and leave to cool.

Bacon snd Egg Muffins

364

For bacon and egg muffins, fold 2 chopped soft boiled eggs into the mixture before baking.

Lemon Muffins with Cream Cheese Icing

Orange Muffins with Cream Cheese Icing

366

Try this recipe with orange juice and zest in the mixture and orange marmalade in the cream cheese mixture.

Lime Muffins with Cream Cheese Icing

367

Try this recipe with lime juice and zest in the mixture and lime marmalade in the cream cheese mixture.

PREPARATION TIME: 15 MINUTES

COOKING TIME: 25 MINUTES

INGREDIENTS

1 large egg
120 ml / 4 fl. oz / ½ cup sunflower oil
120 ml / 4 fl. oz / ½ cup milk
1 lemon, juiced
375 g / 12 ½ oz / 2 ½ cups self-raising flour, sifted
1 tsp baking powder
200 g / 7 oz / ¾ cup caster (superfine) sugar
1 tbsp lemon zest, finely grated
To decorate
225 g / 8 oz / 1 cup cream cheese
110 g / 4 oz / ½ cup butter, softened
225 g / 8 oz / 2 cups icing (confectioners') sugar
2 tbsp lemon marmalade

- Preheat the oven to 180°C (160° fan) / 350 F / gas 4 and oil a 12-hole silicone muffin tin.
- Beat the egg in a jug with the oil, milk and lemon juice until well mixed.
- Mix the flour, baking powder, sugar and lemon zest in a bowl, then pour in the egg mixture and stir just enough to combine.
- Divide the mixture between the moulds, then bake in the oven for 20 – 25 minutes.
- Test with a wooden toothpick, if it comes out clean, the muffins are done.
- Transfer the muffins to a wire rack and leave to cool completely.
- To make the icing, beat the cream cheese and butter together with a wooden spoon until light and fluffy then beat in the icing sugar a quarter at a time.
- Add the lemon marmalade then use a whisk to whip the mixture for 2 minutes or until smooth and light.
- Spoon on top of the muffins.

368

MAKES 12

Mini Apple Muffins

PREPARATION TIME: 15 MINUTES

COOKING TIME: 20 MINUTES

INGREDIENTS

1 large egg
120 ml / 4 fl. oz / ½ cup sunflower oil
120 ml / 4 fl. oz / ½ cup milk
375 g / 12 ½ oz / 2 ½ cups self-raising flour, sifted
1 tsp baking powder
200 g / 7 oz / ¾ cup caster (superfine) sugar
150 g / 5 oz / 1 cup apple, grated

- Preheat the oven to 180°C (160° fan) / 350 F / gas 4 and line a 24-hole mini muffin tin with paper cases.
- Beat the egg in a jug with the oil and milk until well mixed.
- Mix the flour, baking powder, sugar and grated apple in a bowl, then pour in the egg mixture and stir just enough to combine.
- Divide the mixture between the paper cases, then bake in the oven for 15 – 20 minutes.
- Test with a wooden toothpick, if it comes out clean, the muffins are done.
- Transfer the muffins to a wire rack and leave to cool completely.

Mini Apple and Cinnamon Muffins

369

For apple and cinnamon mini muffins, add 1 tsp ground cinnamon.

370

MAKES 12

Apricot and Cardamom Muffins

PREPARATION TIME: 15 MINUTES

COOKING TIME: 25 MINUTES

INGREDIENTS

1 large egg
120 ml / 4 fl. oz / ½ cup sunflower oil
120 ml / 4 fl. oz / ½ cup milk
375 g / 12 ½ oz / 2 ½ cups self-raising flour, sifted
1 tsp baking powder
200 g / 7 oz / ¾ cup caster (superfine) sugar
75 g / 2 ½ oz / ½ cup dried apricots, chopped
½ tsp ground cardamom

- Preheat the oven to 180°C (160° fan) / 350 F / gas 4 and oil a 12-hole silicone muffin tin.
- Beat the egg in a jug with the oil and milk until well mixed.
- Mix the flour, baking powder, sugar, apricots and cardamom in a bowl, then pour in the egg mixture and stir just enough to combine.
- Divide the mixture between the paper cases, then bake in the oven for 20 – 25 minutes.
- Test with a wooden toothpick, if it comes out clean, the muffins are done.
- Transfer the muffins to a wire rack and leave to cool completely.

Apricot and Date Muffins

371

Try adding 5 tbsp of chopped dates to the muffin mixture along with the apricots.

372

MAKES 12 Summer Fruit Muffins

- Preheat the oven to 180°C (160° fan) / 350 F / gas 4 and line a 12-hole muffin tin with paper cases.
- Beat the egg in a jug with the oil and milk until well mixed.
- Mix the flour, baking powder, sugar and summer fruits in a bowl, then pour in the egg mixture and stir just enough to combine.
- Divide the mixture between the moulds, then bake in the oven for 20 – 25 minutes.
- Test with a wooden toothpick, if it comes out clean, the muffins are done.
- Transfer the muffins to a wire rack and leave to cool.

PREPARATION TIME: 15 MINUTES

COOKING TIME: 25 MINUTES

INGREDIENTS

1 large egg
120 ml / 4 fl. oz / ½ cup sunflower oil
120 ml / 4 fl. oz / ½ cup milk
375 g / 12 ½ oz / 2 ½ cups self-raising flour, sifted
1 tsp baking powder
200 g / 7 oz / ¾ cup caster (superfine) sugar
150 g / 5 oz / 1 cup mixed summer fruits

With Extra Fruity Flavour 373

Add the grated zest of 1 orange and 1 lemon for an extra citrusy tang.

374

MAKES 12 Sun-dried Tomato and Basil Muffins

- Preheat the oven to 180°C (160° fan) / 350 F / gas 4 and line a 12-hole muffin tin with paper cases.
- Beat the egg in a jug with the oil, yoghurt and cheese until well mixed.
- Mix the sundried tomatoes, basil, flour, raising agents and salt in a bowl, then pour in the egg mixture and stir just enough to combine.
- Divide the mixture between the paper cases, then bake in the oven for 20 – 25 minutes.
- Test with a wooden toothpick, if it comes out clean, the muffins are done.
- Transfer the muffins to a wire rack and leave to cool completely.

PREPARATION TIME: 15 MINUTES

COOKING TIME: 25 MINUTES

INGREDIENTS

2 large eggs
120 ml / 4 fl. oz / ½ cup sunflower oil
180 ml / 6 fl. oz / ¾ cup Greek yogurt
110 g / 4 oz / 1 cup Parmesan, grated
75 g / 2 ½ oz / ½ cup sundried tomatoes, chopped
2 tbsp basil leaves, shredded
225 g / 8 oz / 1 ½ cups plain (all purpose) flour
2 tsp baking powder
½ tsp bicarbonate of (baking) soda
½ tsp salt

Sun-dried Tomato and Feta Muffins 375

Try adding 100 g / 4 oz of feta cheese to the muffin mixture before cooking.

Almond and Cherry Jam Mini Muffins

- Preheat the oven to 180°C (160° fan) / 350 F / gas 4 and oil a 24 small dariole moulds.
- Beat the egg in a jug with the oil and milk until well mixed.
- Mix the flour, baking powder, sugar and ground almonds in a bowl, then pour in the egg mixture and stir just enough to combine.
- Divide half the mixture between the moulds, and top each one with a spoon of cherry jam.
- Top with the rest of the muffin mixture, then bake in the oven for 15 – 20 minutes.
- Test with a wooden toothpick, if it comes out clean, the muffins are done.
- Transfer the muffins to a wire rack and leave to cool.

PREPARATION TIME: 15 MINUTES

COOKING TIME: 20 MINUTES

INGREDIENTS

1 large egg
120 ml / 4 fl. oz / ½ cup sunflower oil
120 ml / 4 fl. oz / ½ cup milk
375 g / 12 ½ oz / 2 ½ cups self-raising flour, sifted
1 tsp baking powder
200 g / 7 oz / ¾ cup caster (superfine) sugar
55 g / 2 oz / ½ cup ground almonds
110 g / 4 oz / ½ cup cherry jam (jelly)
75 g / 2 ½ oz / ½ cup flaked (slivered) almonds

Blackcurrant and Granola Muffins

PREPARATION TIME: 15MINUTES

COOKING TIME: 25 MINUTES

INGREDIENTS

1 large egg
120 ml / 4 fl. oz / ½ cup sunflower oil
120 ml / 4 fl. oz / ½ cup milk
375 g / 12 ½ oz / 2 ½ cups self-raising flour, sifted
1 tsp baking powder
200 g / 7 oz / ¾ cup caster (superfine) sugar
150 g / 5 oz / 1 cup blackcurrants
75 g / 2 ½ oz / ½ cup plain granolaced
basil, to garnish

- Preheat the oven to 180°C (160° fan) / 350 F / gas 4 and line a 12-hole muffin tin with paper cases.
- Beat the egg in a jug with the oil and milk until well mixed.
- Mix the flour, baking powder, sugar and blackcurrants in a bowl, then pour in the egg mixture and stir just enough to combine.
- Divide the mixture between the moulds and sprinkle with granola then bake in the oven for 20 – 25 minutes.
- Test with a wooden toothpick, if it comes out clean, the muffins are done.
- Transfer the muffins to a wire rack and leave to cool completely.

Raspberry and Orange Muffins

PREPARATION TIME: 15 MINUTES

COOKING TIME: 25 MINUTES

INGREDIENTS

1 large egg
120 ml / 4 fl. oz / ½ cup sunflower oil
120 ml / 4 fl. oz / ½ cup milk
1 orange, zest finely grated
375 g / 12 ½ oz / 2 ½ cups self-raising flour, sifted
1 tsp baking powder
200 g / 7 oz / ¾ cup caster (superfine) sugar
150 g / 5 oz / 1 cup raspberries
75 g / 2 ½ oz / ½ cup candied orange peel, chopped

TO DECORATE

12 raspberries

- Preheat the oven to 180°C (160° fan) / 350 F / gas 4 and oil a 12-hole silicone muffin tin.
- Beat the egg in a jug with the oil, milk and orange zest until well mixed.
- Mix the flour, baking powder, sugar, raspberries and candied peel in a bowl, then pour in the egg mixture and stir just enough to combine.
- Divide the mixture between the moulds, then bake in the oven for 20 – 25 minutes.
- Test with a wooden toothpick, if it comes out clean, the muffins are done.
- Transfer the muffins to a wire rack and leave to cool completely.

Chocolate and Coffee Syrup Muffins

379

MAKES 12

- Preheat the oven to 190°C (170° fan) / 375 F / gas 5 and oil a 12-hole silicone cupcake mould.
- Combine the flour, sugar, butter and eggs in a bowl and whisk together for 2 minutes or until smooth.
- Fold in ¾ of the chocolate chips then divide the mixture between the moulds.
- Sprinkle the rest of the chocolate chips on top then bake for 15 – 20 minutes. Transfer the muffins to a wire rack and leave to cool completely.
- To make the syrup, mix the sugar and espresso powder together in a small saucepan with 55ml water. Stir over a medium heat to dissolve the sugar, then boil for 2 minutes or until syrupy.
- Leave to cool and thicken, then drizzle over the cupmuffins.

PREPARATION TIME: 15 MINUTES

COOKING TIME: 20 MINUTES

....

INGREDIENTS

110 g / 4 oz / ½ cup self-raising flour, sifted
110 g / 4 oz / ½ cup caster (superfine) sugar
110 g / 4 oz / ½ cup butter, softened
2 large eggs
1 tsp instant espresso powder
150 g / 5 oz / 1 cup chocolate chips

TO DECORATE

55 g / 2 oz / ¼ cup caster (superfine) sugar
¼ tsp instant espresso powder

Chocolate and Honey Syrup Muffins

380

Replace the coffee powder with 1 tbsp of honey.

Sugar Nib Muffins

381

MAKES 12

- Preheat the oven to 180°C (160° fan) / 350 F / gas 4 and line a 12-hole muffin tin with paper cases.
- Beat the egg in a jug with the oil and milk until well mixed.
- Mix the flour, baking powder and sugar in a bowl, then pour in the egg mixture and stir just enough to combine.
- Divide the mixture between the paper cases and sprinkle with sugar nibs, then bake in the oven for 20 – 25 minutes.
- Test with a wooden toothpick, if it comes out clean, the muffins are done.
- Transfer the muffins to a wire rack and leave to cool completely.

PREPARATION TIME: 15 MINUTES

COOKING TIME: 25 MINUTES

....

INGREDIENTS

1 large egg
120 ml / 4 fl. oz / ½ cup sunflower oil
120 ml / 4 fl. oz / ½ cup milk
375 g / 12 ½ oz / 2 ½ cups self-raising flour, sifted
1 tsp baking powder
200 g / 7 oz / ¾ cup caster (superfine) sugar
1 tsp vanilla extract
75 g / 2 ½ oz / ½ cup sugar nibs

Sugar Nib and Summer Berry Muffins

382

Add 110g / 4 oz / ½ cup of summer berries to the mixture.

383

MAKES 12

Cranberry Muffins

PREPARATION TIME: 15 MINUTES

COOKING TIME: 25 MINUTES

INGREDIENTS

1 large egg
120 ml / 4 fl. oz / ½ cup sunflower oil
120 ml / 4 fl. oz / ½ cup milk
375 g / 12 ½ oz / 2 ½ cups self-raising flour, sifted
1 tsp baking powder
200 g / 7 oz / ¾ cup caster (superfine) sugar
75 g / 2 ½ oz / ½ cup dried cranberries

- Preheat the oven to 180°C (160° fan) / 350 F / gas 4 and oil a 12 metal muffin tins.
- Beat the egg in a jug with the oil and milk until well mixed.
- Mix the flour, baking powder, sugar and cranberries in a bowl, then pour in the egg mixture and stir just enough to combine.
- Divide the mixture between the tins, then bake in the oven for 20 – 25 minutes.
- Test with a wooden toothpick, if it comes out clean, the muffins are done.
- Transfer the muffins to a wire rack and leave to cool completely.

Cranberry and Orange Muffins

 384

Add finely grated zest of 1 orange to the muffin mixture.

385

MAKES 12

Ginger and Marmalade Muffins

PREPARATION TIME: 15 MINUTES

COOKING TIME: 25 MINUTES

INGREDIENTS

1 large egg
120 ml / 4 fl. oz / ½ cup sunflower oil
120 ml / 4 fl. oz / ½ cup milk
2 tbsp marmalade
375 g / 12 ½ oz / 2 ½ cups self-raising flour, sifted
1 tsp baking powder
200 g / 7 oz / ¾ cup caster (superfine) sugar
75 g / 2 ½ oz / ½ cup stem ginger, chopped

TO DECORATE

2 tbsp orange marmalade

- Preheat the oven to 180°C (160° fan) / 350 F / gas 4 and oil a 12-hole silicone muffin tin.
- Beat the egg in a jug with the oil, milk and marmalade until well mixed.
- Mix the flour, baking powder, sugar and stem ginger in a bowl, then pour in the egg mixture and stir just enough to combine.
- Divide the mixture between the paper cases, then bake in the oven for 20 – 25 minutes.
- Test with a wooden toothpick, if it comes out clean, the muffins are done.
- As soon as the muffins come out of the oven, brush them with marmalade to glaze.
- Transfer the muffins to a wire rack and leave to cool completely.

Ginger and Lime Marmalade Muffins

 386

Replace the orange marmalade with lime marmalade.

387

MAKES 24

Pecan Mini Muffins

- Preheat the oven to 180°C (160° fan) / 350 F / gas 4 and oil a 24-hole silicone mini muffin mould.
- Beat the egg in a jug with the oil and milk until well mixed.
- Mix the flour, baking powder, sugar and chopped pecans in a bowl, then pour in the egg mixture and stir just enough to combine.
- Press a pecan half into the top of each cake.
- Divide the mixture between the moulds, then bake in the oven for 15 – 20 minutes.
- Test with a wooden toothpick, if it comes out clean, the muffins are done.
- Transfer the muffins to a wire rack and leave to cool completely.

PREPARATION TIME: 10 MINUTES

COOKING TIME: 20 MINUTES

INGREDIENTS

1 large egg
120 ml / 4 fl. oz / ½ cup sunflower oil
120 ml / 4 fl. oz / ½ cup milk
375 g / 12 ½ oz / 2 ½ cups self-raising flour, sifted
1 tsp baking powder
200 g / 7 oz / ¾ cup caster (superfine) sugar
75 g / 2 ½ oz / ½ cup pecans, chopped
24 pecan halves

Spicy Pecan Muffins

388

Try adding ½ tsp freshly grated nutmeg to add some warming spice.

389

MAKES 12

Mixed Pepper Muffins

- Preheat the oven to 180°C (160° fan) / 350 F / gas 4 and line a 12-hole muffin tin with paper cases.
- Fry the peppers in the olive oil for 10 minutes or until soft.
- Beat the egg in a jug with the oil, yogurt and cheese until well mixed then stir in the peppers.
- Mix the flour, raising agents and salt in a bowl, then pour in the egg mixture and stir just enough to combine.
- Divide the mixture between the paper cases, then bake in the oven for 20 – 25 minutes.
- Test with a wooden toothpick, if it comes out clean, the muffins are done.
- Serve warm.

PREPARATION TIME: 15 MINUTES

COOKING TIME: 25 MINUTES

INGREDIENTS

1 red pepper, deseeded and sliced
1 orange pepper, deseeded and sliced
1 green pepper, deseeded and sliced
2 tbsp olive oil
2 large eggs
120 ml / 4 fl. oz / ½ cup sunflower oil
180 ml / 6 fl. oz / ¾ cup Greek yogurt
110 g / 4 oz / 1 cup Parmesan, grated
225 g / 8 oz / 1 ½ cups plain (all purpose) flour
2 tsp baking powder
½ tsp bicarbonate of (baking) soda
½ tsp salt

Mixed Pepper and Mozzarella Muffins

390

Try adding 2 tbsp of pesto to the mixture before baking. Alternatively, try adding 5 tbsp of cubed mozzarella.

Glace Cherry Muffins

Candied Fruit Muffins   392

Try adding 110g / 4oz / ½ cup chopped candied angelica and 110g / 4oz / ½ cup candied pineapple pieces for a jewelled effect.

Dried Fruit and Nut Muffins   393

Replace the cherries with sultanas and raisins and add 85 g / 3 oz of chopped mixed nuts.

Glace Cherry and Coconut Muffins   394

Add 2 tbsp of desiccated coconut to the muffin mixture before cooking.

PREPARATION TIME: 15 MINUTES

COOKING TIME: 25 MINUTES

INGREDIENTS

1 large egg
120 ml / 4 fl. oz / ½ cup sunflower oil
120 ml / 4 fl. oz / ½ cup milk
375 g / 12 ½ oz / 2 ½ cups self-raising flour, sifted
1 tsp baking powder
200 g / 7 oz / ¾ cup caster (superfine) sugar
150 g / 5 oz / 1 cup glace cherries, halved

- Preheat the oven to 180°C (160° fan) / 350 F / gas 4 and line a 12-hole muffin tin with paper cases.
- Beat the egg in a jug with the oil and milk until well mixed.
- Mix the flour, baking powder, sugar and cherries in a bowl, then pour in the egg mixture and stir just enough to combine.
- Divide the mixture between the moulds, then bake in the oven for 20 – 25 minutes.
- Test with a wooden toothpick, if it comes out clean, the muffins are done.
- Transfer the muffins to a wire rack and leave to cool completely.

395

MAKES 12

Chocolate Fudge Chunk Muffins

- Preheat the oven to 180°C (160° fan) / 350 F / gas 4 and line a 12-hole muffin tin with paper cases.
- Beat the egg in a jug with the oil and milk until well mixed.
- Mix the flour, cocoa, baking powder, sugar, chocolate and fudge in a bowl, then pour in the egg mixture and stir just enough to combine.
- Divide the mixture between the paper cases, then bake in the oven for 20 – 25 minutes.
- Test with a wooden toothpick, if it comes out clean, the muffins are done.
- Transfer the muffins to a wire rack and leave to cool completely.

Vanilla Fudge Chunk Muffins   396

Leave out the cocoa powder and flavour the muffins with 1 tsp of vanilla extract instead.

PREPARATION TIME: 15 MINUTES

COOKING TIME: 25 MINUTES

INGREDIENTS

1 large egg
120 ml / 4 fl. oz / ½ cup sunflower oil
120 ml / 4 fl. oz / ½ cup milk
375 g / 12 ½ oz / 2 ½ cups self-raising flour, sifted
55 g / 2 oz / ½ cup unsweetened cocoa powder, sifted
1 tsp baking powder
200 g / 7 oz / ¾ cup caster (superfine) sugar
110 g / 4 oz / ½ cup dark chocolate, minimum 60% cocoa solids, chopped
110 g / 4 oz / ½ cup fudge, cubed

397

MAKES 36

Banana and Chocolate Chip Muffins

- Preheat the oven to 200°C (180° fan) / 400 F / gas 6 and line a 36-hole mini muffin tin with paper cases.
- Mash 3 of the bananas with a fork then whisk in the sugar, eggs and oil.
- Sieve the flour and bicarbonate of soda into the bowl and add the chocolate chips, then stir just enough to evenly mix all the ingredients together.
- Divide the mixture between the paper cases.
- Slice the last 2 bananas and add a slice to the top of each cake.
- Transfer the tin to the oven and bake for 15 – 20 minutes.
- Test with a wooden toothpick, if it comes out clean, the muffins are done.
- Transfer the muffins to a wire rack and leave to cool completely.

Pear and Chocolate Chip Muffins   398

Replace the bananas with pears .

PREPARATION TIME: 15 MINUTES

COOKING TIME: 20 MINUTES

INGREDIENTS

5 very ripe bananas
110g / 4 oz / 2/3 cup soft light brown sugar
2 large eggs
120ml / 4 fl oz / ½ cup sunflower oil
225g / 8 oz / 1 ½ cups plain (all purpose) flour
1 tsp bicarbonate of (baking) soda
75g / 2 ½ oz / ½ cup chocolate chips

399

MAKES 12

Peanut Butter and Chocolate Muffins

Almond Butter and Chocolate Muffins

400

Replace the peanut butter with almond butter.

Peanut Butter and Hazelnut Muffins

401

Add 110 g / 4 oz of hazelnut chocolate spread.

Peanut Butter and Walnut Muffins

402

Add 85 g / 3 oz of chopped walnuts to the cupcake mixture.

PREPARATION TIME: 15 MINUTES

COOKING TIME: 25 MINUTES

INGREDIENTS

1 large egg
120 ml / 4 fl. oz / ½ cup sunflower oil
120 ml / 4 fl. oz / ½ cup milk
375 g / 12 ½ oz / 2 ½ cups self-raising flour, sifted
1 tsp baking powder
200 g / 7 oz / ¾ cup caster (superfine) sugar
110 g / 4 oz / ⅔ cup chocolate chips
110 g / 4 oz / ½ cup crunchy peanut butter

- Preheat the oven to 180°C (160° fan) / 350 F / gas 4 and oil a 12-hole silicone muffin tin.
- Beat the egg in a jug with the oil and milk until well mixed.
- Mix the flour, baking powder and sugar in a bowl, then pour in the egg mixture and stir just enough to combine.
- Divide the half the mixture between the paper cases.
- Mix the chocolate chips with the peanut butter and put a big spoonful into each muffin case.
- Top with the rest of the muffin mixture then bake in the oven for 20 – 25 minutes.
- Test with a wooden toothpick, if it comes out clean, the muffins are done.
- Transfer the muffins to a wire rack and leave to cool completely.

403

MAKES 12

Chocolate and Cream Muffins

- Preheat the oven to 180°C (160° fan) / 350 F / gas 4 and line a 12-hole muffin tin with paper cases.
- Beat the egg in a jug with the oil and milk until well mixed.
- Mix the flour, cocoa, baking powder, sugar and chocolate in a bowl, then pour in the egg mixture and stir just enough to combine.
- Divide the mixture between the paper cases, then bake in the oven for 20 – 25 minutes.
- Transfer the muffins to a wire rack and leave to cool completely.
- To make the filling, whisk the cream with the icing sugar and vanilla until thick, then fill a piping bag fitted with a large star nozzle.
- Cut each muffin in half horizontally, pipe a swirl of cream onto the bottom halves and sandwich back together again.

Chocolate and Jam Muffins

404

Add a tbsp of cherry jam on top of the cream before sandwiching back together to make a miniature black forest gateau.

PREPARATION TIME: 15 MINUTES

COOKING TIME: 25 MINUTES

INGREDIENTS

1 large egg
120 ml / 4 fl. oz / ½ cup sunflower oil
120 ml / 4 fl. oz / ½ cup milk
375 g / 12 ½ oz / 2 ½ cups self-raising flour, sifted
55 g / 2 oz / ½ cup unsweetened cocoa powder, sifted
1 tsp baking powder
200 g / 7 oz / ¾ cup caster (superfine) sugar
110 g / 4 oz / ⅔ cup dark chocolate, minimum 60% cocoa solids, chopped

TO DECORATE

225 ml / 8 fl. oz / 1 cup double (heavy) cream
2 tbsp icing (confectioners') sugar
½ tsp vanilla extract

405

MAKES 12

Dark Chocolate Muffins

- Preheat the oven to 180°C (160° fan) / 350 F / gas 4 and line a 12-hole muffin tin with paper cases.
- Beat the egg in a jug with the oil and milk until well mixed.
- Mix the flour, cocoa, baking powder, sugar and chocolate in a bowl, then pour in the egg mixture and stir just enough to combine.
- Divide the mixture between the paper cases, then bake in the oven for 20 – 25 minutes.
- Test with a wooden toothpick, if it comes out clean, the muffins are done.
- Transfer the muffins to a wire rack and leave to cool completely.

Dark Chocolate and Raisin Muffins

406

Add 85 g / 3 oz of raisins to the muffin mixture before cooking.

PREPARATION TIME: 10 MINUTES

COOKING TIME: 25 MINUTES

INGREDIENTS

1 egg
120 ml / 4 fl. oz / ½ cup sunflower oil
120 ml / 4 fl. oz / ½ cup milk
375 g / 12 ½ oz / 2 ½ cups self-raising flour, sifted
55 g / 2 oz / ½ cup unsweetened cocoa powder, sifted
1 tsp baking powder
200 g / 7 oz / ¾ cup caster (superfine) sugar
110 g / 4 oz dark chocolate, chopped

407

MAKES 12

Blueberry and Ginger Muffins

PREPARATION TIME: 10 MINUTES

COOKING TIME: 20 MINUTES

....

INGREDIENTS

250 g / 9 oz / 1 ¾ cups self-raising flour
1 tsp bicarbonate of (baking) soda
2 tsp ground ginger
200 g / 8 ½ oz / ½ cup golden syrup
125 g / 4 ½ oz / ½ cup butter
125 g / 4 ½ oz / ¾ cup light brown sugar
2 large eggs, beaten
240 ml / 8 fl. oz / 1 cup milk
150 g / 5 oz / 1 cup blueberries

- Preheat the oven to 190°C (170° fan) / 375 F / gas 5 and line a 12-hole muffin tin with paper cases.
- Sieve the flour, bicarbonate of soda and ground ginger together into a bowl.
- Put the golden syrup, butter and brown sugar in a small saucepan and boil gently for 2 minutes, stirring to dissolve the sugar.
- Pour the butter and sugar mixture onto the flour with the eggs and milk and fold it all together with the blueberries until smooth.
- Divide the mixture between the muffin cases and bake in the oven for 20 – 25 minutes.
- Test with a wooden toothpick, if it comes out clean, the muffins are done.
- Transfer the muffins to a wire rack and leave to cool.

Blueberry and Cinnamon Muffins

408

Replace the ginger with 2 tsp of cinnamon. Mix 1 tsp of ground cinnamon with 1 tbsp of caster sugar and sprinkle over the muffins.

409

MAKES 12

Cheese and Tomato Muffins

PREPARATION TIME: 10 MINUTES

COOKING TIME: 20-25 MINUTES

....

INGREDIENTS

2 large eggs
120 ml / 4 fl. oz / ½ cup sunflower oil
180 ml / 6 fl. oz / ¾ cup Greek yoghurt
110 g / 4 oz / 1 cup cheddar, grated
225 g / 8 oz / 1 ½ cups plain flour
2 tsp baking powder
½ tsp bicarbonate of (baking) soda
½ tsp salt
110 g / 4 oz / 1 cup tomato chutney

- Preheat the oven to 180°C (160° fan) / 350 F / gas 4 and oil a 12-hole silicone muffin mould.
- Beat the egg in a jug with the oil, yoghurt and cheese until well mixed.
- Mix the flour, raising agents and salt in a bowl, then pour in the egg mixture and chutney and stir just enough to combine.
- Divide the mixture between the moulds, then bake in the oven for 20 – 25 minutes.
- Test with a wooden toothpick, if it comes out clean, the muffins are done.
- Transfer the muffins to a wire rack and leave to cool completely.

Stilton and Onion Muffins

410

Replace the cheddar with 110 g of crumbled Stilton and replace the tomato chutney with onion marmalade.

411

MAKES 12

Black Sesame Seed Muffin

- Preheat the oven to 180°C (160° fan) / 350 F / gas 4 and oil a 12-hole silicone muffin tin.
- Beat the egg in a jug with the oil, milk and sesame oil until well mixed.
- Mix the flour, baking powder, sugar and ¾ of the sesame seeds in a bowl, then pour in the egg mixture and stir just enough to combine.
- Divide the mixture between the moulds and sprinkle with the remaining sesame seeds, then bake in the oven for 20 – 25 minutes.
- Test with a wooden toothpick, if it comes out clean, the muffins are done.
- Transfer the muffins to a wire rack and leave to cool completely.

PREPARATION TIME: 10 MINUTES

COOKING TIME: 45 MINUTES

INGREDIENTS

1 large egg
120 ml / 4 fl. oz / ½ cup sunflower oil
120 ml / 4 fl. oz / ½ cup milk
2 tbsp toasted sesame oil
375 g / 12 ½ oz / 2 ½ cups self-raising flour, sifted
1 tsp baking powder
200 g / 7 oz / ¾ cup caster (superfine) sugar
75 g / 2 ½ oz / ¼ cup black sesame seeds

Black Sesame Seed and Candied Peel Muffins

412

Add 75g / 3 oz / ⅓ cup chopped mixed candied peel to the muffin mixture.

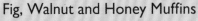

413

MAKES 12

Fig and Honey Muffins

- Preheat the oven to 180°C (160° fan) / 350 F / gas 4 and oil a 12 silicone muffin moulds.
- Beat the egg in a jug with the oil, milk and honey until well mixed.
- Mix the flour, baking powder, sugar and figs in a bowl, then pour in the egg mixture and stir just enough to combine.
- Divide the mixture between the moulds and bake in the oven for 20 – 25 minutes.
- Test with a wooden toothpick, if it comes out clean, the muffins are done.
- Transfer the muffins to a wire rack to cool.

PREPARATION TIME: 10 MINUTES

COOKING TIME: 25 MINUTES

INGREDIENTS

1 large egg
120 ml / 4 fl. oz / ½ cup sunflower oil
120 ml / 4 fl. oz / ½ cup milk
110 g / 4 oz / ½ cup honey
375 g / 12 ½ oz / 2 ½ cups self-raising flour, sifted
1 tsp baking powder
200 g / 7 oz / ¾ cup caster (superfine) sugar
150 g / 5 oz / 1 cup fresh figs, chopped
75 g / 2 ½ oz / ½ cup dried figs, chopped

Fig, Walnut and Honey Muffins

414

Add 75g / 3oz / ⅓ cup of chopped walnuts to the muffin mixture.

415

MAKES 12

Orange and Chocolate Chip Muffins

PREPARATION TIME: 20 MINUTES

COOKING TIME: 20 MINUTES

INGREDIENTS

110 g / 4 oz / 1 cup self-raising flour, sifted
110 g / 4 oz / ½ cup caster (superfine) sugar
110 g / 4 oz / ½ cup butter, softened
2 large eggs
1 orange, zest finely grated
2 tsp ground cinnamon
150 g / 5 oz / 1 cup chocolate chips

FOR THE GLAZE

½ orange, juiced
60 ml / 2 fl. oz / ¼ cup honey
1 cinnamon stick

- Preheat the oven to 190°C (170° fan) / 375 F / gas 5 and line a 12-hole cupcake tin with paper cases.
- Combine the flour, sugar, butter, eggs, orange zest and cinnamon in a bowl and whisk together for 2 minutes or until smooth, then fold in ¾ of the chocolate chips.
- Divide the mixture between the paper cases and sprinkle the rest of the chocolate chips on top, then transfer the tin to the oven and bake for 15 – 20 minutes.
- Test with a wooden toothpick, if it comes out clean, the muffins are done.
- Transfer the muffins to a wire rack and leave to cool completely.
- To make the glaze, combine the ingredients in a small saucepan and boil for 2 minutes or until syrupy.
- Remove the cinnamon stick and leave to cool then spoon on top of the muffins.

Orange, Cinamon and Raisin Muffins

416

Replace the chocolate chips with 110g / 4 oz / ½ cup raisins that have been soaked in the juice of 1 orange for an hour.

417

MAKES 12

Almond and Raspberry Cream Muffins

PREPARATION TIME: 40 MINUTES

COOKING TIME: 25 MINUTES

INGREDIENTS

1 large egg
120 ml / 4 fl. oz / ½ cup sunflower oil
120 ml / 4 fl. oz / ½ cup milk
375 g / 12 ½ oz / 2 ½ cups self-raising flour, sifted
1 tsp baking powder
200 g / 7 oz / ¾ cup caster (superfine) sugar
75 g / 2 ½ oz / ½ cup ground almonds

TO DECORATE

225 ml / 8 fl. oz / 1 cup double (heavy) cream
2 tbsp icing (confectioners') sugar
2 tbsp raspberry syrup
150 g / 5 oz / 1 cup raspberries
75 g / 2 ½ oz / ½ cup toasted, flaked (slivered) almonds

- Preheat the oven to 180°C (160° fan) / 350 F / gas 4 and line a 12-hole muffin tin with paper cases.
- Beat the egg in a jug with the oil and milk until well mixed.
- Mix the flour, baking powder, sugar and ground almonds in a bowl, then pour in the egg mixture and stir just enough to combine.
- Divide the mixture between the paper cases and bake for 20 – 25 minutes. Transfer the muffins to a wire rack and leave to cool completely.
- Whip the cream with the icing sugar and raspberry syrup until thick.
- Spoon the raspberry cream into a piping bag fitted with a large plain nozzle and pipe a big swirl on top of each cake.
- Top with fresh raspberries and flaked almonds.

Almond and Strawberry Cream Muffins

418

Replace the raspberry syrup in the cream with strawberry syrup and top the muffins with fresh strawberries and flaked almond.

419

MAKES 12

Blackberry Crumble Muffins

Spiced Plum Crumble Muffins

420

Replace the blackberries with 3 stoned, chopped plums and add 1 tsp mixed spice and ½ tsp ground cloves.

Cranberry Crumble Muffins

421

Replace the blackberries with cranberries and the cinnamon with vanilla extract.

But and Raisin Crumble Muffins

422

Replace the blackberries with raisins and add 85 g / 4 oz of chopped mixed nuts.

PREPARATION TIME: 45 MINUTES

COOKING TIME: 25 MINUTES

INGREDIENTS

1 large egg
120 ml / 4 fl. oz / ½ cup sunflower oil
120 ml / 4 fl. oz / ½ cup milk
375 g / 12 ½ oz / 2 ½ cups self-raising flour, sifted
1 tsp baking powder
200 g / 7 oz / ¾ cup caster (superfine) sugar
150 g / 5 oz / 1 cup blackberries
2 tsp ground cinnamon

FOR THE CRUMBLE TOPPING

55 g / 2 oz / ¼ cup butter, cubed and chilled
110 g / 4 oz / ¾ cup plain (all purpose) flour
2 tbsp caster (superfine) sugar

- Preheat the oven to 180°C (160° fan) / 350 F / gas 4 and line a 12-hole muffin tin with paper cases.
- Beat the egg in a jug with the oil and milk until well mixed.
- Mix the flour, baking powder, sugar and blackberries in a bowl, then pour in the egg mixture and stir just enough to combine.
- Divide the mixture between the paper cases.
- To make the crumble topping, rub the butter into the flour until the mixture resembles fine breadcrumbs. Stir in the sugar, then clump the mixture together in your hands and crumble it over the top of the muffins.
- Transfer the tin to the oven and bake for 20 - 25 minutes.
- Test with a wooden toothpick, if it comes out clean, the muffins are done.
- Transfer the muffins to a wire rack and leave to cool completely.

423

MAKES 12

Peanut Macaroons

- Oil and line a large baking tray with baking parchment. Grind the ground almonds, hazelnuts and icing sugar together in a food processor to a very fine powder.
- Whisk the egg whites to stiff peaks then carefully fold in the nut and sugar mixture. Spoon the mixture into a piping bag fitted with a large plain nozzle and pipe 2 ½cm / 1" rounds onto the baking tray.
- Sprinkle with chopped hazelnuts then leave the to stand for 30 minutes to form a skin.
- Preheat the oven to 170°C (150° fan) / 325 F / gas 3. Bake for 10 – 15 minutes. Slide the paper onto a cold work surface and leave the macaroons to cool completely.
- Beat the butter until light and fluffy then beat in the icing sugar. Add the milk, then whisk for 2 minutes.
- Spoon the buttercream into a piping bag fitted with a plain nozzle and pipe an even round onto half of the macaroons. Sandwich together with the other half.

**PREPARATION TIME:
1 HOUR 15 MINUTES**

COOKING TIME: 15 MINUTES

INGREDIENTS

110 g / 4 oz / 1 cup ground almonds
55 g / 2 oz / ½ cup ground hazelnuts
175 g / 6 oz / 1 ½ cups icing sugar
2 large egg whites
2 tbsp hazelnuts, finely chopped

TO DECORATE

110 g / 4 oz / ½ cup butter, softened
225 g / 8 oz / 2 cups icing sugar

Plain Almond Macaroons

424

MAKES 18

PREPARATION TIME: 10 MINUTES

COOKING TIME: 45 MINUTES

INGREDIENTS

175 g / 6 oz / 1 ½ cups ground almonds
175 g / 6 oz / 1 ½ cups icing (confectioners') sugar
2 large egg whites

- Oil and line a large baking sheet with baking parchment.
- Grind the ground almonds and icing sugar together in a food processor to a very fine powder.
- Whisk the egg whites to stiff peaks in a very clean bowl then carefully fold in the almond and sugar mixture.
- Spoon the mixture into a piping bag fitted with a large plain nozzle and pipe 2 ½ cm / 1" rounds onto the baking tray.
- Leave the uncooked macaroons to stand for 30 minutes to form a skin.
- Preheat the oven to 170°C (150° fan) / 325 F / gas 3.
- Bake for 10 – 15 minutes or until crisp on the outside and still a bit chewy in the middle.
- Slide the greaseproof paper onto a cold work surface and leave the macaroons to cool completely.

Strawberry Macaroons

425

MAKES 12

**PREPARATION TIME:
1 HOUR 15 MINUTES**

COOKING TIME: 15 MINUTES

INGREDIENTS

175 g / 6 oz / 1 ½ cups ground almonds
175 g / 6 oz / 1 ½ cups icing sugar
2 large egg whites
1 tbsp strawberry syrup
10 drops pink food colouring

TO DECORATE

110 g / 4 oz / ½ cup butter, softened
225 g / 8 oz / 2 cups icing sugar
1 tbsp strawberry syrup

- Oil and line a large baking sheet with baking parchment. Grind the almonds and icing sugar together to a very fine powder.
- Whisk the egg whites to stiff peaks then carefully fold in the almond and sugar mixture with the strawberry syrup and food colouring.
- Spoon the mixture into a piping bag fitted with a large plain nozzle and pipe 2 ½cm / 1" rounds onto the baking tray.
- Leave them to stand for 30 minutes to form a skin. Preheat the oven to 170°C (150° fan) / 325 F / gas 3. Bake for 10 – 15 minutes.
- Slide the paper onto a cold work surface and leave to cool.
- Beat the butter until light and fluffy then beat in the icing sugar. Add the strawberry syrup, then whisk for 2 minutes.
- Spoon the buttercream into a piping bag fitted with a plain nozzle and pipe an even round onto half of the macaroons.
- Sandwich together with the other half.

426
MAKES 18
Golden Chocolate Macaroons

- Oil and line a large baking tray with baking parchment.
- Grind the almonds, icing sugar and cocoa powder together to a very fine powder. Whisk the egg whites to stiff peaks then fold in the almond and sugar mixture.
- Spoon the mixture into a piping bag fitted with a plain nozzle and pipe 2 ½ cm / 1" rounds onto the tray.
- Leave them to stand for 30 minutes to form a skin.
- Preheat the oven to 170°C (150° fan) / 325 F / gas 3.
- Bake for 10 – 15 minutes. Slide the paper onto a cold work surface and leave them to cool completely.
- Beat the butter until light and fluffy then beat in the icing sugar. Mix the milk and cocoa together then add to the buttercream and whisk for 2 minutes.
- Spoon the buttercream into a piping bag fitted with a plain nozzle and pipe an even round onto half of the macaroons. Sandwich together with the other half.
- Carefully apply the gold leaf with a dry brush.

PREPARATION TIME: 10 MINUTES

COOKING TIME: 45 MINUTES

INGREDIENTS

175 g / 6 oz / 1 ½ cups ground almonds
175 g / 6 oz / 1 ½ cups icing (confectioners') sugar
2 tbsp unsweetened cocoa powder
2 large egg whites

TO DECORATE

110 g / 4 oz / ½ cup butter, softened
225 g / 8 oz / 2 cups icing (confectioners') sugar
1 tbsp milk
1 tbsp unsweetened cocoa powder
3 sheets of gold leaf

Golden Almond Macaroons — 427

Add 2 tsp of almond extract for an instene almond flavour.

428
MAKES 24
Cocoa Meringues with White Chocolate Cream

- Preheat the oven to 140°C (120° fan) / 275 F / gas 1 and oil and line a large baking tray with greaseproof paper.
- Whisk the egg whites until stiff, then gradually whisk in half the sugar until the mixture is very shiny.
- Fold in the remaining sugar with the cocoa then spoon the mixture into a piping bag fitted with a large plain nozzle.
- Pipe 24 rounds onto the baking tray, then bake in the oven for 35 minutes or until the meringues are crisp.
- Leave to cool completely.
- To make the white chocolate cream, melt the white chocolate in a microwave or bain marie and leave to cool a little.
- Whisk the cream until it forms soft peaks, then fold in the chocolate and spoon into glasses.
- Serve with the cocoa meringues.

PREPARATION TIME: 10 MINUTES

COOKING TIME: 45 MINUTES

INGREDIENTS

4 large egg whites
110 g / 4 oz / 1 cup caster (superfine) sugar
1 tbsp cocoa powder

TO DECORATE

110 g / 4 oz / ½ cup white chocolate, chopped
225 ml / 8 fl. oz / 1 cup double cream

Cocoa Meringues with Milk Chocolate Cream — 429

You can make a milk chocolate cream by replacing the white chocolate with milk chocolate and marbling it through the whipped cream.

430

MAKES 18

Orange Crunch Macaroons

PREPARATION TIME:
1 HOUR 15 MINUTES

COOKING TIME: 15 MINUTES

....

INGREDIENTS

175 g / 6 oz / 1 ½ cups ground
almonds
175 g / 6 oz / 1 ½ cups icing
(confectioners') sugar
2 large egg whites
2 tsp orange zest, finely grated
8 drops orange food colouring

TO DECORATE
110 g / 4 oz / ½ cup butter, softened
225 g / 8 oz / 2 cups icing
(confectioners') sugar
1 tbsp orange juice
2 tbsp cornflakes, crushed
55 g / 2 oz dark chocolate
1 tsp ground pistachios
basil, to garnish

- Oil and line a large baking tray with baking parchment.
- Grind the almonds and icing sugar together to a very fine powder. Whisk the egg whites to stiff peaks then fold in the almond and sugar mixture with the orange zest and food colouring.
- Spoon the mixture into a piping bag fitted with a plain nozzle and pipe 2 ½cm / 1" rounds onto the baking tray.
- Leave the m to stand for 30 minutes to form a skin.
- Preheat the oven to 170°C (150° fan) / 325 F / gas 3.
- Bake for 10 – 15 minutes or until crisp on the outside and still a bit chewy in the middle.
- Slide the greaseproof paper onto a cold work surface and leave the macaroons to cool completely.
- Beat the butter until light and fluffy then beat in the icing sugar. Add the orange juice, then whisk for 2 minutes. Spoon the buttercream into a piping bag fitted with a plain nozzle and pipe an even round onto half of the macaroons.
- Sandwich together with the other half then dip the edges in the crushed cornflakes.
- Melt the chocolate in a microwave or bain marie and fill a small piping bag.
- Decorate the macaroons with the chocolate and finish with a sprinkling of ground pistachios.

431

MAKES 6

Giant Lemon and Raspberry Macaroons

PREPARATION TIME: 10 MINUTES

COOKING TIME: 45 MINUTES

....

INGREDIENTS

175 g / 6 oz / 1 ½ cups ground
almonds
175 g / 6 oz / 1 ½ cups icing
(confectioners') sugar
2 large egg whites
1 tbsp raspberry syrup

TO DECORATE
110 g / 4 oz / ½ cup lemon curd
150 g / 5 oz / 1 cup raspberries
chocolate sprinkles

- Oil and line a large baking tray with baking parchment.
- Grind the almonds and icing sugar to a fine powder. Whisk the egg whites to stiff peaks in a then fold in the almond and sugar mixture with the raspberry syrup.
- Spoon the mixture into a piping bag fitted with a large plain nozzle and pipe 12 circles of 8m / 3" onto the baking tray.
- Leave them to stand for 30 minutes to form a skin.
- Preheat the oven to 170°C (150° fan) / 325 F / gas 3.
- Bake for 15 - 20 minutes or until crisp on the outside and still a bit chewy in the middle.
- Slide the greaseproof paper onto a cold work surface and leave the macaroons to cool completely.
- Divide the lemon curd between 6 of the macaroons and dot round the edge with raspberries.
- Top with the final 6 macaroons.

Giant Lime and Raspberry Macaroons

432

Replace the lemon curd with lime marmalade.

MAKES 18

Chocolate and Raspberry Macaroons

433

Chocolate and Strawberry Macaroons

434

Replace the raspberry jam with strawberry jam.

Chocolate and Plum Macaroons

435

Replace the raspberry jam with plum jam.

Chocolate and Fig Macaroons

436

Replace the raspberry jam with fig jam.

**PREPARATION TIME:
1 HOUR 15 MINUTES**

COOKING TIME: 15 MINUTES

....

INGREDIENTS

175 g / 6 oz / 1 ½ cups ground almonds
175 g / 6 oz / 1 ½ cups icing (confectioners') sugar
2 tbsp unsweetened cocoa powder
2 large egg whites

TO DECORATE

55 g / 2 oz / ¼ cup butter, softened
110 g / 4 oz / 1 cup icing (confectioners') sugar
2 tsp milk
2 tbsp raspberry jam (jelly)

- Oil and line a large baking sheet with baking parchment.
- Grind the ground almonds, icing sugar and cocoa powder together in a food processor to a very fine powder.
- Whisk the egg whites to stiff peaks in a very clean bowl then carefully fold in the almond and sugar mixture.
- Spoon the mixture into a piping bag fitted with a small plain nozzle and pipe 36 heart shapes onto the tray.
- Leave the uncooked macaroons to stand for 30 minutes to form a skin.
- Preheat the oven to 170°C (150° fan) / 325 F / gas 3.
- Bake for 10 – 15 minutes or until crisp on the outside and still a bit chewy in the middle.
- Slide the greaseproof paper onto a cold work surface and leave the macaroons to cool completely.
- Beat the butter with a wooden spoon until light and fluffy then beat in the icing sugar a quarter at a time.
- Use a whisk to incorporate the milk into the buttercream then whisk for 2 minutes or until smooth and well whipped.
- Fold the jam into the buttercream until it looks marbled and use it to sandwich the macaroons together in pairs.

MAKES 18

Morello Cherry Macaroons

Cherry and Chocolate Hazelnut Macaroons

438

Add a layer of chocolate hazelnut spread between the macaroons.

PREPARATION TIME:
1 HOUR 15 MINUTES

COOKING TIME: 10 - 15 MINUTES

INGREDIENTS

175 g / 6 oz / 1 ½ cups ground almonds
175 g / 6 oz / 1 ½ cups icing (confectioners') sugar
2 large egg whites
1 tbsp cherry syrup
a few drops of pink food colouring

TO DECORATE

110 g / 4 oz / ½ cup butter, softened
225 g / 8 oz / 2 cups icing (confectioners') sugar
1 tbsp cherry syrup
a few drops of pink food colouring
9 fresh morello cherries with stalks

- Oil and line a large baking sheet with baking parchment.
- Grind the almonds and icing sugar together in a food processor to a fine powder.
- Whisk the egg whites in a bowl, then fold in the almond and sugar mixture with the cherry syrup and food colouring.
- Spoon the mixture into a piping bag and pipe 2 ½ cm / 1" rounds onto the baking tray.
- Leave the uncooked macaroons to stand for 30 minutes.
- Preheat the oven to 170⁰°C (150⁰ fan) / 325 F / gas 3.
- Bake for 10 – 15 minutes.
- Place the greaseproof paper onto a work surface and leave the macaroons to cool.
- Beat the butter until fluffy then beat in the icing sugar a quarter at a time.
- Mix the cherry syrup and food colouring, then whisk for 2 minutes.
- Spoon the buttercream into a piping bag and pipe an even round onto the back of the macaroons, then halve and stone the cherries.
- Top half of the macaroons with half a cherry and sandwich together with the other half of the macaroons.

439

MAKES 18

Matcha Green Tea Macaroons

- Oil and line a large baking tray with baking parchment.
- Grind the almonds, icing sugar and half the matcha powder together to a very fine powder.
- Whisk the egg whites to stiff peaks then fold in the almond and sugar mixture.
- Spoon the mixture into a piping bag fitted with a plain nozzle and pipe 2 ½cm / 1" rounds onto the baking tray.
- Sprinkle with matcha powder then leave them to stand for 30 minutes to form a skin.
- Preheat the oven to 170°C (150° fan) / 325F / gas 3.
- Bake for 10 – 15 minutes or until crisp on the outside and still a bit chewy in the middle.
- Slide the greaseproof paper onto a cold work surface and leave the macaroons to cool completely.
- Beat the butter until light and fluffy then beat in the icing sugar.
- Use a whisk to incorporate the milk and matcha powder, then whisk for 2 minutes or until smooth and well whipped.
- Spoon the buttercream into a piping bag fitted with a medium plain nozzle and pipe an even round onto half of the macaroons.
- Sandwich together with the other half.

PREPARATION TIME:
1 HOUR 15 MINUTES

COOKING TIME: 15 MINUTES

INGREDIENTS

175 g / 6 oz / 1 ½ cups ground almonds
175 g / 6 oz / 1 ½ cups icing (confectioners') sugar
2 tsp matcha green tea powder
2 large egg whites

TO DECORATE

110 g / 4 oz / ½ cup butter, softened
225 g / 8 oz / 2 cups icing (confectioners') sugar
1 tbsp milk
1 tsp matcha green tea powder

440

MAKES 18

Coffee and Walnut Macaroons

- Oil and line a large baking tray with baking parchment.
- Grind the almonds, walnuts and icing sugar together to a very fine powder. Whisk the egg whites to stiff peaks then carefully fold in the nut and sugar mixture.
- Spoon the mixture into a piping bag fitted with a plain nozzle and pipe 2 ½ cm / 1" rounds onto the baking tray. Leave them to stand for 30 minutes to form a skin.
- Preheat the oven to 170°C (150° fan) / 325 F / gas 3.
- Bake for 10 – 15 minutes. Slide the greaseproof paper onto a cold work surface and leave to cool completely.
- Beat the butter until light and fluffy then beat in the icing sugar. Add the milk and espresso powder, then whisk for 2 minutes or until smooth and well whipped.
- Spoon the buttercream into a piping bag fitted with a medium plain nozzle and pipe an even round onto half of the macaroons.
- Sandwich together with the other hal

PREPARATION TIME:
1 HOUR 15 MINUTES

COOKING TIME: 15 MINUTES

INGREDIENTS

110 g / 4 oz / ½ cup ground almonds
55 g / 2 oz / ½ cup ground walnuts
175 g / 6 oz / 1 ½ cups icing (confectioners') sugar
2 large egg whites

TO DECORATE

110 g / 4 oz / ½ cup butter, softened
225 g / 8 oz / 2 cups icing (confectioners') sugar
1 tbsp milk
1 tbsp instant espresso powder

Maple Syrup Macaroons

441

Try filling the macaroons with maple buttercream – just replace the milk and espresso powder with 2 tbsp of maple syrup.

BROWNIES AND MINI CAKES

MAKES 12

442

Nutty Chocolate Brownies

PREPARATION TIME: 25 MINUTES

COOKING TIME: 20 MINUTES

INGREDIENTS

110 g / 4 oz / ½ cup milk chocolate, chopped
85 g / 3 oz / ¾ cup unsweetened cocoa powder, sifted
225 g / 8 oz / 1 cup butter
450 g / 15 oz / 2 ½ cups light brown sugar
4 large eggs
110 g / 4 oz / 1 cup self-raising flour
75 g / 2 ½ oz / ½ cup almonds, chopped
75 g / 2 ½ oz / ½ cup walnuts, chopped
75 g / 2 ½ oz / ½ cup cashews, chopped

- Preheat the oven to 170°C (150° fan) / 325 F / gas 3 and oil and line a 20cm x 20cm / 8" x 8" square cake tin.
- Melt the chocolate, cocoa and butter together in a saucepan, then leave to cool a little.
- Whisk the sugar and eggs together with an electric whisk for 3 minutes or until very light and creamy.
- Pour in the chocolate mixture and sieve over the flour, then fold everything together until evenly mixed.
- Scrape into the tin and sprinkle over the nuts.
- Bake for 35 – 40 minutes or until the outside is set, but the centre is still quite soft, as it will continue to cook as it cools.
- Leave the brownie to cool completely before cutting into 12 rectangles.

Cherry Chocolate Brownies

443

Try adding 75g / 3 oz / ⅓ cup of halved glacé cherries to the mixed nut topping.

MAKES 12

444

Hazelnut Brownies

PREPARATION TIME: 25 MINUTES

COOKING TIME: 20 MINUTES

INGREDIENTS

110 g / 4 oz / ½ cup dark chocolate, chopped
85 g / 3 oz / ¾ cup unsweetened cocoa powder, sifted
225 g / 8 oz / 1 cup butter
110 g / 4 oz / ½ cup chocolate hazelnut spread
450 g / 15 oz / 2 ½ cups light brown sugar
4 large eggs
110 g / 4 oz / 1 cup self-raising flour
75 g / 2 ½ oz / ½ cup hazelnuts

- Preheat the oven to 170°C (150° fan) / 325 F / gas 3 and oil and line a 20cm x 20cm / 8" x 8" square cake tin.
- Melt the chocolate, cocoa and butter together in a saucepan, then leave to cool a little before stirring in the chocolate hazelnut spread.
- Whisk the sugar and eggs together with an electric whisk for 3 minutes or until very light and creamy.
- Pour in the chocolate mixture and sieve over the flour, then fold everything together with the hazelnuts until evenly mixed.
- Scrape into the tin and bake for 35 – 40 minutes or until the outside is set, but the centre is still quite soft, as it will continue to cook as it cools.
- Leave the brownie to cool completely before cutting into 12 rectangles.

Hazelnut and Raisin Brownies

445

Add 85 g / 3 oz of raisins to the mixture for a fruity twist.

446

MAKES 9

Marbled Brownies

- Preheat the oven to 170°C (150 fan) / 325 F / gas 3 and oil and line a 20cm x 20cm / 8" x 8" square cake tin.
- Melt the dark chocolate, cocoa and butter together in a saucepan, then leave to cool a little.
- Whisk the sugar and eggs together with an electric whisk for 3 minutes or until very light and creamy.
- Pour in the chocolate mixture and sieve over the flour, then fold everything together until evenly mixed.
- Make the white chocolate mixture in the same way, folding in the ground almonds with the flour at the end.
- Put alternate spoonfuls of each mixture into the prepared tin, then marble together by drawing a toothpick through the mixture.
- Bake for 35 – 40 minutes until the outside is set.
- Leave the brownie to cool completely before cutting into squares.

Nutty Marbled Brownies

 447

Add 75g / 3 oz / ⅓ cup of chopped mixed nuts to the dark chocolate brownie mixture.

PREPARATION TIME: 25 MINUTES

COOKING TIME: 20 MINUTES

INGREDIENTS

55 g / 2 oz / ¼ cup dark chocolate, minimum 60% cocoa solids, chopped
40 g / 1 ½ oz / ⅓ cup unsweetened cocoa powder, sifted
110 g / 4 oz / ½ cup butter
225 g / 7 ½ oz / 1 ¼ cups light brown sugar
2 large eggs
55 g / 2 oz / ½ cup self-raising flour

FOR THE WHITE CHOCOLATE MIXTURE

55 g / 2 oz / ¼ cup white chocolate, chopped
110 g / 4 oz / ½ cup butter
225 g / 7 ½ oz / 1 ¼ cups light brown sugar
2 large eggs
55 g / 2 oz / ½ cup self-raising flour
2 tbsp ground almonds

448

MAKES 9

Chocolate and Ginger Brownies

- Preheat the oven to 170°C (150° fan) / 325 F / gas 3 and oil and line a 20cm x 20cm / 8" x 8" square cake tin.
- Melt the chocolate, cocoa and butter together in a saucepan, then leave to cool a little.
- Whisk the sugar and eggs together with an electric whisk for 3 minutes or until very light and creamy.
- Pour in the chocolate mixture and sieve over the flour and ground ginger, then fold everything together with the stem ginger until evenly mixed.
- Scrape into the tin and bake for 35 – 40 minutes or until the outside is set, but the centre is still quite soft, as it will continue to cook as it cools.
- Leave the brownie to cool completely before cutting into 9 squares and topping with the cake sprinkles.

Star Anise Brownies

 **449**

Try replacing the milk chocolate with dark chocolate and use 1 tsp of ground star anise instead of the ground ginger.

PREPARATION TIME: 25 MINUTES

COOKING TIME: 20 MINUTES

INGREDIENTS

110 g / 4 oz / ½ cup milk chocolate, chopped
85 g / 3 oz / ¾ cup unsweetened cocoa powder, sifted
225 g / 8 oz / 1 cup butter
450 g / 15 oz / 2 ½ cups light brown sugar
4 large eggs
110 g / 4 oz / 1 cup self-raising flour
2 tsp ground ginger
75 g / 2 ½ oz / ½ cup stem ginger, finely chopped

TO DECORATE

Hundreds and thousands

450

MAKES 9

Almond and Chocolate Brownies

PREPARATION TIME: 25 MINUTES

COOKING TIME: 20 MINUTES

INGREDIENTS

110 g / 4 oz / ½ cup dark chocolate, minimum 60% cocoa solids, chopped
85 g / 3 oz / ¾ cup unsweetened cocoa powder, sifted
225 g / 8 oz / 1 cup butter
450 g / 15 oz / 2 ½ cups light brown sugar
4 large eggs
110 g / 4 oz / 1 cup self-raising flour
75 g / 2 ½ oz / ½ cup flaked (slivered) almonds

TO DECORATE

75 g / 2 ½ oz / ½ cup flaked (slivered) almonds
Icing (confectioners') sugar to dust

- Preheat the oven to 170°C (150° fan) / 325 F / gas 3 and oil and line a 20cm x 20cm / 8" x 8" square cake tin.
- Melt the chocolate, cocoa and butter together in a saucepan, then leave to cool a little.
- Whisk the sugar and eggs together with an electric whisk for 3 minutes or until very light and creamy.
- Pour in the chocolate mixture and sieve over the flour, then fold everything together with the flaked almonds until evenly mixed.
- Scrape into the tin and bake for 35 – 40 minutes or until the outside is set, but the centre is still a quite soft, as it will continue to cook as it cools.
- Leave the brownie to cool completely before cutting into 9 squares and topping with more flaked almonds and a dusting of icing sugar.

Marzipan Brownies

451

For extra almond flavour, add 110g / 4oz / ½ cup of marzipan in cubes to the brownie mixture.

452

MAKES 24

Mini Chocolate Brownies

PREPARATION TIME: 25 MINUTES

COOKING TIME: 20 MINUTES

INGREDIENTS

110 g / 4 oz / ⅔ cup dark chocolate, minimum 60% cocoa solids, chopped
85 g / 3 oz / ¾ cup unsweetened cocoa powder, sifted
225 g / 8 oz / 1 cup butter
450 g / 15 oz / 2 ½ cups light brown sugar
4 large eggs
110 g / 4 oz / 1 cup self-raising flour

- Preheat the oven to 170°C (150° fan) / 325 F / gas 3 and line a 24-hole muffin tin with paper cases.
- Melt the chocolate, cocoa and butter together in a saucepan, then leave to cool a little.
- Whisk the sugar and eggs together with an electric whisk for 3 minutes or until very light and creamy.
- Pour in the chocolate mixture and sieve over the flour, then fold everything together until evenly mixed.
- Spoon into the muffin cases and bake for 15 – 20 minutes or until the outside is set, but the centre is still a quite soft, as they will continue to cook as they cool.

MAKES 6

Chestnut Cream Refrigerator Cakes

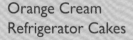

Chocolate Cream Refrigerator Cakes

454

Replace the chestnut puree with melted milk chocolate. Decorate with milk chocolate curls.

Orange Cream Refrigerator Cakes

455

Replace the chestnut puree in the chestnut cream with 1 tbsp grated orange zest. Decorate with candied peel.

PREPARATION TIME: 25 MINUTES

COOKING TIME : 15 MINUTES

INGREDIENTS

2 plain cakes
55 g / 2 oz / ¼ cup chestnut puree

FOR THE CHOCOLATE GANACHE
110 g / 4 oz / ½ cup dark chocolate, minimum 60% cocoa solids
110 ml / 4 fl. oz / ½ cup double (heavy) cream

FOR THE CHESTNUT CREAM
225 ml / 8 fl. oz / 1 cup double (heavy) cream
2 tbsp icing (confectioners') sugar
½ tsp vanilla extract
110 g / 4 oz / ½ cup chestnut puree
2 tbsp mixed nuts, finely chopped
Gold leaf

- Put the cakes in a food processor and process to fine crumbs.
- Stir in the chestnut puree and press the mixture into the bottom of 6 sundae glasses.
- Chop the chocolate and transfer to a mixing bowl.
- Heat the cream until it starts to simmer, then pour over the chopped chocolate and stir until the mixture has cooled and thickened.
- Spoon on top of the cake mixture and chill until firm.
- Whip the cream with the icing sugar and vanilla extract, then whisk in the chestnut puree.
- Spoon the chestnut cream on top of the chocolate ganache and top with chopped nuts and gold leaf.

456

MAKES 12

Basil and Mozzarella Mini Loaf Cakes

Mozzarella and Tomato Loaf Cakes

457

Try marbling the muffin mixture with 2 tbsp of sun-dried tomato paste.

Mozzarella and Oregano Loaf Cakes

458

Replace the basil with fresh oregano.

PREPARATION TIME: 25 MINUTES

COOKING TIME: 20 MINUTES

....

INGREDIENTS

2 large eggs
120 ml / 4 fl. oz / ½ cup sunflower oil
180 ml / 6 fl. oz / ¾ cup Greek yogurt
110 g / 4 oz / 1 cup mozzarella, cubed
28 g / 1 oz / 1 cup basil leaves, shredded
225 g / 8 oz / 1 ½ cups plain (all purpose) flour
2 tsp baking powder
½ tsp bicarbonate of (baking) soda
½ tsp salt

- Preheat the oven to 180°C (160° fan) / 350 F / gas 4 and oil 12 mini loaf tins.
- Beat the egg in a jug with the oil, yogurt, cheese and basil until well mixed.
- Mix the flour, raising agents and salt in a bowl, then pour in the egg mixture and stir just enough to combine.
- Divide the mixture between the tins, then bake in the oven for 20 – 25 minutes.
- Test with a wooden toothpick, if it comes out clean, the cakes are done.
- Serve warm.

459

MAKES 12

Apricot, Date and Hazelnut Cakes

- Preheat the oven to 180°C (160° fan) / 350 F / gas 4 and oil a 12-hole silicone muffin tin.
- Beat the egg in a jug with the oil and milk until well mixed.
- Mix the flour, baking powder, sugar, apricots, dates and hazelnuts in a bowl, then pour in the egg mixture and stir just enough to combine.
- Divide the mixture between the moulds, then bake in the oven for 20 – 25 minutes.
- Test with a wooden toothpick, if it comes out clean, the cakes are done.
- Transfer the cakes to a wire rack and leave to cool completely.

PREPARATION TIME: 25 MINUTES

COOKING TIME: 25 MINUTES

INGREDIENTS

1 large egg
120 ml / 4 fl. oz / ½ cup sunflower oil
120 ml / 4 fl. oz / ½ cup milk
375 g / 12 ½ oz / 2 ½ cups self-raising flour, sifted
1 tsp baking powder
200 g / 7 oz / ¾ cup caster (superfine) sugar
75 g / 2 ½ oz / ½ cup dried apricots, chopped
75 g / 2 ½ oz / ½ cup dates, stoned and chopped
75 g / 2 ½ oz / ½ cup hazelnuts (cob nuts), chopped

Oaty Cakes

460

Try adding 2 tbsp rolled oats to the mixture to boost the fibre content.

461

MAKES 12

Almond and Raspberry Jam Mini Cakes

- Preheat the oven to 190°C (170° fan) / 375 F / gas 5 and oil a 36-hole silicone mini cupcake mould.
- Combine the flour, baking powder, ground almonds, sugar, butter, eggs and almond essence in a bowl and whisk together for 2 minutes or until smooth.
- Divide half of the mixture between the moulds, then add a small spoonful of raspberry jam in the centre of each one.
- Top with the rest of the cake mixture then transfer the tin to the oven and bake for 10 – 15 minutes.
- Test with a wooden toothpick, if it comes out clean, the cakes are done.
- Transfer the cakes to a wire rack and leave to cool.

PREPARATION TIME: 20 MINUTES

COOKING TIME: 15 MINUTES

INGREDIENTS

55 g / 2 oz / ½ cup self-raising flour, sifted
2 tsp baking powder
55 g / 2 oz / ½ cup ground almonds
110 g / 4 oz / ½ cup caster (superfine) sugar
110 g / 4 oz / ½ cup butter, softened
2 large eggs
1 tsp almond essence
110 g / 4 oz / ½ cup raspberry jam (jelly)

Almond Drizzle Cakes

462

Try making an almond drizzle to ice the cakes: mix 225g / 8 oz / 1 cup icing sugar with ½ tsp almond essence and just enough boiling water to make a runny glaze.

463

MAKES 9

Chocolate and Pecan Brownies

PREPARATION TIME: 25 MINUTES

COOKING TIME: 40 MINUTES

....

INGREDIENTS

110 g / 4 oz / ½ cup dark chocolate,
minimum 60% cocoa solids,
chopped

85 g / 3 oz / ¾ cup unsweetened
cocoa powder, sifted

225 g / 8 oz / 1 cup butter

450 g / 15 oz / 2 ½ cups light brown
sugar

4 large eggs

110 g / 4 oz / 1 cup self-raising flour

75 g / 2 ½ oz / ½ cup pecan nuts,
chopped

TO DECORATE

18 pecan halves

- Preheat the oven to 170°C (150° fan) / 325 F / gas 3 and oil and line a 20cm x 20cm / 8" x 8" square cake tin.
- Melt the chocolate, cocoa and butter together in a saucepan, then leave to cool a little.
- Whisk the sugar and eggs together with an electric whisk for 3 minutes or until very light and creamy.
- Pour in the chocolate mixture and sieve over the flour, then fold everything together with the chopped pecans until evenly mixed.
- Scrape into the tin and bake for 35 – 40 minutes or until the outside is set, but the centre is still quite soft, as it will continue to cook as it cools.
- Leave the brownie to cool completely before cutting into 9 squares.
- Top each square with 2 pecan nuts.

Chocolate And Pistachio Brownies   **464**

Replace the pecan nuts with 75g / 3 oz / ⅓ cup of whole pistachio nuts and dust with unsweetened cocoa powder before serving.

465

MAKES 12

Peanut and Caramel Brownie Slices

PREPARATION TIME: 25 MINUTES

COOKING TIME: 40 MINUTES

....

INGREDIENTS

110 g / 4 oz milk chocolate

85 g / 3 oz / ¾ cup unsweetened
cocoa powder, sifted

225 g / 8 oz / 1 cup butter

450 g / 15 oz / 2 ½ cups light brown
sugar

4 large eggs

110 g / 4 oz / ½ cup self-raising flour

150 g / 5 oz / ⅔ cup peanuts, chopped

TO DECORATE

85 g / 3 oz / ½ cup butter

85 ml / 3 fl. oz / ⅓ cup double
(heavy) cream

85 g / 3 oz / ¼ cup golden syrup

85 g / 3 oz / ½ cup dark brown sugar

110 g / 4 oz dark chocolate,
minimum 60% cocoa solids

75 g / 2 ½ oz / ½ cup peanuts,
roughly chopped

- Preheat the oven to 170°C (150° fan) / 325 F / gas 3 and oil and line a 20cm x 20cm / 8" x 8" square cake tin.
- Melt the chocolate, cocoa and butter together in a saucepan, then leave to cool a little.
- Whisk the sugar and eggs together for 3 minutes.
- Pour in the chocolate mixture and sieve over the flour, then fold everything together with the chopped peanuts until evenly mixed.
- Scrape into the tin and bake for 35 – 40 minutes or until the outside is set, but the centre is still quite soft, as it will continue to cook as it cools.
- Leave the brownie to cool completely in the tin.
- Put the butter, cream, golden syrup and brown sugar in a small saucepan and boil for 2 minutes, stirring to dissolve the sugar.
- Pour the caramel over the brownie and leave to set in the fridge until firm.
- Melt the chocolate in a microwave or bain marie and pour over the caramel layer.
- Scatter over the peanuts and cut into 12 slices.

466

MAKES 24

Almond and Orange Mini Cakes

Almond and Lemon Cakes

467

Replace the orange juice with lemon juice and the orange zest with lemon zest.

Iced Almond and Orange Mini Cakes

468

Decorate these little cakes with a drizzle of plain white icing: mix 200 g of icing sugar with just enough boiling water to make a thin icing.

PREPARATION TIME: 25 MINUTES

COOKING TIME: 20 MINUTES

INGREDIENTS

1 large egg
120 ml / 4 fl. oz / ½ cup sunflower oil
120 ml / 4 fl. oz / ½ cup milk
2 tbsp orange juice
375 g / 12 ½ oz / 2 ½ cups self-raising flour, sifted
1 tsp baking powder
200 g / 7 oz / ¾ cup caster (superfine) sugar
55 g / 2 oz / ½ cup ground almonds
1 tbsp orange zest, finely grated
75 g / 2 ½ oz / ½ cup flaked (slivered) almonds
icing sugar to dust

- Preheat the oven to 180°C (160° fan) / 350F / gas 4 and oil a 24-hole silicone mini muffin mould.
- Beat the egg in a jug with the oil, milk and orange juice until well mixed.
- Mix the flour, baking powder, sugar, ground almonds and orange zest in a bowl, then pour in the egg mixture and stir just enough to combine.
- Divide the mixture between the moulds and sprinkle with flaked almonds, then bake in the oven for 15 – 20 minutes.
- Test with a wooden toothpick, if it comes out clean, the cakes are done.
- Transfer the cakes to a wire rack and dust with icing sugar.

469

MAKES 24

Plain Mini Cakes

PREPARATION TIME: 25 MINUTES

COOKING TIME: 20 MINUTES

INGREDIENTS

1 large egg
120 ml / 4 fl. oz / ½ cup sunflower oil
120 ml / 4 fl. oz / ½ cup milk
375 g / 12 ½ oz / 2 ½ cups self raising flour, sifted
1 tsp baking powder
200 g / 7 oz / ¾ cup caster (superfine) sugar

- Preheat the oven to 180°C (160° fan) / 350 F / gas 4 and line a 24-hole mini muffin tin with paper cases.
- Beat the egg in a jug with the oil and milk until well mixed.
- Mix the flour, baking powder and sugar in a bowl, then pour in the egg mixture and stir just enough to combine.
- Divide the mixture between the paper cases, then bake in the oven for 15 – 20 minutes.
- Test with a wooden toothpick, if it comes out clean, the cakes are done.
- Transfer the cakes to a wire rack and leave to cool completely.

Sesame Seed Cakes

470

Add 85 g / 3 oz of sesame seeds to the mixture before cooking.

471

MAKES 4

Chocolate Soufflé Cups

PREPARATION TIME: 35 MINUTES

COOKING TIME: 15 MINUTES

INGREDIENTS

110 g / 4 oz / ⅔ cup dark chocolate, minimum 60% cocoa solids, chopped
4 large eggs
85 g / 3 oz / ⅓ cup caster (superfine) sugar

- Preheat the oven to 200°C (180° fan) / 400 F / gas 6 and put a baking tray in to heat.
- Oil 4 small mugs then dust the insides with a little caster sugar.
- Melt the chocolate in a microwave or bain marie and leave to cool.
- Separate the eggs and stir the egg yolks into the melted chocolate.
- Whip the egg whites to stiff peaks, then stir ¼ of the egg whites into the chocolate mixture.
- Pour the chocolate mixture into the egg white bowl and carefully fold together until evenly mixed.
- Divide the mixture between the mugs and level the tops, then transfer them to the heated baking tray and bake for 12 – 15 minutes or until well risen.
- Serve immediately.

MAKES 12

Plum and Vanilla Cakes

- Preheat the oven to 190°C (170° fan) / 375 F / gas 5 and oil a 12-hole silicone cupcake mould.
- Combine the flour, sugar, butter, eggs and vanilla extract in a bowl and whisk together for 2 minutes or until smooth.
- Fold in the plums.
- Divide the mixture between the moulds, then transfer the tin to the oven and bake for 15 – 20 minutes.
- Test with a wooden toothpick, if it comes out clean, the cakes are done.
- Transfer the cakes to a wire rack and leave to cool before dusting with icing sugar.

PREPARATION TIME: 25 MINUTES

COOKING TIME: 20 MINUTES

INGREDIENTS

110 g / 4 oz / ½ cup self-raising flour, sifted
110 g / 4 oz / ½ cup caster (superfine) sugar
110 g / 4 oz / ½ cup butter, softened
2 large eggs
1 tsp vanilla extract
12 plums, stoned and sliced
Icing (confectioners') sugar to dust

Plum and Cinnamon Cakes

473

Try replacing the vanilla with 2 tsp ground cinnamon.

MAKES 24

Mini Hazelnut Choux Buns

- Oil and line a large baking tray with greaseproof paper, then spray it with a little water.
- Put the butter in a saucepan with 150 ml cold water and heat until the butter melts and the water starts to boil.
- Turn off the heat and immediately beat in the flour with a wooden spoon.
- Continue to beat the mixture until it forms a smooth ball of pastry and leaves the sides of the saucepan clean.
- Stir in the beaten egg a little at a time until you have a glossy paste.
- Spoon the pastry into a piping bag with a large plain nozzle and pipe 2.5 cm / 1" buns onto the prepared baking tray.
- Bake for 10 minutes, then increase the heat to 220°C (200° fan) / 425 F / gas 7 and bake for another 10 minutes.
- Transfer the choux buns to a wire rack and make a small hole in the underneath of each one with a skewer so the steam can escape.
- Leave to cool completely then cut the buns in half horizontally.
- Whip the cream with the icing sugar and vanilla until thick, then fold in the ground hazelnuts.
- Spoon the hazelnuts into a piping bag fitted with a large star nozzle and fill the bottom halves of the choux buns.
- Put the tops back on and dust with pink icing sugar.

PREPARATION TIME: 20 MINUTES

COOKING TIME: 10 - 15 MINUTES

INGREDIENTS

55 g / 2 oz / butter, cubed
70 g / 2 ½ oz / strong white bread flour, sieved
2 large eggs, beaten

TO DECORATE
225 ml / 8 fl. oz / 1 cup double (heavy) cream
2 tbsp icing (confectioners') sugar
½ tsp vanilla extract
55 g / 2 oz / ½ cup ground hazelnuts
pink icing sugar to dust

MAKES 12

Coconut and Raspberry Mini Loaf Cakes

Orange and Raspberry Mini Loaf Cakes 476

Try adding 1 tbsp finely grated orange zest to the cake mixture.

Coconut and Cherry Mini Loaf Cakes 477

Replace the raspberries with stoned cherries.

Coconut and Sultana Mini Loaf Cakes 478

Replace the raspberries with sultanas.

PREPARATION TIME: 20 MINUTES

COOKING TIME: 20 MINUTES

....

INGREDIENTS

110 g / 4 oz / ½ cup self-raising flour, sifted
110 g / 4 oz / ½ cup caster (superfine) sugar
110 g / 4 oz / ½ cup butter, softened
2 large eggs
1 tsp vanilla extract
28 g / 1 oz / ⅛ cup desiccated coconut
150 g / 5 oz / 1 cup raspberries

- Preheat the oven to 190°C (170° fan) / 375 F / gas 5 and oil 12 silicone mini loaf cake moulds.
- Combine the flour, sugar, butter and eggs in a bowl and whisk together for 2 minutes or until smooth.
- Fold in the coconut then divide the mixture between the moulds.
- Stud each cake with raspberries then bake for 15 – 20 minutes.
- Test with a wooden toothpick, if it comes out clean, the cakes are done.
- Transfer the cakes to a wire rack and leave to cool completely.

479

MAKES 12

Chocolate and Walnut Mini Brownies

- Preheat the oven to 170°C (150° fan) / 325 F / gas 3 and line a 12-hole cupcake tin with paper cases.
- Melt the chocolate, cocoa and butter together in a saucepan, then leave to cool a little.
- Whisk the sugar and eggs together with an electric whisk for 3 minutes or until very light and creamy.
- Pour in the chocolate mixture and sieve over the flour, then fold everything together until evenly mixed.
- Spoon into the cake cases and top each one with 3 walnut halves.
- Bake for 10 – 15 minutes or until the outside is set, but the centres are still quite soft, as they will continue to cook as they cool.

PREPARATION TIME: 25 MINUTES

COOKING TIME: 15 MINUTES

INGREDIENTS

110 g / 4 oz / 1 cup dark chocolate, minimum 60% cocoa solids, chopped
85 g / 3 oz / ¾ cup unsweetened cocoa powder, sifted
225 g / 8 oz / 1 cup butter
450 g / 15 oz / 2 ½ cups light brown sugar
4 large eggs
110 g / 4 oz / 1 cup self-raising flour
36 walnut halves

Maple Syrup and Walnut Brownies

 480

Try adding 2 tbsp of maple syrup to the brownie mixture.

481

MAKES 12

Candied Fruit Cakes

- Preheat the oven to 180°C (160° fan) / 350 F / gas 4 and line a 12-hole muffin tin with paper cases.
- Beat the egg in a jug with the oil and milk until well mixed.
- Mix the flour, baking powder, sugar, mixed spice and ¾ of the candied fruit in a bowl, then pour in the egg mixture and stir just enough to combine.
- Divide the mixture between the moulds, sprinkle with the rest of the candied fruit and bake in the oven for 20 – 25 minutes.
- Test with a wooden toothpick, if it comes out clean, the cakes are done.
- Transfer the cakes to a wire rack and leave to cool completely.

PREPARATION TIME: 25 MINUTES

COOKING TIME: 25 MINUTES

INGREDIENTS

1 large egg
120 ml / 4 fl. oz / ½ cup sunflower oil
120 ml / 4 fl. oz / ½ cup milk
375 g / 12 ½ oz / 2 ½ cups self-raising flour, sifted
1 tsp baking powder
200 g / 7 oz / ¾ cup caster (superfine) sugar
2 tsp mixed spice
75 g / 2 ½ oz / ½ cup candied pineapple, chopped
75 g / 2 ½ oz / ½ cup candied papaya, chopped
75 g / 2 ½ oz / ½ cup candied mixed peel, chopped

Honey Glazed Fruit Cakes

 482

Try brushing the hot cakes with honey for a glossy finish.

483

MAKES 12

Ratatouille Cakes

PREPARATION TIME: 25 MINUTES

COOKING TIME: 20-25 MINUTES

INGREDIENTS

1 shallot, chopped
1 medium courgettes (zucchini), sliced
½ aubergine, chopped
1 yellow pepper, chopped
4 tbsp olive oil
1 clove of garlic, chopped
2 large eggs
120 ml / 4 fl. oz / ½ cup sunflower oil
180 ml / 6 fl. oz / ¾ cup Greek yoghurt
225 g / 8 oz / 1 ½ cups plain flour
2 tsp baking powder
½ tsp bicarbonate of (baking) soda
½ tsp salt

- Fry the shallot, courgette, aubergine and pepper in the olive oil for 10 minutes until softened.
- Add the garli°C and continue to cook, stirring occasionally for 2 minutes, then leave to cool.
- Preheat the oven to 180°°C (160⁰ fan) / 350 F / gas 4 and oil a 12-hole silicone muffin tin.
- Beat the egg in a jug with the oil, yoghurt and fried vegetables until well mixed.
- Mix the flour, raising agents and salt in a bowl, then pour in the egg mixture and stir just enough to combine.
- Divide the mixture between the moulds, then bake in the oven for 20 – 25 minutes.
- Test with a wooden toothpick, if it comes out clean, the cakes are done.
- Serve warm.

Ratatouille and Goats Cheese Cakes

 484

Add 100 g of cubed goats cheese and 2 tbsp fresh oregano leaves to the muffin mixture.

485

MAKES 12

Coconut and Chocolate Mini Loaf Cakes

PREPARATION TIME: 20 MINUTES

COOKING TIME: 20 MINUTES

INGREDIENTS

110 g / 4 oz / ½ cup self-raising flour, sifted
110 g / 4 oz / ½ cup caster (superfine) sugar
110 g / 4 oz / ½ cup butter, softened
2 large eggs
1 tsp vanilla extract
28 g / 1 oz / ⅛ cup desiccated coconut
150 g / 5 oz / 1 cup chocolate chips

- Preheat the oven to 190°C (170° fan) / 375 F / gas 5 and oil a 12-hole silicone mini loaf cake mould.
- Combine the flour, sugar, butter and eggs in a bowl and whisk together for 2 minutes or until smooth.
- Fold in the coconut and chocolate chips then divide the mixture between the moulds.
- Transfer the mould to the oven and bake for 15 – 20 minutes.
- Test with a wooden toothpick, if it comes out clean, the cakes are done.
- Transfer the cakes to a wire rack and leave to cool completely.

White Chocolate and Coconut Mini Loaf Cakes

 486

Try covering the cakes in melted white chocolate and rolling them in desiccated coconut before leaving to set on a wire rack.

487

MAKES 12

Orange Mini Loaf Cakes

Marmalade-glazed Mini Loaf Cakes

488

For a simple but effective glaze, heat 4 tbsp marmalade in a small saucepan and spoon over the cakes when they come out of the oven.

PREPARATION TIME: 20 MINUTES

COOKING TIME: 20 MINUTES

INGREDIENTS

110 g / 4 oz / ½ cup self-raising flour, sifted

110 g / 4 oz / ½ cup caster (superfine) sugar

110 g / 4 oz / ½ cup butter, softened

2 large eggs

1 orange, zest finely grated

- Preheat the oven to 190°C (170° fan) / 375 F / gas 5 and oil a 12-hole silicone mini loaf cake mould.
- Combine the flour, sugar, butter, eggs and orange zest in a bowl and whisk together for 2 minutes or until smooth.
- Divide the mixture between the moulds then transfer the mould to the oven and bake for 15 – 20 minutes.
- Test with a wooden toothpick, if it comes out clean, the cakes are done.
- Transfer the cakes to a wire rack and leave to cool completely.

MAKES 12

Crab and Coriander Mini Loaf Cakes

PREPARATION TIME: 25 MINUTES

COOKING TIME: 20 MINUTES

INGREDIENTS

2 large eggs
120 ml / 4 fl. oz / ½ cup sunflower oil
180 ml / 6 fl. oz / ¾ cup Greek yogurt
110 g / 4 oz / 1 cup fresh crab meat
1 shallot, finely chopped
1 green chilli, finely chopped
2 tbsp fresh coriander (cilantro), chopped
225 g / 8 oz / 1 ½ cups plain (all purpose) flour
2 tsp baking powder
½ tsp bicarbonate of (baking) soda
½ tsp salt

- Preheat the oven to 180°C (160° fan) / 350 F / gas 4 and line 12 mini loaf tins with paper cases.
- Beat the egg in a jug with the oil, yogurt, cheese, crab, shallots, chilli and coriander until well mixed.
- Mix the flour, raising agents and salt in a bowl, then pour in the egg mixture and stir just enough to combine.
- Divide the mixture between the tins, then bake in the oven for 20 – 25 minutes.
- Test with a wooden toothpick, if it comes out clean, the cakes are done.
- Serve warm.

Crab and Coriander Mini Loaf Cakes with Guacamole

490

Try splitting open the warm loaf cakes and filling with a dollop of guacamole.

491

MAKES 24

Carrot, Saffron and Sultana Mini Cakes

PREPARATION TIME: 25 MINUTES

COOKING TIME: 20 MINUTES

INGREDIENTS

120 ml / 4 fl. oz / ½ cup milk
1 pinch of saffron
1 large egg
120 ml / 4 fl. oz / ½ cup sunflower oil
375 g / 12 ½ oz / 2 ½ cups self-raising flour, sifted
1 tsp baking powder
200 g / 7 oz / ¾ cup caster (superfine) sugar
150 g / 5 oz / 1 cup carrot, coarsely grated
75 g / 2 ½ oz / ½ cup sultanas

- Preheat the oven to 180°C (160° fan) / 350 F / gas 4 and oil a 24-hole silicone mini muffin mould.
- Heat the milk until it starts to simmer, then take off the heat, add the saffron and leave to infuse for 20 minutes.
- Beat the egg in a jug with the oil and saffron milk until well mixed.
- Mix the flour, baking powder, sugar, carrot and sultanas in a bowl, then pour in the egg mixture and stir just enough to combine.
- Divide the mixture between the moulds, then bake in the oven for 15 – 20 minutes.
- Test with a wooden toothpick, if it comes out clean, the cakes are done.
- Transfer the cakes to a wire rack and leave to cool completely.

Spiced Mini Cakes

492

Try adding ½ tsp freshly grated nutmeg to add some warming spice.

MAKES 12

493

Cherry Brandy Cakes

- Preheat the oven to 190°°C (170° fan) / 375 F / gas 5 and oil 12 mini pudding basins.
- Combine the flour, ground almonds, sugar, butter, eggs and almond essence in a bowl and whisk together for 2 minutes or until smooth.
- Divide the mixture between the basins and top with the cherries.
- Sit the pudding basins on a baking tray and bake in the oven for 15 – 20 minutes.
- Test with a wooden toothpick, if it comes out clean, the cakes are done.
- Spoon over the cherry brandy and leave to cool.

PREPARATION TIME: 20 MINUTES

COOKING TIME: 15-20 MINUTES

INGREDIENTS

55 g / 2 oz / ½ cup self-raising flour, sifted
55 g / 2 oz / ½ cup ground almonds
110 g / 4 oz / ½ cup caster (superfine) sugar
110 g / 4 oz / ½ cup butter, softened
2 large eggs
1 tsp almond essence
150 g / 5 oz / 1 cup cherries in brandy, drained
60 ml / 2 fl. oz / ¼ cup cherry brandy

Apricot Brandy Cakes

494

Replace the cherries with fresh apricot halves and spoon over apricot brandy when the cakes come out of the oven.

495

MAKES 12

Mini Fruit Cakes

- Oil 6 ramekin dishes and dust the insides with icing sugar.
- Melt the chocolate, butter and sugar together in a saucepan, stirring to dissolve the sugar.
- Leave to cool a little then beat in the eggs and egg yolks and fold in the flour and prunes.
- Divide the mixture between the pudding basins, then chill them for 30 minutes.
- Preheat the oven to 180°C (160° fan) / 350 F / gas 4 and put a baking tray in to heat.
- Transfer the fondants to the heated baking tray and bake in the oven for 8 minutes.
- Serve the fondants immediately.

PREPARATION TIME: 30 MINUTES

COOKING TIME: 8 MINUTES

INGREDIENTS

2 tbsp icing (confectioners') sugar
150g / 6 oz white chocolate, chopped
150g / 6 oz / 2/3 cup butter, chopped
85g / 3 oz / 1/3 cup caster (superfine) sugar
3 large eggs
3 egg yolks
1 tbsp plain (all purpose) flour
75g / 2 ½ oz / ½ cup prunes, stoned and chopped

496

MAKES 6

Milk Chocolate Fondants

White Chocolate and Malt Fondants

497

Replace the milk chocolate with white chocolate and the cocoa powder for powdered malt.

PREPARATION TIME: 50 MINUTES

COOKING TIME: 8 MINUTES

INGREDIENTS

2 tbsp unsweetened cocoa powder
150 g / 6 oz milk chocolate, chopped
150 g / 6 oz / ⅔ cup butter, chopped
85 g / 3 oz / ⅓ cup caster (superfine) sugar
3 large eggs
3 egg yolks
1 tbsp plain (all purpose) flour

- Oil 6 mini pudding basins and dust the insides with cocoa.
- Melt the chocolate, butter and sugar together in a saucepan, stirring to dissolve the sugar.
- Leave to cool a little then beat in the eggs and egg yolks and fold in the flour.
- Divide the mixture between the pudding basins, then chill them for 30 minutes.
- Preheat the oven to 180°C (160° fan) / 350 F / gas 4 and put a baking tray in to heat.
- Transfer the fondants to the heated baking tray and bake in the oven for 8 minutes.
- Leave the fondants to cool for 2 minutes, then turn them out of their moulds and serve immediately.

498

MAKES 6

Tuile Cups with Bananas

Tuile Cups with Fruits

 499

Replace the bananas with mixed summer berries and top with plain whipped cream.

Tuile Cups with Raisins

 500

Replace the bananas with raisins and top with plain whipped cream.

PREPARATION TIME:
1 HOUR 15 MINUTES

COOKING TIME: 8 – 10 MINUTES

· ·

INGREDIENTS

55 g / 2 oz / ½ cup plain (all-purpose) flour
55 g / 2 oz / ¼ cup caster (superfine) sugar
2 large egg whites
55 g / 2 oz / ¼ cup butter, melted

TO DECORATE

225 ml / 8 fl. oz / 1 cup double (heavy) cream
6 bananas, chopped
2 tbsp hazelnuts, chopped

- Beat together the flour, sugar and egg whites until smooth, then beat in the melted butter.
- Refrigerate for 30 minutes.
- Preheat the oven to 180°°C (160° fan) / 350 F / gas 4 and oil a large baking tray.
- Spoon teaspoonfuls of the mixture onto the baking tray and spread out with the back of the spoon to make 15 cm / 6" circles.
- Bake for 8 – 10 minutes.
- As soon as the biscuits come out of the oven, lift them off the baking tray with a palette knife and mould them around a jam jar.
- When the biscuits are cool and crisp, remove from the jar.
- Whip the cream until thick and spoon into a piping bag fitted with a large star nozzle.
- Fill the tuile cups with chopped banana, then pipe a big swirl of cream on top and sprinkle with nuts.

501

MAKES 12

Caramel Cream Brownies

PREPARATION TIME: 25 MINUTES

COOKING TIME: 40 MINUTES

INGREDIENTS

110 g / 4 oz / ½ milk chocolate, chopped
85 g / 3 oz / ¾ cup unsweetened cocoa powder, sifted
225 g / 8 oz / 1 cup butter
450 g / 15 oz / 2 ½ cups light brown sugar
4 large eggs
110 g / 4 oz / 1 cup self-raising flour

TO DECORATE

85 g / 3 oz / ½ cup butter
85 g / 3 oz / ¼ cup golden syrup
85 g / 3 oz / ½ cup dark brown sugar
225 ml / 8 fl. oz / 1 cup double (heavy) cream

- Preheat the oven to 170°C (150° fan) / 325 F / gas 3 and oil a 12-hole silicone cupcake mould.
- Melt the chocolate, cocoa and butter together in a saucepan, then leave to cool a little.
- Whisk the sugar and eggs together with an electric whisk for 3 minutes or until very light and creamy.
- Pour in the chocolate mixture and sieve over the flour, then fold everything together until evenly mixed.
- Divide the mixture between the moulds and bake for 35 – 40 minutes or until the outside is set, but the centres are still quite soft, as they will continue to cook as they cool.
- Put the butter, golden syrup and brown sugar in a small saucepan and boil for 2 minutes, stirring to dissolve the sugar.
- Leave to cool completely.
- Whip the cream until thick, then fold in the cooled caramel mixture.
- Spoon into a piping bag fitted with a large star nozzle and pipe a generous swirl on top of each brownie.

502

MAKES 12

Rosemary and Sultana Cakes

PREPARATION TIME: 25 MINUTES

COOKING TIME: 25 MINUTES

INGREDIENTS

1 large egg
120ml / 4 fl oz / ½ cup sunflower oil
120ml / 4 fl oz / ½ cup milk
375g / 12 ½ oz / 2 ½ cups self-raising flour, sifted
1 tsp baking powder
200g / 7 oz / ¾ cup caster (superfine) sugar
2 tsp fresh rosemary, chopped
75g / 2 ½ oz / ½ cup sultanas

TO DECORATE

12 golden sultanas
12 rosemary leaves

- Preheat the oven to 180C (160C fan) / 350F / gas 4 and oil a 12-hole silicone muffin tin.
- Beat the egg in a jug with the oil and milk until well mixed.
- Mix the flour, baking powder, sugar, rosemary and sultanas in a bowl, then pour in the egg mixture and stir just enough to combine.
- Divide the mixture between the moulds, then bake in the oven for 20 – 25 minutes.
- Test with a wooden toothpick, if it comes out clean, the cakes are done.
- Transfer the cakes to a wire rack and leave to cool completely.
- Top each cake with a sultana and a rosemary leaf.

Apricot and Lemon Thyme Cakes

503

Replace the sultanas with chopped dried apricots and replace the chopped rosemary with fresh lemon thyme leaves.

504

MAKES 24

Wholemeal Nutmeg and Orange Mini Cakes

PREPARATION TIME: 25 MINUTES

COOKING TIME: 15-20 MINUTES

INGREDIENTS

1 large egg
120 ml / 4 fl. oz / ½ cup sunflower oil
120 ml / 4 fl. oz / ½ cup milk
375 g / 12 ½ oz / 2 ½ cups wholemeal flour
2 tsp baking powder
200 g / 7 oz / ¾ cup caster (superfine) sugar
1 tbsp orange zest, finely grated
1 tsp freshly grated nutmeg

- Preheat the oven to 180°°C (160° fan) / 350 F / gas 4 and oil a 24-hole silicone mini muffin mould.
- Beat the egg in a jug with the oil and milk until well mixed.
- Mix the flour, baking powder, sugar, orange zest and nutmeg in a bowl, then pour in the egg mixture and stir just enough to combine.
- Divide the mixture between the moulds then bake in the oven for 15 – 20 minutes.
- Test with a wooden toothpick, if it comes out clean, the cakes are done.
- Transfer the cakes to a wire rack and leave to cool.

505

MAKES 12

Lemon and Almond Cakes

PREPARATION TIME: 20 MINUTES

COOKING TIME: 20 MINUTES

INGREDIENTS

55 g / 2 oz / ½ cup self-raising flour, sifted
2 tsp baking powder
55 g / 2 oz / ½ cup ground almonds
110 g / 4 oz / ½ cup caster (superfine) sugar
110 g / 4 oz / ½ cup butter, softened
2 large eggs
1 lemon, finely grated zest

TO DECORATE
12 pieces of candied lemon peel

- Preheat the oven to 190°C (170° fan) / 375 F / gas 5 and oil a 12-hole silicone cupcake mould.
- Combine the flour, baking powder, ground almonds, sugar, butter, eggs and lemon zest in a bowl and whisk together for 2 minutes or until smooth.
- Divide the mixture between the moulds and bake for 15 – 20 minutes.
- Test with a wooden toothpick, if it comes out clean, the cakes are done.
- Turn out the cakes onto a wire rack and leave to cool then decorate with a strip of candied lemon peel.

Grapefruit Cakes 506

These cakes work really well with grapefruit zest in the cake mixture and a strip of candied grapefruit peel.

507

MAKES 12

Pistachio Mini Cakes

PREPARATION TIME: 25 MINUTES

COOKING TIME: 15 MINUTES

INGREDIENTS

55 g / 2 oz / ¼ cup self-raising flour, sifted
2 tsp baking powder
55 g / 2 oz / ¼ cup ground pistachios
110 g / 4 oz / ½ cup caster (superfine) sugar
110 g / 4 oz / ½ cup butter, softened
2 large eggs
1 tsp almond essence

- Preheat the oven to 190°C (170° fan) / 375 F / gas 5 and oil a 36-hole silicone mini cupcake mould.
- Combine the flour, baking powder, ground pistachios, sugar, butter, eggs and almond essence in a bowl and whisk together for 2 minutes or until smooth.
- Divide the mixture between the moulds, then bake in the oven for 10 – 15 minutes.
- Test with a wooden toothpick, if it comes out clean, the cakes are done.
- Transfer the cakes to a wire rack and leave to cool.

Pistachio Mini Sandwiches 508

Try splitting these cakes in half horizontally before sandwiching together with cherry jam (jelly) and whipped cream.

MAKES 9

Chocolate and Marshmallow Brownies

Marshmallow Brownies

510

Try folding 110g / 4oz / ½ cup of untoasted mini marshmallows into the brownie mixture as well for extra marshmallow flavour.

PREPARATION TIME: 25 MINUTES

COOKING TIME: 40 MINUTES

INGREDIENTS

110 g / 4 oz / ½ cup marshmallows
110 g / 4 oz / ½ cup dark chocolate, minimum 60% cocoa solids, chopped
85 g / 3 oz / ¾ cup unsweetened cocoa powder, sifted
225 g / 8 oz / 1 cup butter
450 g / 15 oz / 2 ½ cups light brown sugar
4 large eggs
110 g / 4 oz / 1 cup self-raising flour

TO DECORATE
110 g / 4 oz / ½ cup marshmallows

- Preheat the oven to 170°C (150° fan) / 325 F / gas 3 and oil and line a 20cm x 20cm / 8" x 8" square cake tin.
- Spread the marshmallows out on a baking tray and bake in the oven for 4 – 5 minutes or until gooey and golden brown.
- Melt the chocolate, cocoa and butter together in a saucepan, then stir in the melted marshmallows and leave to cool a little.
- Whisk the sugar and eggs together with an electric whisk for 3 minutes or until very light and creamy.
- Pour in the chocolate mixture and sieve over the flour, then fold everything together until evenly mixed.
- Scrape into the tin and bake for 35 – 40 minutes or until the outside is set, but the centre is still quite soft, as it will continue to cook as it cools.
- Leave the brownie to cool completely before cutting into 9 squares.
- To decorate, divide the remaining marshmallows between the brownies and toast the tops briefly under a hot grill or with a cooks' blow torch.

511
MAKES 12

Lemon Curd Cakes

PREPARATION TIME: 15 MINUTES

COOKING TIME: 20 MINUTES

INGREDIENTS

110 g / 4 oz / ½ cup self-raising flour, sifted

110 g / 4 oz / ½ cup caster (superfine) sugar

110 g / 4 oz / ½ cup butter, softened

2 large eggs

1 lemon, zest finely grated

110 g / 4 oz / ½ cup lemon curd

TO DECORATE

225 g / 8 oz / 2 cups icing (confectioners') sugar

4 tsp lemon juice

- Preheat the oven to 190°C (170° fan) / 375 F / gas 5 and grease 12 dariole moulds.
- Combine the flour, sugar, butter, eggs and lemon zest in a bowl and whisk together for 2 minutes or until smooth.
- Divide half the mixture between the moulds, and top with a spoonful of lemon curd.
- Divide the rest of the cake mixture between the moulds then bake in the oven for 15 – 20 minutes.
- Transfer the cakes to a wire rack and leave to cool completely.
- Sieve the icing sugar into a bowl, then slowly stir in the lemon juice a few drops at a time until you have a thick icing.
- Pop the cakes out of their moulds and spoon over the icing.

Passion Fruit Cakes

512

Try this recipe with passion fruit curd in the centre and spoon some passion fruit seeds on top of the icing at the end.

513
MAKES 12

Strawberry Madeleines

PREPARATION TIME: 15 MINUTES

COOKING TIME: 15 MINUTES

INGREDIENTS

110 g / 4 oz / ½ cup butter

55 g / 2 oz / ⅓ cup plain (all purpose) flour

55 g / 2 oz / ½ cup ground almonds

110 g / 4 oz / 1 cup icing (confectioners') sugar

3 large egg whites

3 strawberries, quartered

- Heat the butter until it foams and starts to smell nutty, then leave to cool.
- Combine the flour, ground almonds and icing sugar in a bowl and whisk in the eggs whites.
- Pour the cooled butter through a sieve into the bowl and whisk into the mixture until evenly mixed.
- Leave the cake mixture to rest in the fridge for an hour.
- Preheat the oven to 170°C (150° fan) / 325 F / gas 3 and oil and flour a 12-hole Madeleine mould.
- Spoon the mixture into the moulds and press a strawberry quarter into the top of each one, then transfer the tin to the oven and bake for 10 – 15 minutes.
- Transfer the cakes to a wire rack to cool for 5 minutes. before serving in paper cupcake cases.

Raspberry Madeleines

514

Try this recipe with a fresh raspberries instead of the strawberries.

515

MAKES 12

Mirabelle Cakes

- Preheat the oven to 180°C (160° fan) / 350 F / gas 4 and oil a 12-hole silicone muffin tin.
- Beat the egg in a jug with the oil and milk until well mixed.
- Mix the flour, baking powder, sugar and Mirabelles in a bowl, then pour in the egg mixture and stir just enough to combine.
- Divide the mixture between the moulds, then bake in the oven for 20 – 25 minutes.
- Test with a wooden toothpick, if it comes out clean, the cakes are done.
- Transfer the cakes to a wire rack and leave to cool completely.

PREPARATION TIME: 25 MINUTES

COOKING TIME: 25 MINUTES

INGREDIENTS

1 large egg
120 ml / 4 fl. oz / ½ cup sunflower oil
120 ml / 4 fl. oz / ½ cup milk
375 g / 12 ½ oz / 2 ½ cups self-raising flour, sifted
1 tsp baking powder
200 g / 7 oz / ¾ cup caster (superfine) sugar
150 g / 5 oz / 1 cup Mirabelle plums, stoned and quartered

Mirabelle and Almond Cakes

 516

Add 2 tbsp ground almonds to the mixture for extra moist cakes.

517

MAKES 12

Almond and Apricot Mini Cakes

- Preheat the oven to 180°C (160° fan) / 350 F / gas 4 and oil a 24-hole mini muffin tin.
- Beat the egg in a jug with the oil and milk until well mixed.
- Mix the flour, baking powder, sugar, ground almonds and apricots in a bowl, then pour in the egg mixture and stir just enough to combine.
- Divide the mixture between the moulds and scatter with flaked almonds, then bake in the oven for 15 – 20 minutes.
- Test with a wooden toothpick, if it comes out clean, the cakes are done.
- Transfer the cakes to a wire rack and leave to cool.

PREPARATION TIME: 25 MINUTES

COOKING TIME: 20 MINUTES

INGREDIENTS

1 large egg
120 ml / 4 fl. oz / ½ cup sunflower oil
120 ml / 4 fl. oz / ½ cup milk
375 g / 12 ½ oz / 2 ½ cups self-raising flour, sifted
1 tsp baking powder
200 g / 7 oz / ¾ cup caster (superfine) sugar
55 g / 2 oz / ½ cup ground almonds
75 g / 2 ½ oz / ½ cup dried apricots, chopped
2 tbsp flaked (slivered) almonds

Almond Drizzle Mini Cakes

 518

Try making an almond drizzle icing by mixing 225g / 8 oz / 1 cup icing sugar with ½ tsp almond essence and just enough boiling water to make a runny glaze.

519

MAKES 24

Vanilla Cranberry Cakes

PREPARATION TIME: 25 MINUTES

COOKING TIME: 25 MINUTES

INGREDIENTS

175 g/ 6 oz/ ¾ cup unsalted butter, softened
175 g/ 6oz/ 1 1/8 th cups self-raising flour
1 tsp baking powder
3 medium eggs lightly beaten
175g/6 oz/ ¾ cup golden caster sugar
75g/ 2 ½ oz/ ½ cup dried cranberries, chopped
1 tsp vanilla extract
24 paper cases

TO DECORATE

400g/ 7oz/ 1 cup unsalted butter
800g/ 14oz/ 3 cups icing sugar, sifted
a little pink food colouring
75g/ 2 ½ oz/ ½ cup dried cranberries, chopped

- Preheat oven to 180°C (160° fan) 375F, gas 5.
- Line cupcake tin with paper cases.
- Cream together in a food processor the sugar and butter until pale and fluffy.
- Add the eggs a little at a time if the mixture starts to curdle add a little of the measured flour.
- Add the vanilla extract to the mixture together with the dried cranberries.
- Spoon the mixture into the cases and bake for 18-20 minutes until risen and golden.
- Leave to cool on a wire rack.
- To decorate, beat the butter until soft. Add the icing sugar and beat again.
- Add a little pink food colouring and spoon onto the cooled cakes.
- Decorate with the chopped, dried cranberries

520

MAKES 24

Marmalade And Chocolate Mini Cakes

- Preheat the oven to 180°C (160° fan) / 350 F / gas 4 and oil a 24-hole silicone mini muffin mould.
- Beat the egg in a jug with the oil, milk and marmalade until well mixed.
- Mix the flour, baking powder, sugar and chocolate chunks in a bowl, then pour in the egg mixture and stir just enough to combine.
- Divide the mixture between the moulds, then bake in the oven for 15 – 20 minutes.
- Test with a wooden toothpick, if it comes out clean, the cakes are done.
- Transfer the cakes to a wire rack and leave to cool.

PREPARATION TIME: 25 MINUTES

COOKING TIME: 20 MINUTES

....

INGREDIENTS

1 large egg
120 ml / 4 fl. oz / ½ cup sunflower oil
120 ml / 4 fl. oz / ½ cup milk
110 g / 4 oz / ½ cup thick cut marmalade
375 g / 12 ½ oz / 2 ½ cups self-raising flour, sifted
1 tsp baking powder
200 g / 7 oz / ¾ cup caster (superfine) sugar
150 g / 5 oz / ⅔ cup dark chocolate, minimum 60% cocoa solids, chopped

Marmalade and Orange Chocolate Chunk Mini Cakes

521

Try using orange flavoured chocolate for the chunks for an even zestier taste.

522

MAKES 24

Almond Mini Cakes

- Preheat the oven to 180°C (160° fan) / 350 F / gas 4 and oil a 24-hole silicone mini muffin mould.
- Beat the egg in a jug with the oil, milk and honey until well mixed.
- Mix the flour, baking powder, sugar and ground almonds in a bowl, then pour in the egg mixture and stir just enough to combine.
- Divide the mixture between the moulds, then bake in the oven for 15 – 20 minutes.
- Test with a wooden toothpick, if it comes out clean, the cakes are done.
- Transfer the cakes to a wire rack and leave to cool.

PREPARATION TIME: 25 MINUTES

COOKING TIME: 20 MINUTES

....

INGREDIENTS

1 large egg
120 ml / 4 fl. oz / ½ cup sunflower oil
120 ml / 4 fl. oz / ½ cup milk
2 tbsp honey
375 g / 12 ½ oz / 2 ½ cups self-raising flour, sifted
1 tsp baking powder
200 g / 7 oz / ¾ cup caster (superfine) sugar
55 g / 2 oz / ½ cup ground almonds

Decorated Almond Mini Cakes

523

Try decorating these little cakes with a drizzle of plain white icing and a whole blanched almond on each one.

524

MAKES 6

Chocolate, Coconut And Almond Cakes

PREPARATION TIME: 20 MINUTES

COOKING TIME: 20 MINUTES

INGREDIENTS

55 g / 2 oz / ½ cup self-raising flour, sifted
55 g / 2 oz / ½ cup ground almonds
28 g / 1 oz / ¼ cup unsweetened cocoa powder, sifted
28 g / 1 oz / ¼ cup desiccated coconut
110 g / 4 oz / ½ cup caster (superfine) sugar
110 g / 4 oz / ½ cup butter, softened
2 large eggs

TO DECORATE

2 tbsp desiccated coconut

- Preheat the oven to 190°C (170° fan) / 375 F / gas 5 and oil a 6-hole silicone tartlet mould or 6 individual tartlet tins.
- Combine all of the cake ingredients in a bowl and whisk together for 2 minutes or until smooth.
- Divide the mixture between the tins then transfer the cakes to the oven and bake for 20 – 25 minutes.
- Test with a wooden toothpick, if it comes out clean, the cakes are done.
- Transfer the cakes to a wire rack to cool, then sprinkle over a little desiccated coconut.

Extra Almond Cakes

525

To increase the almond flavour in these cakes, add ½ tsp of almond essence to the cake mixture and sprinkle the cakes with flaked almonds before baking.

526

MAKES 12

Wholemeal Dairy-Free Banana Cakes

PREPARATION TIME: 25 MINUTES

COOKING TIME: 25 MINUTES

INGREDIENTS

3 very ripe bananas
110 g / 4 oz / ⅔ cup soft light brown sugar
2 large eggs
120 ml / 4 fl. oz / ½ cup sunflower oil
225 g / 8 oz / 1 ½ cups wholemeal flour
2 tsp bicarbonate of (baking) soda

TO DECORATE

dried banana chips

- Preheat the oven to 200°C (180° fan) / 400 F / gas 6 and line a 12-hole cupcake tin with paper cases.
- Mash the bananas with a fork then whisk in the sugar, eggs and oil.
- Sieve the flour and bicarbonate of soda into the bowl and stir just enough to evenly mix all the ingredients together.
- Divide the mixture between the paper cases, then transfer the tin to the oven and bake for 15 – 20 minutes.
- Test with a wooden toothpick, if it comes out clean, the cakes are done.
- Transfer the cakes to a wire rack and leave to cool completely.
- Top with dried banana chips to finish.

Dark Chocolate Banana Cakes

527

For a touch of luxury, stir in 110g / 4oz / ⅔ cup dark chocolate chunks before baking.

528

MAKES 12

Apple Crumble Cakes

- Preheat the oven to 190°C (170° fan) / 375 F / gas 5 and line a 12-hole muffin tin with paper cases.
- Whisk the sugar, eggs and oil together for 3 minutes until thick.
- Fold in the flour, baking powder and cinnamon, followed by the grated and chopped apple and the sultanas.
- Divide the mixture between the paper cases.
- To make the crumble topping, rub the butter into the flour until the mixture resembles fine breadcrumbs. Stir in the sugar, then clump the mixture together in your hands and crumble it over the top of the cakes.
- Transfer the tin to the oven and bake for 20 - 25 minutes.
- Test with a wooden toothpick, if it comes out clean, the cakes are done.
- Transfer the cakes to a wire rack and leave to cool.

Rhubarb Crumble Cakes   529

This recipe works brilliantly with rhubarb too – substitute the chopped and grated apple for 150g / 5 oz finely chopped rhubarb.

PREPARATION TIME: 20 MINUTES

COOKING TIME: 20 MINUTES

INGREDIENTS

175 g / 6 oz / 1 cup light brown sugar
2 eggs
150 ml / 5 fl. oz / ¾ cup sunflower oil
175 g / 6 oz / 1 ¼ cups wholemeal flour
3 tsp baking powder
2 tsp ground cinnamon
110 g / 4 oz apples, coarsely grated
110 g / 4 oz apples, chopped
175 g / 6 oz / ¾ cup sultanas

FOR THE CRUMBLE TOPPING
55 g / 2 oz / ¼ cup butter, cubed and chilled
110 g / 4 oz / ¾ cup plain (all purpose) flour
2 tbsp caster (superfine) sugar

530

MAKES 12

White Chocolate and Frangipane Cakes

- Preheat the oven to 190°C (170° fan) / 375 F / gas 5 and line a 12-hole cupcake tin with paper cases.
- Combine the flour, ground almonds, sugar, butter, eggs and almond essence in a bowl and whisk together for 2 minutes or until smooth.
- Divide the mixture between the cases.
- Melt the chocolate in a microwave or bain marie and spoon it into a small piping bag.
- Pipe a design on top of the cakes then transfer the tin to the oven and bake for 15 – 20 minutes.
- Test with a wooden toothpick, if it comes out clean, the cakes are done.
- Transfer the cakes to a wire rack to cool.

White Chocolate   531
Apricot Cakes

Try pressing half a fresh apricot into the centre of each cake before baking.

PREPARATION TIME: 20 MINUTES

COOKING TIME: 20 MINUTES

INGREDIENTS

55 g / 2 oz / ½ cup self-raising flour, sifted
55 g / 2 oz / ½ cup ground almonds
110 g / 4 oz / ½ cup caster (superfine) sugar
110 g / 4 oz / ½ cup butter, softened
2 large eggs
1 tsp almond essence
110 g / 4 oz white chocolate, chopped

532

MAKES 12

Mini Pavlovas

Mini Chocolate Pavlovas

533

Dip the base of the meringues in melted white or dark chocolate.

PREPARATION TIME: 20 MINUTES

COOKING TIME: 35 MINUTES

....

INGREDIENTS

4 large egg whites
110 g / 4 oz / 1 cup caster (superfine) sugar
1 tsp cornflour (cornstarch)

TO DECORATE

225 ml / 8 fl. oz / 1 cup double (heavy) cream
2 tbsp icing (confectioners') sugar
½ tsp vanilla extract
4 tsp raspberry jam (jelly)
4 raspberries
4 tsp chocolate spread
4 tsp white chocolate spread
white and dark chocolate curls, to garnish

- Preheat the oven to 140°C (120° fan) / 275 F / gas 1 and oil and line a baking tray with greaseproof paper.
- Whisk the egg whites until stiff, then gradually whisk in half the sugar until the mixture is very shiny.
- Fold in the remaining sugar and the cornflour then spoon the mixture into a large piping bag fitted with a large star nozzle.
- Pipe 12 small swirls onto the baking tray, then bake in the oven for 30 minutes or until the meringues are crisp on the outside, but still a bit chewy in the middle.
- Leave to cool completely.
- To make the topping, whisk the cream with the icing sugar and vanilla until thick.
- Spoon the mixture into a piping bag fitted with a large star nozzle and pipe a ring on top of each meringue.
- Fill the centres with jam or chocolate spread and add a corresponding topping of raspberries or chocolate curls.

534

MAKES 24

Mini Mincemeat Tarts

- Sieve the flour into a mixing bowl then rub in the butter until the mixture resembles fine breadcrumbs.
- Stir in just enough cold water to bring the pastry together into a pliable dough.
- Roll out the pastry on a floured surface and cut out 24 circles then use them to line a 24 mini tartlet tins and crimp around the edges.
- Leave the pastry to chill the fridge for 30 minutes.
- Preheat the oven to 200°C (180° fan) / 400 F / gas 6.
- Fill the pastry cases ¾ full with mincemeat then bake for 15 – 20 minutes.

PREPARATION TIME: 35 MINUTES

COOKING TIME: 15 MINUTES

....

INGREDIENTS

225 g / 8 oz / 1 ½ cups plain (all-purpose) flour
110 g / 4 oz / ½ cup butter, cubed and chilled
225 g / 8 oz / 1 cup mincemeat

Mini Mincemeat Tarts with Marzipan Stars

535

Roll out 225g / 8 oz / 1 cup marzipan and cut out 24 stars and put on top of the tarts before baking.

536

MAKES 6

Rum and Raisin Giant Babas

- Oil a 6-hole silicone muffin mould.
- Combine the flour, yeast, sugar and salt in a bowl and gradually whisk in half of the beaten egg.
- Continuing to whisk, incorporate half of the butter, followed by the rest of the egg.
- Beat the remaining butter in and incorporate the raisins, then divide the mixture between the moulds.
- Leave the babas to prove in a warm, draught-free place for 1 hour or until they have doubled in size.
- Preheat the oven to 200°C (180° fan) / 400 F / gas 6.
- Bake the babas for 15 – 20 minutes or until golden brown and cooked through, then turn them out onto a wire rack.
- Put the sugar in a saucepan with 675ml / 1 ¼ pints / 3 cups water and stir over a medium heat to dissolve the sugar.
- Boil the sugar water for 5 minutes or until it starts to turn syrupy, then stir in the rum
- Transfer the babas to a mixing bowl, pour over the syrup and leave to soak until cold, turning occasionally.

PREPARATION TIME: 1 HOUR 15 MINUTES

COOKING TIME: 20 MINUTES

....

INGREDIENTS

150 g / 5 oz / 1 cup plain (all purpose) flour
2 tsp dried easy-blend yeast
1 tbsp caster (superfine) sugar
½ tsp salt
3 large eggs, lightly beaten
75 g / 2 ½ oz / ⅓ cup butter, softened
75 g / 2 ½ oz / ½ cup raisins
For the soaking syrup
450 g / 1 lb / 2 cups caster (superfine) sugar
240 ml / 8 fl. oz / 1 cup rum

MAKES 6

Peach Melba Cakes

537

PREPARATION TIME: 25 MINUTES

COOKING TIME: 20 MINUTES

INGREDIENTS

110 g / 4 oz / ½ cup self-raising flour, sifted
110 g / 4 oz / ½ cup caster (superfine) sugar
110 g / 4 oz / ½ cup butter, softened
2 large eggs
6 canned peach halves, drained
110 g / 4 oz / ½ cup raspberry jam (jelly)
Icing sugar (congfectioners') for dusting

- Preheat the oven to 190°C (170° fan) / 375 F / gas 5 and grease a 6-hole silicone Yorkshire pudding mould.
- Combine the flour, sugar, butter and eggs in a bowl and whisk together for 2 minutes or until smooth.
- Cut each peach half into thirds and arrange in the bottom of the moulds.
- Add 3 dollops of raspberry jam and top with the cake mixture.
- Transfer the mould to the oven and bake for 15 – 20 minutes.
- Test with a wooden toothpick, if it comes out clean, the cakes are done.
- Un-mould the cakes onto serving plates and dust with a little icing sugar.

Peach Melba Cakes with Raspberry Sauce

538

Serve with a hot raspberry sauce: press 150g / 5 oz / ⅔ cup of raspberries through a sieve and heat the pulp in a pan with 2 tbsp of caster sugar. Stir until the sugar dissolves.

539

MAKES 6

Rose Jam Cakes

PREPARATION TIME: 25 MINUTES

COOKING TIME: 10 MINUTES

INGREDIENTS

4 plain cakes
55 g / 2 oz / ¼ cup desiccated coconut
75 g / 2 ½ oz / ½ cup walnuts, chopped
75 g / 2 ½ oz / ½ cup currants
110 g / 4 oz / ½ cup rose petal jam (jelly)
To decorate
55 g / 2 oz / ¼ cup rose petal jam (jelly)
6 rose petals

- Put the cakes in a food processor and process to fine crumbs.
- Stir in the coconut, walnuts and currants then bind together with the rose petal jam.
- Press the mixture into the bottom of 6 ring moulds and chill until firm.
- Remove the moulds and top with rose petal jam and a fresh rose petal.

Hazelnut Chocolate Cakes

540

Replace the walnuts with chopped hazelnuts and leave out the currants. Bind the mixture with 110g / 4 oz / ½ cup chocolate hazelnut (cob nut) spread instead of the rose petal jam.

541

MAKES 12 # Chocolate Chip Madeleines

- Heat the butter until it foams and starts to smell nutty, then leave to cool.
- Combine the flour, ground almonds and icing sugar in a bowl and whisk in the eggs whites.
- Pour the cooled butter through a sieve into the bowl and whisk into the mixture until evenly mixed.
- Fold in the chocolate chips.
- Leave the cake mixture to rest in the fridge for an hour.
- Preheat the oven to 170°C (150° fan) / 325 F / gas 3 and oil and flour a 12-hole Madeleine mould.
- Spoon the mixture into the moulds, then transfer the tin to the oven and bake for 10 – 15 minutes.
- Test with a wooden toothpick, if it comes out clean, the cakes are done.
- Transfer the cakes to a wire rack to cool for 5 minutes before serving.

PREPARATION TIME:
1 HOUR 30 MINUTES

COOKING TIME: 15 MINUTES

INGREDIENTS

110 g / 4 oz / ½ cup butter
55 g / 2 oz / ⅓ cup plain (all purpose) flour
55 g / 2 oz / ½ cup ground almonds
110 g / 4 oz / 1 cup icing (confectioners') sugar
3 large egg whites
2 tbsp chocolate chips

White Chocolate Chip Madeleines

542

Replace the milk chocolate chips with white chocolate chips.

543

MAKES 12 # Plain Madeleines

- Heat the butter until it foams and starts to smell nutty, then leave to cool.
- Combine the flour, ground almonds and icing sugar in a bowl and whisk in the eggs whites.
- Pour the cooled butter through a sieve into the bowl and whisk into the mixture until evenly mixed.
- Leave the cake mixture to rest in the fridge for an hour.
- Preheat the oven to 170°C (150° fan) / 325 F / gas 3 and oil and flour a 12-hole Madeleine mould.
- Spoon the mixture into the moulds, then transfer the tin to the oven and bake for 10 – 15 minutes.
- Test with a wooden toothpick, if it comes out clean, the cakes are done.
- Transfer the cakes to a wire rack to cool for 5 minutes before serving.

PREPARATION TIME:
1 HOUR 30 MINUTES

COOKING TIME: 15 MINUTES

INGREDIENTS

110 g / 4 oz / ½ cup butter
55 g / 2 oz / ⅓ cup plain (all purpose) flour
55 g / 2 oz / ½ cup ground almonds
110 g / 4 oz / 1 cup icing (confectioners') sugar
3 large egg whites

Chocolate Madeleines

544

Melt 110g / 4oz / ½ cup of milk chocolate and dip the Madeleines in as you eat them.

Raspberry Madeleines

PREPARATION TIME: 1 HOUR
30 MINUTES

COOKING TIME: 15 MINUTES

INGREDIENTS

110 g / 4 oz / ½ cup butter
55 g / 2 oz / ⅓ cup plain (all purpose)
flour
55 g / 2 oz / ½ cup ground almonds
110 g / 4 oz / 1 cup icing
(confectioners') sugar
3 large egg whites
12 raspberries

- Heat the butter until it foams and starts to smell nutty, then leave to cool.
- Combine the flour, ground almonds and icing sugar in a bowl and whisk in the eggs whites.
- Pour the cooled butter through a sieve into the bowl and whisk into the mixture until evenly mixed.
- Leave the cake mixture to rest in the fridge for an hour.
- Preheat the oven to 170°C (150° fan) / 325 F / gas 3 and oil and flour a 12-hole Madeleine mould.
- Spoon the mixture into the moulds and press a raspberry into each, then transfer the tin to the oven and bake for 10 – 15 minutes.
- Test with a wooden toothpick, if it comes out clean, the cakes are done.
- Transfer the cakes to a wire rack to cool for 5 minutes before serving.

Raspberry Madeleines with White Chocolate Dip

546

Heat 225ml / 8 fl. oz / 1 cup double cream until boiling then pour over 225g / 8 oz / 1 cup chopped white chocolate and stir until smooth.

Wholemeal Salted Caramel Tarts

PREPARATION TIME: 1 HOUR

COOKING TIME: 12-15 MINUTES

INGREDIENTS

225 g / 8 oz / 1 ½ cups wholemeal
flour
110 g / 4 oz / ½ cup butter, cubed and
chilled
To decorate
85 g / 3 oz / ½ cup butter
85 ml / 3 fl. oz / ⅓ cup double cream
85 g / 3 oz / ¼ cup golden syrup
85 g / 3 oz / ½ cup dark brown sugar
½ tsp sea salt flakes
225 ml / 8 fl. oz / 1 cup double
(heavy) cream

- Preheat the oven to 200°°C (180° fan) / 400 F / gas 6.
- Sieve the flour into a bowl then rub in the butter until the mixture resembles fine breadcrumbs.
- Stir in cold water to bring the pastry together into a pliable dough.
- Roll out the pastry and cut 6 circles then use them to line a 6 tartlet tins.
- Line the tins with clingfilm, then fill with baking beans and bake for 10 minutes.
- Remove the film and beans and return the cases to the oven for 2 minutes or until cooked through. Leave to cool.
- Put the butter, cream, golden syrup and brown sugar in a small saucepan and boil for 2 minutes, stirring to dissolve the sugar.
- Stir in the sea salt flakes, then divide half of the caramel between the pastry cases.
- Leave the rest of the caramel to cool completely.
- Whip the cream until thick, then fold in the cooled caramel.
- Spoon the cream into a piping bag fitted with a large star nozzle and pipe a big swirl on top of each tart.

548

MAKES 24

Rose and Pomegranate Cakes

- Preheat the oven to 180°°C (160° fan) / 350 F / gas 4 and oil a 24-hole silicone mini muffin mould.
- Beat the egg in a jug with the oil, milk and rose water until well mixed.
- Mix the flour, baking powder, sugar, ground almonds and pomegranate seeds in a bowl, then pour in the egg mixture and stir just enough to combine.
- Divide the mixture between the moulds and bake in the oven for 15 – 20 minutes.
- Test with a wooden toothpick, if it comes out clean, the cakes are done.
- Transfer the cakes to a wire rack and leave to cool before dusting with icing sugar.
- Sieve the icing sugar into a bowl and add just enough rose water to make a thick icing.
- Spoon the icing over the cakes and crumble over some crystallised rose petals.

Lavender and Blueberry Cakes

549

Replace the pomegranate seeds in the muffin mixture with fresh blueberries and replace the rose water with 2 drops of lavender essence.

PREPARATION TIME: 25 MINUTES

COOKING TIME: 15-20 MINUTES

INGREDIENTS

1 large egg
120 ml / 4 fl. oz / ½ cup sunflower oil
120 ml / 4 fl. oz / ½ cup milk
1 tbsp rose water
375 g / 12 ½ oz / 2 ½ cups self-raising flour, sifted
1 tsp baking powder
200 g / 7 oz / ¾ cup caster (superfine) sugar
55 g / 2 oz / ½ cup ground almonds
75 g / 2 ½ oz / ½ cup fresh pomegranate seeds
icing sugar to dust

TO DECORATE

225 g / 8 oz / 2 cups icing (confectioners') sugar
2 – 4 tsp rose water
crystallised rose petals

550

MAKES 12

Chocolate Filled Madeleines

- Heat the butter until it foams and starts to smell nutty, then leave to cool.
- Combine the flour, ground almonds and icing sugar in a bowl and whisk in the eggs whites.
- Pour the cooled butter through a sieve into the bowl and whisk into the mixture until evenly mixed.
- Leave the cake mixture to rest in the fridge for an hour.
- Preheat the oven to 170°C (150° fan) / 325 F / gas 3 and oil and flour a 12-hole Madeleine mould.
- Spoon the mixture into the moulds.
- Break the chocolate into squares and press a square into the top of each Madeleine, then transfer the tin to the oven and bake for 10 minutes.
- Transfer the cakes to a wire rack to cool for 2 minutes before serving.

Orange Chocolate Madeleines

551

Try stirring 1 tbsp finely grated orange zest into the Madeleine mixture.

PREPARATION TIME: 1 HOUR 30 MINUTES

COOKING TIME: 10 MINUTES

INGREDIENTS

110 g / 4 oz / ½ cup butter
55 g / 2 oz / ⅓ cup plain (all purpose) flour
55 g / 2 oz / ½ cup ground almonds
110 g / 4 oz / 1 cup icing (confectioners') sugar
3 large egg whites
100 g / 4 oz / ½ cup dark chocolate, minimum 60% cocoa solids

552

MAKES 6

Sultana Scones

Cheese Scones

553

Replace the sultanas with 150 g / 4 oz of grated cheese. Add a little grated cheese to the top of each scone to achieve a golden crust.

Chocolate Chip Scones

554

Replace the sultanas with 85 g / 3 oz of chocolate chips.

Cherry Scones

555

Replace the sultanas with 85 g / 3 oz of glacé cherries.

PREPARATION TIME: 25 MINUTES

COOKING TIME: 10-15 MINUTES

INGREDIENTS

225 g / 8 oz / 1 ½ cups self-raising flour
55 g / 2 oz / ¼ cup butter
75 g / 2 ½ oz / ½ cup sultanas
150 ml / 5 fl. oz / ⅔ cup milk

- Preheat the oven to 220°°C (200° fan) / 425 F / gas 7 and oil a large baking sheet.
- Sieve the flour into a bowl and rub in the butter until the mixture resembles fine breadcrumbs.
- Add the sultanas and stir in enough milk to bring the mixture together into a soft dough.
- Press the dough out with your hands on a floured work surface until 2.5 cm / 1" thick.
- Use a pastry cutter to cut out 12 circles and transfer them to the prepared baking sheet.
- Bake in the oven for 10 – 15 minutes or until golden brown and cooked through.
- Transfer the scones to a wire rack to cool a little and serve warm.

MAKES 12

Chocolate and Hazelnut Mini Loaf Cakes

556

- Preheat the oven to 180°C (160° fan) / 350 F / gas 4 and line 12 mini loaf cake tins with cases.
- Beat the egg in a jug with the oil and milk until well mixed.
- Mix the flour, cocoa, baking powder, sugar, chocolate and nuts in a bowl, then pour in the egg mixture and stir just enough to combine.
- Divide the mixture between the paper cases, then bake in the oven for 20 – 25 minutes.
- Test with a wooden toothpick, if it comes out clean, the cakes are done.
- Transfer the cakes to a wire rack and leave to cool completely.

PREPARATION TIME: 25 MINUTES

COOKING TIME: 25 MINUTES

INGREDIENTS

1 large egg
120 ml / 4 fl. oz / ½ cup sunflower oil
120 ml / 4 fl. oz / ½ cup milk
375 g / 12 ½ oz / 2 ½ cups self-raising flour, sifted
55 g / 2 oz / ½ cup unsweetened cocoa powder, sifted
1 tsp baking powder
200 g / 7 oz / ¾ cup caster (superfine) sugar
110 g / 4 oz / ½ cup dark chocolate, minimum 60% cocoa solids, chopped
75 g / 2 ½ oz / ¼ cup hazelnuts (cob nuts), chopped

Hazelnut Topped Mini Loaf Cakes

557

For a simple but effective topping, spread the cakes with chocolate hazelnut spread and sprinkle with chopped hazelnuts.

MAKES 12

Green Olive and Thyme Mini Loaf Cakes

558

- Preheat the oven to 180°C (160 fan) / 350 F / gas 4 and oil 12 mini loaf tins.
- Beat the egg in a jug with the oil, yogurt and cheese until well mixed.
- Mix the flour, raising agents, salt, olives and thyme in a bowl, then pour in the egg mixture and stir just enough to combine.
- Divide the mixture between the tins and bake in the oven for 20 – 25 minutes.
- Test with a wooden toothpick, if it comes out clean, the cakes are done.
- Transfer the cakes to a wire rack and leave to cool.

PREPARATION TIME: 25 MINUTES

COOKING TIME: 20 MINUTES

INGREDIENTS

2 large eggs
120 ml / 4 fl. oz / ½ cup sunflower oil
180 ml / 6 fl. oz / ¾ cup Greek yogurt
110 g / 4 oz / 1 cup Parmesan, grated
225 g / 8 oz / 1 ½ cups plain (all purpose) flour
2 tsp baking powder
½ tsp bicarbonate of (baking) soda
½ tsp salt
75 g / 2 ½ oz / ½ cup green olives, pitted
2 tbsp fresh thyme leaves

Camembert Mini Loaf Cakes

559

Try stirring 110g / 4 oz / ½ cup chopped ripe Camembert into the mixture before baking

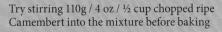

560

MAKES 12

Chocolate Mini Logs

PREPARATION TIME: 25 MINUTES

COOKING TIME: 25 MINUTES

INGREDIENTS

1 large egg
120 ml / 4 fl. oz / ½ cup sunflower oil
120 ml / 4 fl. oz / ½ cup milk
375 g / 12 ½ oz / 2 ½ cups self-raising flour, sifted
55 g / 2 oz / ¼ cup unsweetened cocoa powder, sifted
1 tsp baking powder
200 g / 7 oz / ¾ cup caster (superfine) sugar
110 g / 4 oz / ½ cup dark chocolate, minimum 60% cocoa solids, chopped

TO DECORATE

225 g / 8 oz / 1 cup dark chocolate, minimum 60% cocoa solids, chopped
1 tube of Smarties (TM?)

- Preheat the oven to 180°C (160° fan) / 350 F / gas 4 and oil 12 mini loaf cake tins.
- Beat the egg in a jug with the oil and milk until well mixed.
- Mix the flour, cocoa, baking powder, sugar and chocolate in a bowl, then pour in the egg mixture and stir just enough to combine.
- Divide the mixture between the tins, then bake in the oven for 20 – 25 minutes.
- Test with a wooden toothpick, if it comes out clean, the cakes are done.
- Transfer the cakes to a wire rack and leave to cool completely.
- Melt the chocolate in a microwave or bain marie and coat the cakes evenly on all sides.
- Use a fork to comb a bark pattern in the surface of the cakes and decorate with Smarties.

White Chocolate Mini Logs

561

Replace the dark chocolate in the cake mixture with white chocolate and leave out the Smarties in the decoration in favour of a light dusting of icing sugar.

562

MAKES 16

Coconut Mini Cakes

PREPARATION TIME: 20 MINUTES

COOKING TIME: 25 MINUTES

INGREDIENTS

110 g / 4 oz / ½ cup self-raising flour, sifted
110 g / 4 oz / ½ cup caster (superfine) sugar
110 g / 4 oz / ½ cup butter, softened
2 large eggs
28 g / 1 oz / ⅛ cup desiccated coconut

TO DECORATE

225 g / 8 oz / 1 cup icing (confectioners') sugar
1 – 2 tbsp coconut milk
28 g / 1 oz / ⅛ cup dried coconut slices

- Preheat the oven to 190°C (170° fan) / 375 F / gas 5 and oil and line a 20cm x 30cm / 8" x 12" cake tin with greaseproof paper.
- Combine the flour, sugar, butter, eggs and coconut in a bowl and whisk together for 2 minutes or until smooth.
- Spoon the mixture into the tin and bake in the oven for 20 – 25 minutes.
- Test with a wooden toothpick, if it comes out clean, the cake is done.
- Transfer the cake to a wire rack and leave to cool completely then cut into 16 pieces.
- To make the icing, sieve the icing sugar into a bowl and stir in just enough coconut milk to make a thin icing.
- Coat the cakes in the icing, then roll in the coconut and leave to set on a wire rack.

Almond Mini Cakes

563

Replace the desiccated coconut with ground almonds and make the icing with boiling water instead of the coconut milk. Roll the cakes in flaked (slivered) almonds.

MAKES 12 564

Cream and Jam Mini Cakes

- Preheat the oven to 190°C (170° fan) / 375 F / gas 5 and oil a 12-hole straight-sided silicone mould.
- Combine the flour, sugar, butter, eggs and vanilla extract in a bowl and whisk together for 2 minutes or until smooth.
- Divide the mixture between the moulds, then transfer the tin to the oven and bake for 15 – 20 minutes.
- Test with a wooden toothpick, if it comes out clean, the cakes are done.
- Transfer the cakes to a wire rack and leave to cool completely.
- Whip the cream to soft peaks.
- Cut each cake in half horizontally and top the bottom halves with a tsp of raspberry jam.
- Top with a tsp of whipped cream and put the tops back on the cakes.

PREPARATION TIME: 20 MINUTES

COOKING TIME: 20 MINUTES

INGREDIENTS

110 g / 4 oz / ½ cup self-raising flour, sifted
110 g / 4 oz / ½ cup caster (superfine) sugar
110 g / 4 oz / ½ cup butter, softened
2 large eggs
1 tsp vanilla extract

TO DECORATE

225 ml / 8 fl. oz / 1 cup double (heavy) cream
110 g / 4 oz / ½ cup raspberry jam (jelly)

Cream and Lemon Curd Cakes   565

Replace the raspberry jam with lemon curd for a zesty twist.

566

MAKES 12

Pear and Chocolate Chip Mini Cakes

- Preheat the oven to 190°C (170° fan) / 375 F / gas 5 and oil a 12-hole silicone mini loaf cake mould.
- Combine the flour, sugar, butter and eggs in a bowl and whisk together for 2 minutes or until smooth.
- Fold in the chocolate chips and the pears then divide the mixture between the moulds.
- Bake in the oven for 15 – 20 minutes.
- Test with a wooden toothpick, if it comes out clean, the cakes are done.
- Transfer the cakes to a wire rack and leave to cool completely.

PREPARATION TIME: 20 MINUTES

COOKING TIME: 20 MINUTES

INGREDIENTS

110 g / 4 oz / 1 cup self-raising flour, sifted
110 g / 4 oz / ½ cup caster (superfine) sugar
110 g / 4 oz / ½ cup butter, softened
2 large eggs
1 tsp vanilla extract
150 g / 5 oz / 1 cup chocolate chips
1 pear, peeled, cored and chopped

Hazelnut Mini Loaf Cakes   567

Try adding 5 tbsp chopped hazelnuts to the mixture for extra crunch.

568
MAKES 12

Red Leicester and Walnut Mini Cakes

PREPARATION TIME: 25 MINUTES

COOKING TIME: 20 MINUTES

INGREDIENTS

2 large eggs
120 ml / 4 fl. oz / ½ cup sunflower oil
180 ml / 6 fl. oz / ¾ cup Greek yogurt
225 g / 8 oz / 2 cups Red Leicester, grated
225 g / 8 oz / 1 cup plain (all purpose) flour
2 tsp baking powder
½ tsp bicarbonate of (baking) soda
½ tsp salt
75 g / 2 ½ oz / ½ cup walnuts, chopped

- Preheat the oven to 180°C (160° fan) / 350 F / gas 4 and oil 12 mini loaf tins.
- Beat the egg in a jug with the oil, yoghurt and half the cheese until well mixed.
- Mix the flour, raising agents, salt and walnuts in a bowl, then pour in the egg mixture and stir just enough to combine.
- Divide the mixture between the tins and sprinkle with the rest of the cheese, then bake in the oven for 20 – 25 minutes.
- Test with a wooden toothpick, if it comes out clean, the cakes are done.
- Transfer the cakes to a wire rack and leave to cool.

Red Leicester and Sun-dried Tomato Mini Loaf Cakes   569

Stir 5 tbsp chopped sundried tomatoes into the mixture before baking.

570
MAKES 12

Cherry and Almond Madeleines

PREPARATION TIME:
1 HOUR 30 MINUTES

COOKING TIME: 15 MINUTES

INGREDIENTS

110 g / 4 oz / ½ cup butter
55 g / 2 oz / ⅓ cup plain (all purpose) flour
55 g / 2 oz / ½ cup ground almonds
110 g / 4 oz / 1 cup icing (confectioners') sugar
3 large egg whites
2 tbsp black cherries in syrup, drained and chopped
2 tbsp almonds, chopped

- Heat the butter until it foams and starts to smell nutty, then leave to cool.
- Combine the flour, ground almonds and icing sugar in a bowl and whisk in the eggs whites.
- Pour the cooled butter through a sieve into the bowl and whisk into the mixture until evenly mixed.
- Fold in the cherry pieces then leave the cake mixture to rest in the fridge for an hour.
- Preheat the oven to 170°C (150° fan) / 325 F / gas 3 and oil and flour a 12-hole Madeleine mould.
- Spoon the mixture into the moulds and sprinkle with chopped almonds, then transfer the tin to the oven and bake for 10 – 15 minutes.
- Test with a wooden toothpick, if it comes out clean, the cakes are done.
- Transfer the cakes to a wire rack to cool .

Almond Madeleines   571

For extra almond flavour, add 1 tsp of almond essence to the mixture.

MAKES 12

Breakfast Cereal Mini Loaf Cakes

Cereal and Orange Mini Loaf Cakes

573

To carry on the breakfast theme, add 2 tbsp orange juice to the wet ingredients before mixing.

Cereal and Coconut Mini Loaf Cakes

574

Add 1 tbsp of coconut milk and 1 tsp of desiccated coconut to the mixture.

PREPARATION TIME: 25 MINUTES

COOKING TIME: 20 MINUTES

INGREDIENTS

1 large egg
120 ml / 4 fl. oz / ½ cup sunflower oil
120 ml / 4 fl. oz / ½ cup milk
375 g / 12 ½ oz / 2 ½ cups self-raising flour, sifted
1 tsp baking powder
200 g / 7 oz / ¾ cup caster (superfine) sugar
150 g / 5 oz / 1 cup muesli
75 g / 2 ½ oz / ½ cup crushed cornflakes
75 g / 2 ½ oz / ½ cup dried cranberries

- Preheat the oven to 180°C (160° fan) / 350 F / gas 4 and oil 12 mini loaf tins.
- Beat the egg in a jug with the oil and milk until well mixed.
- Mix the flour, baking powder, sugar, muesli, cornflakes and cranberries in a bowl, then pour in the egg mixture and stir just enough to combine.
- Divide the mixture between the tins and bake in the oven for 15 – 20 minutes.
- Test with a wooden toothpick, if it comes out clean, the cakes are done.
- Transfer the cakes to a wire rack and leave to cool completely.

575

MAKES 12

Orange and Vanilla Madeleines

PREPARATION TIME:

1 HOUR 30 MINUTES

COOKING TIME: 15 MINUTES

INGREDIENTS

110 g / 4 oz / ½ cup butter
55 g / 2 oz / ⅓ cup plain (all purpose) flour
55 g / 2 oz / ½ cup ground almonds
110 g / 4 oz / 1 cup icing (confectioners') sugar
3 large egg whites
1 orange, zest finely grated
1 vanilla pod, seeds only

- Heat the butter until it foams and starts to smell nutty, then leave to cool.
- Combine the flour, ground almonds and icing sugar in a bowl and whisk in the eggs whites, orange zest and vanilla seeds.
- Pour the cooled butter through a sieve into the bowl and whisk into the mixture until evenly mixed.
- Leave the cake mixture to rest in the fridge for an hour.
- Preheat the oven to 170°C (150° fan) / 325 F / gas 3 and oil and flour a 12-hole Madeleine mould.
- Spoon the mixture into the moulds, then transfer the tin to the oven and bake for 10 – 15 minutes.
- Test with a wooden toothpick, if it comes out clean, the cakes are done.
- Transfer the cakes to a wire rack to cool for 5 minutes before serving.

Grapefruit and Vanilla Madeleines **576**

Try replacing the orange zest with grapefruit zest for a piquant flavour.

577

MAKES 12

Pistachio Madeleines

PREPARATION TIME:

1 HOUR 30 MINUTES

COOKING TIME: 15 MINUTES

INGREDIENTS

110 g / 4 oz / ½ cup butter
55 g / 2 oz / ⅓ cup plain (all purpose) flour
55 g / 2 oz / ½ cup ground pistachio nuts
110 g / 4 oz / 1 cup icing (confectioners') sugar
3 large egg whites

- Heat the butter until it foams and starts to smell nutty, then leave to cool.
- Combine the flour, ground pistachios and icing sugar in a bowl and whisk in the eggs whites.
- Pour the cooled butter through a sieve into the bowl and whisk into the mixture until evenly mixed.
- Leave the cake mixture to rest in the fridge for an hour.
- Preheat the oven to 170°C (150° fan) / 325 F / gas 3 and oil and flour a 12-hole Madeleine mould.
- Spoon the mixture into the moulds, then transfer the tin to the oven and bake for 10 – 15 minutes.
- Test with a wooden toothpick, if it comes out clean, the cakes are done.
- Transfer the cakes to a wire rack to cool for 5 minutes before serving.

Hazelnut Madeleines **578**

These little cakes are also lovely made with ground hazelnuts (cob nuts) instead of the pistachios.

Index

Index

Index

Index